TABLE OF CONTENTS

PREFACE

We have a problem. Far too many members of our churches find it far too easy to live without clear evidence of their faith. Examples are easy to find. I think of a young couple I know who live together without the benefit of matrimony and attend church faithfully! I suspect they never question whether they are saved. I think of an elderly man who tells me about how he was converted, baptized, and joined the church in his teens but has not been in church, except for special occasions, in years. He appears to suffer no doubts about his eternal destiny. Yet another young mother left her husband and children to live with another man and shows neither shame nor remorse. I wonder if she even thinks about where she will spend eternity. She has been a church member ever since childhood and that may satisfy her.

These examples are real, but citing them may lead our discussion in the wrong direction. Their offences are finally no more serious than many others who appear upright but nurse secret indulgences or are dominated by sins of the spirit like pride or greed.

Are such folks really Christians? They seem to think so. Indeed, their Christian loved ones often apparently think so, too. They pray for their spiritual recovery, to be sure, but they give little if any thought to the possibility they will go to hell.

Why does this state of affairs prevail? I'm not entirely sure, but I suspect that we who have preached and taught the church bear a large part of the blame. One possibility is we have made it much too easy to wear the name *Christian*. After all, the word serves to modify almost anything: Christian education, Christian political parties, Christian magazines, Christian theme parks, Christian cruises, Christian business practices, Christian radio, Christian rock (music), Christian night clubs—you name it.

I am not saying all the people I know as Christians are inconsistent. Far from it: I know many who are dedicated to Jesus and "walk in the light"—as 1 John puts it.

Nor am I suggesting things are much worse now, within the church, than they used to be. That is always easy to say and never helpful.

At any rate, these considerations have driven me to study again what the New Testament has to say about what is required for eternal life. Perhaps we need to jettison *Christian* entirely and find a narrower word. Among younger believers in our culture, there is already a tendency for some of them to identify themselves as "Christ-followers." They may be on the right track. The biblical word for that is *disciple*.[1]

Regardless, glibly identifying persons as Christians may grow out of an over-emphasis on how simple and undemanding it is to be saved. One must "only believe" (as one of the choruses of my youth expressed it) in Jesus as one's Savior, and salvation is settled. After all, this was arguably the battle cry of the Reformation, expressed as *sola fide*—faith alone. And the Bible sometimes seems to support this simplicity: to the Philippian jailer Paul said, "Believe on the Lord Jesus Christ, and thou shalt be saved" (Acts 16:31). The idea that faith is the sole requirement for salvation is well supported. Is it possible that we have failed to make sure people understand what this means or—worse still—that we have not realized what it means?

The other thing that occurs to me grows out of that. We have so emphasized salvation by faith alone that we have based assurance of salvation on the mere *profession* of faith. Intentionally or not, we have led people to believe that once they have "trusted Jesus" there is no further danger to their souls.

All this has led me to examine afresh the teaching of our Lord and His apostles about salvation. To explain the results of that study is the work of this book, not of this preface. Even so, I began with an assumption that had been forming for a number of years: namely, there are two somewhat different ways in the New Testament—two "models" if you will—of defining personal salvation. My purpose in this book was to explore that, and to do this based on a fresh investigation of what the New Testament has to say about the subject, as though looking at this for the first time and with no prior decisions about it in mind. My training was in the text of the Greek New Testament, and I have interpreted and taught it for more than fifty-five years. My promise to the reader is to show what the whole New Testament, not just parts of it, has to say about how to acquire eternal life. My intention is to take the text seriously, to read out what is there, rather than to read into it what I might want it to say, even when it seems to go against our traditional ways of understanding the gospel.

Is there, in fact, more than one biblical model for conceiving salvation? If so, are they in some ways contradictory, or can they be reconciled in a way that is both biblical and applicable to human experience?

The study begins with a rehearsal of the most common way of understanding salvation, as found especially in the writings of Paul. This is properly represented as justification by faith, and it is the model for understanding salvation that has predominated in the Protestant churches since Luther championed it in sixteenth-century Europe. That understanding, however, can be defective in some ways.

The next chapter examines how our Lord expressed the requirements for eternal life in the Synoptic Gospels. Paul is, of course, the one who gave the Christian faith its first (and inspired) systematic formulation. It is possible, however, that we have let his definition so shape our thinking that we have neglected to grapple with the formulations of Jesus Himself.

Those two chapters set forth the two models just referred to, and all the rest proceeds from there. In turn, I have focused in subsequent chapters on how the issues are framed in the Gospel of John and then in John's first epistle, on whether Paul knows anything of the model suggested in the Synoptics and on the possible reconciliation of the two models in James and Hebrews. The final chapters will attempt to suggest implications of this study for what it means to be a disciple of Jesus, for the grounds of assurance of salvation, and for how to present the gospel to unbelievers.

Meanwhile, I should indicate the reason for two more chapters before the final one. The fact is that there is much discussion about the spiritual condition of professed believers whose lives are characterized by sinful practice. Some say they were never saved. Some say they were saved and still are. Some would agree to this if the persons have not consciously renounced their faith. Some say they were saved, are now lost, and may yet be saved again. One can hardly pursue the question of what is required for eternal life without investigating what the New Testament has to say about sin in the life of a believer.

Specifically, how can we distinguish—if we can—between the sins of a professing Christian who is really unsaved and the sins of a genuine Christian? Then, closely related, what bearing does sanctification have on the issue? This is the reason that two chapters on sanctification and sin have also been included.

As to my overall purpose, two clarifications are needed. First, I did not begin or pursue this project with the differences between Calvinism and Arminianism in mind. Readers who know me are aware I am not a Calvinist and hold to a nuanced kind of Arminianism I call Reformation Arminianism. I am satisfied, however, that the basic thesis of this book should meet with approval from both sides of that theological aisle. There may be a few observations, scattered here and there, where one may detect that this difference could play a part in how things are worded, but I have not purposely pointed my words in the direction of that divide. Nothing I say is meant as an argument for one or the other. The Calvinist may think of faith as entirely a work of God in the wills of the elect that logically flows from regeneration and of the "obedience of faith" as likewise the infallible work of God in the lives of those whom He has regenerated. The classical, evangelical Arminian, on the other hand, may think of faith as a person's willing response to God enabled by the gracious, pre-regenerating work of God, and of that person's "obedience of faith" as likewise impossible without the enabling work of the Spirit. But both of us can agree on what saving faith entails. I will cite numerous Calvinists who support my conclusions.

My second clarification is that I did not begin or pursue this project with the "lordship salvation" issue in mind. When I had finished the second chapter—what Jesus taught that one must do to have eternal life, as represented in the Synoptic Gospels—it occurred to me if my conclusions were correct that the lordship issue was settled. I decided, however, not to read from any of the principals in that debate until I had finished a draft of the whole. I had never read any of the books written on the subject, and I did not want to be influenced by them. As a result, there are not many references to the lordship salvation sources in the book (and the few that are present were added late in the writing process), but in the final chapter (before the Conclusion) I have included a brief section about the implications for that issue.

I had also given some thought to including a chapter that would survey how the relationship between faith and discipleship has fared in church history. Then I became aware of the treatment of this by Alan P. Stanley and decided that I need not attempt to do again what he has done so well. I believe he succeeds in showing that the position I espouse is essentially that of the pillars of the church.[2]

ENDNOTES

[1] I will not entirely abandon the word *Christian* in this book, but given that it is so widely used (and abused), I will most often use the term *disciple* or some more definite equivalent. If we keep *Christian*, we need to invest it with the meaning of discipleship.

[2] Alan P. Stanley, *Did Jesus Teach Salvation by Works? The Role of Works in Salvation in the Synoptic Gospels* (Eugene, OR: Pickwick, 2007), in his chapter "The Role of Works in Salvation in Church History," 19-70.

Chapter One

THE TRANSACTION MODEL: JUSTIFICATION BY FAITH IN PAUL

Regarding the canonical writings of the apostle Paul, I have said elsewhere "his letters form the keystone of Christian theology."[1] I see no need to soften the impact of that observation. Paul, working under the controlling influence of the Holy Spirit like the writing prophets of the Old Testament,[2] was the Christian theologian *par excellence*. His epistles, as situational and personal as they were, provide careful—sometimes even systematic—formulation of the doctrine of salvation. Christian theology has understandably and correctly relied heavily on his teaching and especially on his doctrine of justification by faith.

We must not make Paul a "canon within the canon." Nor should we exalt his letters to the Galatians and Romans over the others as a source for theology. Nevertheless, Paul is the one who most thoroughly defines what one must do to inherit eternal life, and his definition is the one that dominates Christian thinking on the subject.

The purpose of this chapter is to explore what lies at the heart of Paul's exposition of that doctrine and set it down as a starting point. Everything else in this book will proceed from that. When we ask Paul, as did the Philippian jailer, "What must I do to be saved?" the answer is "Believe on the Lord Jesus Christ and you will be saved" (Acts 16:31). Given the pervasiveness of this model in Christian thinking, I can almost assume it here. Consequently, this chapter will be different in two ways from the rest: I will be brief, and I will not interact in detail with other interpreters of the passages I use. I assume, in other words, that what I have to say here echoes the voice of all branches of "reformed" Christianity.

I have no desire to attempt a thorough presentation of Pauline theology, much less to try to settle the debate whether justification by faith was his core truth. Nor will I interact with the so-called "new perspective on Paul." Such questions are irrelevant to my purpose, even though the new perspective could affect our understanding of Paul.[3] What is important is that Paul's teaching on the subject of salvation has become—rightly or not, but surely rightly—the primary source of the evangelical church's way of understanding salvation. As such, it is the basis for what I am calling the "transaction model" of salvation. Because we are already so familiar with this model, I can treat it relatively briefly.

Philip Doddridge's 1755 hymn, *O Happy Day!*, provides the source from which I draw this title. The well-loved third verse (in our hymnals) expresses salvation thus:

> 'Tis done, the great transaction's done—
> I am my Lord's and He is mine;
> He drew me, and I followed on,
> Charmed to confess the voice divine.

I have no idea whether Doddridge would have recognized the description I am about to give. Nor does it matter.

In short, this way of conceiving personal salvation is as a finished transaction, a judicial decision that is settled for good based on the individual's saving faith.[4] This is a view of salvation that focuses on *justification*, a matter of legal standing. It is the model with which we are most familiar and which is easiest to draw from the New Testament. All we have to do to unearth the biblical basis for this model is to turn to Paul, to any number of passages in his inspired letters.

Romans

We begin with Paul's longest and most theological epistle. No sooner does he turn from focusing on mankind's lost estate (chapters one to three) than he reveals how lost people can have eternal life: "A man is justified by faith apart from the deeds of the law," he concludes (Romans 3:28). When he expands and supports this, he speaks of Abraham as one who "believed God, and it was counted to him for righteousness" (Romans 4:3). He draws deliberately on Genesis 15:6 and explains that for one who "works not, but believes on him who justifies the ungodly, his faith is counted for righteousness" (Romans 4:5). "Count" (Greek *logizomai*) means to reckon or even to impute. The Louw and Nida lexicon suggests as a translation "to put into one's account, to charge one's account," and explains that it means, "to keep records of commercial accounts."[5] This certainly conjures up an accounting *transaction*.

Then Paul brings into evidence (Romans 4:6-8) the words of David, who, he says, "describes the blessedness of the man to whom God imputes righteousness apart from works" in these words from Psalm 32:2: "Blessed is the man to whom the Lord will not impute sin."

In short, the passage is clear: people who have faith in Christ have righteousness imputed to them. In the book God keeps, there is a transaction entered: they are justified and credited with righteousness; no sin is charged to their account. This transaction is based solely on faith, it is not by works.

Two words characterize Romans: *righteousness* (justification) and *faith*. Indeed, Paul speaks easily of "the righteousness of faith" (Romans 4:13), apparently meaning the righteousness one possesses by faith. That righteousness before God should be obtained this way is necessary, he says, in order that salvation may be by grace (Romans 4:16). Citing Abraham again, Paul marvels at the patriarch's faith and repeats that this was the reason "it was imputed to him for righteousness" (Romans 4:22).

From this point, Paul moves into the implications of this for understanding the Christian life (chapters five to eight). I will return to this section of Romans in a later chapter, but everything in them builds on the foundation laid in chapters three and four, a point Paul marks well with his transitional "Therefore being justified by faith, we have peace with God" (Romans 5:1).

In chapters nine to eleven Paul turns to the question of the place of Jews and Gentiles in salvation history. Delving into his discussion of God's sovereignty here goes beyond the purposes of this survey, but Paul firmly concludes that Gentiles "have attained to righteousness, even the righteousness which is by faith" (Romans 9:30), while Israelites have not attained this: "Why not? Because they sought it not by faith, but as it were by the works of the law" (Romans 9:32). Indeed, says Paul, "Christ is the end of the law for righteousness to everyone that believes" (Romans 10:4), and this leads him to the axiom, "That if you will confess with your mouth the Lord Jesus, and believe in your heart that God has raised him from the dead, you will be saved" (Romans 10:9).

Galatians

Shorter but equally clear and powerful is Galatians, which was apparently the very basis for Martin Luther's Reformation battle cry, justification by faith. The letter, from beginning to end, is a defense of the gospel of salvation by faith that Paul preached, which he insists was revealed to him by Jesus Christ (Galatians 1:12). Indeed, he yielded nothing to the leading apostles, illustrated by his rebuke of Peter's inconsistency. Recalling this leads him to affirm that a man is not justified by the works of the law, but by "the faith of Jesus Christ" (Galatians 2:16, A.V.). That this means faith *in* Christ (an objective genitive in Greek), rather than some mysterious faith that Jesus had or gives, seems to me to be beyond question.[6]

So Paul cites Abraham and Genesis 15:6 again[7] (Galatians 3:6) and makes the almost outrageous claim that God Himself was "preaching the gospel" in Genesis 12:3 when (in stating the Abrahamic covenant) He promised to bless *all nations* in Abraham (Galatians 3:8). As if that were not startling enough Paul cites Habakkuk 2:4—"the just shall live by faith"—as grounds for insisting "no man is justified in the sight of God by the law" (Galatians 3:11). At best, the law was a "schoolmaster," a *pedagogue*, "to bring us to Christ, that we might be justified by faith" (Galatians 3:24).

Indeed, justification is not the only soteriological fruit of faith. Faith is the grounds on which the life-giving Holy Spirit is shared with human beings: we "receive the promise of the Spirit [the promised Spirit] through faith" (Galatians 3:14). Furthermore, Paul affirms that people are "children of God by faith in Christ Jesus" (Galatians 3:26). The transaction, then, involves not only justification but also the regenerating presence of the Holy Spirit and the legal standing of membership in God's family as His children and heirs—adoption, in other words. By faith, not by works, we are God's sons and daughters experiencing His confirming and life-giving presence.

The Prison Epistles

These great letters—Colossians, Ephesians, Philemon, and Philippians—know this doctrine also. I do not take the time to analyze that blessed, doctrinal benediction of praise in Ephesians 1:3-14,[8] but the repeated "in Christ," "in him," "in the beloved," "in whom" makes clear that spiritual riches are ours by virtue of our union with Christ. And it is equally clear this union is by faith: Paul identifies his readers as those who trusted—believed, exercised faith—in Christ when they heard the gospel, and that when they *believed* they were sealed with the promised Holy Spirit, the earnest of our inheritance (Ephesians 1:13-14).

Ephesians 2:8-9 is perhaps the most well-known passage: "For by grace you have been saved through faith; and that not of yourselves: it is the gift of God: not of works, lest any man should boast." I note in passing that objective interpreters will acknowledge that the word "that" does not refer back to "faith"; the two do not agree in grammatical gender.[9] Instead, "that" refers to the whole truth of the preceding clause. Regardless, the verses make abundantly clear any works of our own did not achieve our salvation relationship with God; instead, it is a gift of God to us received by faith.

The transaction takes place by the gracious gift of God. We are only to believe Him, to trust His offer of salvation in Christ, and to rest our salvation on the meritorious work of Christ in confidence. At root, that is the nature of faith.

Philippians draws out the very same picture in Paul's own personal testimony. Citing all the achievements of his illustrious career as a rabbinic Jewish Pharisee, he renounces it all and longs in faith to "be found in him, not having my own righteousness, which is of the law, but that which is through the faith of Christ [faith *in* Christ, again], the righteousness which is of God by faith" (Philippians 3:9).

In this context, there is a statement in Colossians that sums up well the transaction model. Paul describes his Christian readers in several phrases (Colossians 2:11-13) as having been "circumcised with the circumcision made without hands," "buried with him [Christ] in baptism," "risen with him," "made alive together with him," and having been "forgiven" all their trespasses. All of this, he says, was accomplished through faith in the working of the God who raised Jesus from the dead.[10]

Elsewhere in Paul

The rest of Paul's letters do not focus as much on the theology of salvation. Even so, justification by faith is never far removed from Paul's written proclamation of the gospel, even when the problems he addresses are primarily practical or involve other doctrinal issues. To the Corinthians, for example, Paul expresses the eternal good pleasure of God to "save those who believe" (1 Corinthians 1:21). He distinguishes between the saved and the lost as those who believe versus those who do not believe (as in 1 Corinthians 7:12-15). Describing their response to the gospel

Paul says, "So we preach, and so you believed" (1 Corinthians 15:11). Such passing references tend to show that the church in Paul's day might already have been using *believer* and *unbeliever* in much the same way as in our day, and this usage depends on the model of salvation by faith.

The marvelous passage in 2 Corinthians 5:17-21 certainly reflects this model. There we read, "God was in Christ, reconciling the world to himself, not imputing their trespasses to them" (v. 19). The climactic words are in verse 21: "He has made him who knew no sin to be sin for us, that we might be made the righteousness of God in him." Although the word *faith* does not appear here, this "double imputation" is at the heart of the transaction model of salvation and must necessarily be accomplished by faith.

In the Thessalonian correspondence, when Paul mentions those who will suffer the judgment of God at the end of the age, he blames this on the fact they "did not believe the truth" (2 Thessalonians 2:12). In the Pastoral letters he addresses a Christian reader as a "man or woman that believes" (1 Timothy 5:16)—*a believer*, as we would put it. False teachers attempt to "overthrow the faith of some" (2 Timothy 2:18). The Scriptures are able to make a person "wise unto salvation through faith which is in Christ Jesus" (2 Timothy 3:15). And in Titus 3:7 Paul uses the phrase "being justified by his [God's] grace" in a way that (in light of Romans 4:16 above) means essentially the same thing as being justified by faith, and this is the grounds on which we are made heirs of God who have hope for eternal life.

Conclusion

Although additional passages might be cited, these are sufficient for my purpose. Any of us will be able to fill in the details of mortar that ties these great theological building blocks together. We are well acquainted with this model, and I have no doubt Paul would have gladly sung Doddridge's hymn: "'Tis done, the great transaction's done." The righteousness of Christ—Christ's own right standing with the Father—was on his account by faith. It is ours, if we have faith in Christ.

In summary, the transaction model views personal salvation primarily from the judicial perspective of justification, conceiving salvation as imputation of the righteousness of Christ or as a legal standing in the family of God. The one who is exercising faith in Christ—with whatever that implies, which will be more fully developed in the following chapters—is in possession of this standing. For us to have standing as children of God by virtue of union with Christ is to be counted by

God as clothed in the righteousness of Christ, to be counted in right standing with God, to have no sins counted against us.

This model rests on widespread biblical evidence. To understand the gospel one must understand this. To take this lightly is to put our own souls in peril. The rest of the New Testament may well flesh out our understanding (or correct our misunderstanding) of what this means, but it must surely not contradict it, lest Scripture be broken after all and Jesus err (John 10:35).

ENDNOTES

[1] Robert E. Picirilli, *Paul the Apostle* (Chicago: Moody, 1986), vii.

[2] "Holy men of God spoke as they were borne along by the Holy Spirit" (2 Peter 1:21).

[3] I am satisfied that proponents of the new perspective have, like proponents of the old one, interpreted Paul too narrowly as though all those he opposed were of one single persuasion about the role of the law. But that need not occupy us here. My view of Paul's soteriology will be clear in what follows. For a thorough, evangelical appraisal of the new perspective, see D. A. Carson, Peter T. O'Brien, and Mark A. Seifrid, eds., *Complexities of Second Temple Judaism*, vol. 1 (Grand Rapids: Baker, 2001); for a less technical, but helpful, response see Alan P. Stanley, *Did Jesus Teach Salvation by Works? The Role of Works in Salvation in the Synoptic Gospels* (Eugene, OR: Pickwick, 2006), 80-115.

[4] It is cumbersome to have to continue to speak of "saving faith." From this point on I will resist the temptation to add a modifier to *faith*; the reader should know that whenever I refer to faith, I mean genuine, saving faith, not some "easy" belief or mere intellectual persuasion. The book will provide opportunity to define this faith more fully.

[5] Johannes P. Louw and Eugene A. Nida, eds., *Greek-English Lexicon of the New Testament Based on Semantic Domains*, 2nd edition (New York: United Bible Societies, 1988, 1989), 1.583.

[6] Any number of commentators, including many thorough going Calvinists, can be cited to demonstrate this. I am aware of some recent efforts to resurrect the idea that the genitive *faith* is not objective and refers to Christ's own faith or faithfulness, but I do not find them convincing and see no need to pursue the matter here.

[7] Whether he cited this first in Romans or in Galatians depends on which was written first, a question that has not been finally resolved by New Testament scholars.

[8] For a grammatical exegesis of the passage, one may consult my "Commentary on Ephesians" in *The Randall House Bible Commentary: Galatians through Colossians* (Nashville: Randall House, 1988), 132-144.

[9] At least this is true of interpreters whom I judge to be objective! I realize some sincere interpreters would disagree, but I see no need to pursue this here.

[10] Another objective genitive following *faith*, as above in Galatians 2:16 and Philippians 3:9.

Chapter Two

THE DISCIPLESHIP MODEL:
THE CALL OF JESUS IN THE SYNOPTIC GOSPELS

Were we to ask Jesus our basic question—How can I have eternal life?—how would He answer? In fact, some of those He encountered asked and He responded.

In the previous chapter, I have set forth what I think most who read this will agree to: one is saved by faith in Christ alone. I have called this the *transaction* model, and it represents what I assume is the most basic theological understanding of what it means to be a Christian.[1] In this model, personal salvation is conceived as a finished transaction, a judicial decision that is settled for good.[2]

This view of salvation focuses on *justification*, a matter of legal standing. The biblical basis for this is found especially in Paul, in any number of passages in his inspired letters, including Romans 3:20-28; 4:1-8; Galatians 2:16; 3:6-14; Ephesians 2:8-9; Philippians 3:8-9; and others. In summary, people who have faith in Christ have His righteousness imputed to them. In the book God keeps, there is a transaction entered: they are justified and credited with righteousness; no sin is charged to their account. This transaction, known in short as justification, is based solely on faith and includes the believer's legal standing of membership in God's family as His child. This transaction takes place by the gracious gift of God. We are only to believe Him, to trust His offer of salvation in Christ, and to rest our salvation confidently on the meritorious work of Christ and not on our own works.

The question I am raising in this chapter is whether there is any other biblical way of understanding what it means to have eternal life. In particular, I have been carefully reading the Synoptic Gospels with this question in mind, and that has led me to propose just such a model, one I will call the *discipleship* model.[3] The two most fundamental questions that arise out of this are: (1) Is being a *disciple* of Jesus the same thing as being a *Christian*? Does the New Testament support the equation of the two terms? (2) If so what does it mean to be a disciple or to be a Christian?

Disciples and Christians in Acts

Before giving specific attention to Jesus' requirements for being a disciple, I first offer an observation made by the inspired physician Luke: "The disciples were called Christians first in Antioch" (Acts 11:26). I mention this because it seems to justify thinking that *disciples* and *Christians* are synonyms, two names for the same persons.

Will this implication hold up under scrutiny? That is the question I am exploring, and a survey of the appearances of the word *disciple(s)* in Acts may help answer it.

- 1:15: Peter stood in the midst of the 120 *disciples*;
- 6:1, 7: the number of *disciples* was multiplied (after increasing by 3,000 at Pentecost and subsequently to 5,000 men, 2:41; 4:4);
- 6:2: the twelve called the multitude of *disciples* together;
- 9:1: Saul threatened the *disciples* of the Lord;
- 9:10, 36: individual *disciples* named Ananias and Tabitha are identified;
- 9:19: after his conversion Saul was with the *disciples* at Damascus, who later (9:25) helped him escape arrest there;
- 9:26: Saul attempted to identify himself with the *disciples* in Jerusalem, who did not at first believe Saul had become a *disciple*;
- 9:38: the *disciples* at Joppa sent to Lydda for Peter;
- 13:52: the *disciples* at Antioch were filled with joy;
- 14:20: the *disciples* at Lystra stood around Paul, left for dead after the stoning there;
- 15:10: Peter warns the Jerusalem Council against putting a yoke on the neck of the *disciples*;
- 18:23: on the third journey Paul toured Galatia and Phrygia, strengthening "all the *disciples*";
- 19:9: Paul separated the *disciples* from the Jewish synagogue in Ephesus;
- 20:7: At Troas the *disciples* gathered on the first day of the week to break bread.
- See also 11:29; 14:22, 28; 16:1; 18:27; 19:1, 30; 20:1, 30; and 21:4, 16.

This leaves me in no doubt that, as far as Luke the historian was concerned in writing Acts, *disciple* was synonymous with *Christian*, thus putting Acts 11:26 into its proper perspective. Indeed, it is interesting that Luke does not take up the word *Christian* but continues to refer to Christians as disciples for the rest of his volume.[4] Indeed, *Christian* (Greek *Christianos*) occurs only three times in the New Testament, the other two being Acts 26:28 and 1 Peter 4:16, and these may reflect more the name used by outsiders than the name believers used for themselves. We may not need to scrap that word entirely, but *disciple* seems a far more meaningful term.

Even so, Luke's usage alone is not enough to serve as a full and final answer to the questions I am raising. Other aspects of New Testament usage, especially in the Synoptic Gospels, must be explored.

The Hard Sayings of Jesus about Discipleship

Crucial to this investigation is what Jesus said, as reported in the Synoptic Gospels. I think we already know He had very little to say about justification in the forensic sense prominent in Paul and as expressed in the transaction model outlined in chapter one. He spoke of righteousness, but never of the righteousness of Christ or of the imputation of righteousness or of righteousness by faith. However, He did have a great deal to say about discipleship, and my first purpose is to examine some of those sayings, beginning with Luke 14:26-27:

> If anyone comes to me, and does not hate his father, and mother,
> and wife, and children, and brothers, and sisters—yes, and his own
> life also—he cannot be my disciple. And whoever does not bear his
> cross, and come after me, cannot be my disciple.

Verse 33, following a couple of parabolic illustrations, summarizes: "Every one of you who does not forsake all that he has cannot be my disciple."

The immediate question, forgetting for the moment what we have found in Acts (above), is whether *Christian* might correctly be substituted for *disciple* in these verses, without affecting the meaning. Is it so that if a person does not hate his family and his own life, and forsake all he possesses, he cannot be a *Christian*?

Indeed, is there any alternative to this extreme view? The only one that occurs to me is perhaps *disciple* is at a higher level than a mere Christian?[5] In that case, one could be a Christian without being a disciple; a *disciple* is more fully committed to following Christ, someone who walks consistently in the ways of Jesus, while a *Christian* is more basic: someone who has received Christ by faith and had the justification transaction entered on his account with God.

Can we get by with that? Not if *disciple* and *Christian* are synonyms. We have to take the words to mean what they say. One cannot be a Christian (literally, twice, "is not able to be my disciple") unless he (1) hates family, (2) hates his own life, and (3) bears his cross; furthermore he must (4) forsake all he has, (5) come to Christ (*erchetai pros me*) and (6) come after Christ (*erchetai opisō mou*). These words merit some additional exegesis—although doing so will not soften the demand.[6]

A *disciple* (*mathētēs*) is a follower or pupil. The noun is from a verb (*manthanō*) that means to learn or be instructed. Then a disciple is "a person who learns from another by instruction, whether formal or informal."[7] A saying that reflects this perspective is Luke 6:40: "The disciple is not above his master," where *master* is the common word for *teacher* (*didaskalos*). Indeed, it is likely that by the time of Jesus *disciple* had taken on the conscious meaning of devotion or commitment, thus referring to an *adherent* of another person and his teaching.[8]

To *hate* someone, in the Bible, often has the practical meaning of rejecting that person or that person's claims.[9] So to hate one's family is to reject any claim they might have to first place in the disciple's life. And to hate one's own life is the same thing: to reject all one's own self-interest—including the desire to stay alive!—as the primary interest one must fulfill. Forsaking all one has is "saying a final 'good-bye' to one's possessions."[10]

Bearing one's cross expands on hating one's life. A cross, in the New Testament culture, was a place of execution, and so of death. Disciples have renounced any Lordship except that of Christ, any primary claim to their lives except that of Jesus. They carry about with them—we may paraphrase—the lethal injection that others, at their pleasure, may use to execute them! They have *come to* Christ as their Savior, Lord, and Teacher; and they *come after* Him, follow where He leads and learn from Him. Jesus claims such a primary allegiance from them it is as though there is no commitment to anyone or anything else. Even their self-sacrificing love for their families is a manifestation of their commitment to Jesus and their obedience to His commands—and He certainly commands that!

Again, then, can it be that without this one cannot be a Christian? And, if so, do any of us have eternal life? Before we draw a hasty conclusion, we must consider parallel passages in the gospels; they may add some light.

In Luke 9:23 (also Matthew 16:24; Mark 8:34) Jesus makes the same demand: if anyone will come after Him he must deny himself, take up his cross every day, and follow Him. No doubt denying self is the equivalent of hating one's own life, and although the word *disciple* is not used, coming after Him substitutes precisely for it and is the very same expression as in Luke 14:27, made even more specific by the words "follow me." The same instrument of death—the cross—is required: "the position of the man who is already condemned to death."[11]

It seems likely that the tenses of the three verbs in the requirement are significant, especially the obvious change in tense: both *deny* and *take up* (Greek aorist) look at actions as wholes, in this context suggesting settled decisions—although "daily" may mean the matter will have to be "settled" again and again. But *follow* (Greek present) looks at action in progress, in this context suggesting an on-going way of life:[12] "The call to follow Jesus is constant, growing out of the base commitment."[13] Though briefer, then, this saying lays down the same requirement for being a disciple of Jesus.

Perhaps Matthew 10:37-38—although the context is not the same—is parallel:

> The one loving father or mother more than me is not worthy of me: and the one loving son or daughter more than me is not worthy of me. And he who does not take his cross and follow after me is not worthy of me.

Two things are expressed differently here, although the demand is the same. Instead of speaking of "hate," Jesus expresses the matter as loving family more than Him. Just as *hate* practically means to reject, so *love* means to choose—the other side of the same coin. Unless people choose Jesus' claims above those of family, they are not worthy of Him. We may like this way of putting it better than the other, but the requirement is no easier.

The other difference is that Jesus says "is not worthy of me" instead of "cannot be my disciple"—three times each in the two passages. Perhaps this makes clear that the meaning is the same as being a Christian. Surely anyone "not worthy of" Jesus is not one of His. I cannot imagine anyone saying that someone can be a Christian and yet be judged by Jesus as unworthy of Him. This passage does nothing to soften the hard saying.

Nor does the parallel Mark 8:34-38, where Jesus' conclusion to the same hard saying is this:

> For whoever is ashamed of me and of my words in this adulterous
> and sinful generation; of him also will the Son of man be ashamed
> when he comes in the glory of his Father with the holy angels.

The *for* connects this to the hard saying (v. 34): the one who is ashamed of Jesus is the one who does not deny himself and take up his cross and follow Him. And for Jesus to be ashamed of such a one, when He comes, is the same as "not being worthy of him" (above). Indeed, Jesus often linked His future coming in glory to what I will call the "second-coming judgment," and that seems clearly to be the implication here. The point is the same as in Matthew 10:32-33 (or Luke 12:8-9):

> Therefore every one whoever will confess me before men, him will
> I confess also before my Father who is in heaven. But whoever will
> deny me before men, him will I also deny before my Father who
> is in heaven.

In that case, the conclusion is a serious one, indeed, and speaks pointedly to our question what one must do to have eternal life: if Jesus is ashamed of someone at the judgment, there is no hope for his final salvation.[14] And those of whom He will not be thus ashamed are those who have met the demands of discipleship. "To acknowledge [Jesus] is to be acknowledged by God; to disown him is to face disownment later."[15]

So far, then, the case appears to be at least worthy of serious consideration: what we mean by *Christian* is what the New Testament means by *disciple*. Otherwise, we have to acknowledge there can be "Christians" whom Jesus will deny before God at the judgment. Christians who are ashamed of Christ and do not confess Him before men and are unworthy of Him. Christians who love members of their families more than Jesus. Christians who do not take up their crosses to follow Him. Christians who do not deny their own self-interest to prefer His—in short, Christians who are not disciples. That possibility seems very unlikely, indeed.

Jesus and the Rich Young Ruler

In the hard sayings above, Jesus stated the rigorous demands of discipleship in general terms. At times He applied these to specific situations, and His encounter with the rich young ruler—found in Luke 18:18-23, Mark 10:17-22 and Matthew 19:16-22—is one of the most instructive. Although He does not use the word "disciple," specifically, Jesus appears to speak directly about what is required for eternal life.

The young man asked the question the very way we might express it: "What shall I do to inherit eternal life?"[16] In response, Jesus first pointed to the commandments (Luke 18:20), naming those that deal primarily with one's relationship to others: adultery, murder, theft, false witness, and honoring one's parents. To this, the man replied that he had kept these since childhood.[17] Jesus proceeded to the heart of the problem: "You lack one more thing," He said, "Sell everything, distribute the proceeds to the poor—and you will have treasure in heaven (cf. 12:21)—and come, follow me." "Jesus' question exposed that he had other gods who offered him more than he thought heaven could give."[18]

That Jesus was calling the man to discipleship is clear in the words, "Come, follow me"; that He was answering the question about eternal life is clear from the words "You will have treasure in heaven."[19] And He was requiring exactly the same thing as in the hard sayings about discipleship discussed above: to be a disciple he must hate everything else and follow Jesus.

I am satisfied Jesus made this demand because the young man loved his possessions more than he loved God. He trusted in his riches, his treasure was on earth. To be a disciple of Christ he had to give that up. This was the way to heaven. The *substance* of the requirement is the same for everyone, even if the *form* it took was adapted to the young man's personal situation.

The comments of Jesus that grew out of this encounter (Luke 18:24-30; Mark 10:23-31; Matthew 19:23-30) are likewise instructive and lead to the same conclusions. Those who are wealthy find it hard to enter the kingdom of God (Luke 18:24), Jesus said. Those who heard Him responded with alarm: "Then who can be saved?" (Luke 18:26). God can make this possible, said Jesus, and Peter affirmed they had left everything to follow Jesus. Then Jesus gave these encouraging, but definitive, words (paraphrased): Those who have left the things that meant most to them for My sake and the kingdom of God will receive in this life many times more than they have given up *and in the age to come will receive eternal life.*

Would it do justice to Jesus' words to read them as saying that Christians who do *not* forsake everything will receive eternal life? The answer seems obvious. Surely, the clear implication is those who receive eternal life are those who have denied everything else, the same as being His disciples.[20]

The Synoptic Picture of What It Means to Be Saved

Does the rest of what Jesus had to say about being saved mesh well with what we have seen so far in His definition of the essentials of being a disciple? To attempt to answer this I have re-read the three Gospels in order to consider every instance when Jesus appeared to speak about what is required for eternal salvation. Space does not permit a full discussion of all of these, but I will highlight those that seem to be most significant. In doing so, it will become clear that there are several expressions Jesus used that appear to be equivalent to being a disciple.[21] These include, entering or receiving the Kingdom of God, to have or inherit eternal life, to be forgiven for one's sins, to have "treasure in heaven," or to "be saved."[22]

Before beginning this survey of the Synoptics, however, I must first make a brief excursus that speaks to one's hermeneutical approach to the teachings of Jesus.

The Dispensational Framework for Interpreting the Gospels

My purpose does not permit a detailed treatment, here, of the hermeneutics of dispensationalism.[23] This movement has developed an intricate framework for interpreting and applying the Scriptures, a framework built around distinguishing several dispensations or periods of time when God has dealt differently with His people. The number of these dispensations may differ, from one proponent to another, but three are especially important: the period when the Mosaic law was in force, the period of the Christian Church that followed the finished, redemptive work of Jesus Christ, and the earth-based millennial Kingdom that will follow Christ's second coming.

Essential to this viewpoint is the proposition that Israel and the Church are two entirely different entities addressed in the Scriptures in two entirely different ways. Thus Israel is addressed by law and the Church is addressed by the gospel; the two must never be confused. This is a key to "rightly dividing the Word," and it is especially important in interpreting the Gospels since Jesus was on earth and taught at the crucial conjunction of two dispensations. Some of what He said (especially in the Synoptic Gospels) was for Israel and some (especially in the Gospel of John) was for the Church. The skillful interpreter will distinguish the two.

Indeed, according to dispensationalism, Jesus actually offered to Israel the establishment of the earthly, Messianic kingdom. Therefore, much of what He said—especially during the early part of His ministry—was spoken in this context and represented principles of law that would have applied if the kingdom had come to fruition then. But Israel rejected the offer and the kingdom was postponed until after His second coming, when once again much of what Jesus taught will be appropriate in that context. Meanwhile, the dispensation of the Church— essentially unforeseen by the Old Testament prophets—was ushered in, during which salvation is by grace through faith alone, and that faith is not necessarily expressed in any sense as obedience to the laws of God, not even the moral law. (It is for this reason that many dispensationalists strongly resist what they mockingly refer to as "Lordship salvation.")

By this hermeneutic, then, much of the Synoptic Gospels is not for Christians in the age of grace, including a large part of what I will treat below. This applies to what John and Jesus preached about repentance and the kingdom of God (Mark 1:4-5, 14-15), the Sermon on the Mount (and the sermon on the plain), the Lord's Prayer and the requirement to forgive others, the way Jesus dealt with the rich, young ruler or other inquirers, and the judgment depicted in Matthew 25.

The older dispensationalists—like J. N. Darby,[24] C. I. Scofield,[25] Lewis Sperry Chafer,[26] and others—tended to the view that the *principle* on which the salvation of Israelites was based was the necessity of keeping the Mosaic law. Thus, anything that sounds like this in the Bible is meant for Israel, not for the Church. The notes in the *Scofield Bible* are certainly open to this charge. More recent dispensationalists— like Charles Ryrie[27] and the editors of the *New Scofield Bible*[28]—are more careful, clarifying that even Old Testament saints were saved by faith. But the basic framework for interpretation, as just outlined, remains essentially the same.

I find the dispensational framework, with its neat—to me, artificial— distinctions unacceptable. Instead, I will interact seriously with all of the teachings of Jesus in which He appears to discuss what is required to have eternal life, and my view of the unity of His teaching is such that I will treat them as appropriate for Christians of all time. I will only occasionally interact (mostly in notes), for the sake of illustration, with dispensationalism. Meanwhile, for a thorough treatment of the issues involved, see Daniel P. Fuller's work subtitled *The Hermeneutics of Dispensationalism and Covenant Theology.*[29]

The Preaching of Jesus and the Requirement of Repentance

What seems indisputable is that Jesus, following directly in the pattern established by John the Forerunner, proclaimed that repentance is essential to salvation.

We start with what John preached, summarized in Luke 3:3 (and Mark 1:4-5) as "a baptism of repentance for the forgiveness of sins." Sidestepping the precise relationship of baptism to repentance, it is clear that *repentance* is the key word in this, and that in John's view it was the ingredient essential for forgiveness—and so for eternal life; "forgiveness was unthinkable without repentance."[30]

What Jesus preached is summarized in Mark 1:14-15: Jesus was "preaching the kingdom of God," and in doing so He would say "The kingdom of God is at hand: repent and believe the gospel." That the kingdom of God—the domain of His rule—was "at hand" means that access into it was readily available, and repentance and faith were the means for entrance.[31] No doubt, this is the reason Jesus is sometimes represented, simply, as "preaching the gospel of the kingdom" (Matthew 4:23): that it is at hand and accessible is certainly "good news."[32]

If salvation is by faith—and it is—the faith cannot be separated from repentance. The two are Siamese twins that no theological surgeon is skillful enough to divide. Indeed, in the parallel Matthew 3:2 (also 4:17), only *repent* is commanded, but we need not doubt that Mark's "and believe the gospel" is accurate.

In Luke 13:3, 5 Jesus speaks about being saved in a way that is more like our contemporary usage: "Unless you repent, you will all likewise perish," where "perish" is to be lost and is the opposite of being saved. Repentance is essential to eternal life.[33] Indeed, Jesus indirectly refers to the same essential requirement when He affirms He did not come "to call the righteous, but sinners to repentance" (Luke 5:32, as in Mark 2:17, Matthew 9:13). In His famous parables of the lost sheep and lost coin (Luke 15:7, 10), Jesus makes the application when He explains there will be joy in heaven "over one sinner who repents." In the account of the rich man and Lazarus and their afterlives, even the rich man in hell understood that repentance was the issue of concern (Luke 16:30), where repentance apparently would be to "take seriously what the law and the prophets say."[34]

Not only did John and Jesus preach repentance, Jesus charged the apostles to preach the same. When He sent them out on a preaching mission, their message was "that men should repent" (Mark 6:12), and Luke 9:6 indicates that this was "preaching the gospel." Indeed, at the end of His earthly ministry He commissioned them—and all of us, apparently—"that repentance and remission of sins should be preached in his name among all nations" (Luke 24:47). Repentance and forgiveness go together as "response" and "effect."[35] One of the best biblical definitions is found in 1 Thessalonians 1:9: "You turned to God from idols to serve a living and true God."

Repentance is not possible without faith, of course, but it includes—as the word (*metanoia*) implies—a fundamental change in one's way of life, the kind of change that reflects turning away from sin and turning to God.[36] Mark 1:5 (Matthew 3:6) emphasizes that when John practiced his "baptism of repentance" people *confessed their sins.* And as John developed this theme he spoke pointedly about *fruits worthy of repentance* and warned that any trees that do not bear good fruit will be cut down and burned (Luke 3:8-9; Matthew 3:8-10). When people asked him what to do to fulfill this he cited specific, practical things (Luke 3:11-14)[37]: they should share what they had with those in need, tax-collectors should collect only what was properly assessed, and soldiers should not be guilty of violence or false accusations and should be content with their wages.[38]

Although the word *repentance* does not appear in Luke 19:1-10, the passage must surely serve as an apt illustration of this grace, and it speaks directly to "salvation": Jesus urges that salvation of the lost is the reason He had come into the world (v. 10). And He declares that salvation had come to the house of Zacchaeus (v. 9). What made this clear? Zacchaeus's own affirmation that he was giving half his goods to the poor and making fourfold restoration to anyone he had cheated (v. 8).[39] If Zacchaeus was saved by faith, it was a faith that was expressed in the form of righteous actions, actions that demonstrated repentance.[40]

A number of closely-related conclusions seem well justified then. The faith that saves is inseparably linked to a repentance that brings about such a change that practical fruit evidencing it will be manifested in a person's life. This is essential to salvation, to the forgiveness of sins and entrance into the Kingdom of God. It is likewise essential to the gospel we preach.

The "Sermons" of Jesus

To be sure, Jesus' preaching consisted of much more than the brief summations just noted. We may rightly ask whether His longer, more ethical teaching (more lessons than sermons) yields any grist for our mill, any added clarification of what He presented as essential to being a disciple or possessing eternal life. Probably the two best-known examples of such teaching are the "sermon on the mount" (Matthew 5-7) and the "sermon on the plain" (Luke 6:20-49).[41]

Some may say that what Jesus is doing in these lessons is describing the character of those who are citizens in the kingdom, rather than laying down requirements for being in the kingdom. No doubt, that is generally true, but some of the things He says certainly appear to be the latter. In the Beatitudes, for example, when He says "Blessed are the pure in heart: for they shall see God," it seems likely this means to be with God in the eternal state. But any practical implications of this are not immediately developed, so we must look elsewhere in the sermon for things that more directly address what is essential to being a disciple of Jesus.[42]

Matthew 5:20 is certainly more direct, and Jesus spoke pointedly: only those whose righteousness exceeds that of the scribes and Pharisees will enter the Kingdom of God.[43] When one considers the extremes to which the members of that Jewish sect went to keep the Mosaic law and rabbinic traditions, one wonders how our righteousness might exceed theirs! Perhaps the answer is that the imputed righteousness of Christ, put on our account by faith, is the only way. In that case, we are at once back to the Pauline, transaction model. But given that Jesus never talked about this elsewhere, there is room to doubt that this was on His mind at the time. It seems far more likely that He is speaking of righteousness in conduct *that is rooted in the heart* rather than in external, legal observance.[44]

Many things in the "sermon" tend in that direction, and the saying about being "pure in heart" sets the stage for this—as well as hungering and thirsting for righteousness (5:6). Indeed, Jesus develops this pointed saying by a series of "you have heard" sayings versus "but I say" extensions; and all of them focus on the heart. True righteousness involves what we have in our hearts and speech toward others, not just avoiding murder (v. 22); in avoiding lust, not just adultery (v. 28); avoiding divorce, not just executing it legally (v. 32); speaking so as to be believed without any oaths (vv. 34-37); turning the other cheek instead of exacting what the law allowed (vv. 39-42). Most of all, it means manifesting the character of the Father and so loving even those who spitefully treat us (vv. 43-47). In this way, righteousness can exceed that of the scribes and Pharisees, and without this there is no entrance into the Kingdom of God![45]

The lesson in Matthew includes Jesus' warning about laying up for oneself treasures on earth (Matthew 6:19-21). Some may interpret this as a warning to Christians about their values and rewards, but more likely it is intended to make a contrast between the saved and the lost. Those who lay up for themselves treasures on earth live according to the values of the world, while disciples treasure what is valued in heaven and what may get them there. For, says Jesus, one's heart is with what he values most.

One reason for seeing this contrast in this light is what Jesus adds as explanation in verse 24: "No man can serve two masters ... You cannot serve God and mammon!" The choice is absolute. Then verse 33 puts on the finishing touch: "Seek ye first the kingdom of God."

Near the end of the sermon Jesus states the clincher: "Not everyone who says to me, Lord, Lord, shall enter into the kingdom of heaven, but he that does the will of my Father who is in heaven" (Matthew 7:21; compare Luke 6:46-49). That appears to be a requirement for entering eternal life. Jesus adds (vv. 22-23) that there will be many to whom He must say, in the judgment, "I never knew you," and that "working iniquity" was both the mark of their estrangement from Him and the reason for their eternal departure from His presence.

In Luke's similar and shorter lesson (6:20-49), Jesus is addressing disciples (v. 20) and pronouncing blessing on them, thus speaking more about their experience than the basis of their spiritual blessedness. Even so, as in Matthew 5-7, it is hard to avoid the conclusion that some of what He says to His disciples has the nature of being essential to their standing as disciples. In verse 35 (as in Matthew 5:45-48), for example, He seems to condition being *children of the Highest* on loving their enemies, doing good, and lending without expecting anything in return.[46] In verse 37, He appears to condition being forgiven on being forgiving. One does not have to paraphrase Him much to indicate that without good fruit a tree cannot be pronounced good (v. 43): "The product of one's life is a litmus test of the heart."[47]

The very least that can be said about these excerpts from Jesus' teaching is that one cannot truthfully claim to be a disciple of Jesus—a Christian, as we have usually expressed it—if one's way of life does not manifest the character Jesus described. It is essential that one manifest a righteousness that comes from a righteous and pure heart, that he give the welfare of the Kingdom of God first place in his pursuits, that he choose to serve God rather than mammon, and that he do the will of God as taught by Jesus.

Laying Up Treasure in Heaven

I have already referred to two passages where this expression occurs. The rich, young ruler asked, pointedly, what he must do in order to have eternal life. At the

end, Jesus said he must sell everything and follow Him and if he did so he would
"have treasure in heaven." In Matthew 6:19-21, Jesus warned against living to lay up
treasures on earth and then advised the opposite: "lay up for yourselves treasures
in heaven," confirming this with a reason: "Where your treasure is, there your heart
will also be." The parable of the rich fool (Luke 12:16-21) picks up this same theme:
Jesus applies it thus: "So is he that lays up treasure for himself, and is not rich
toward God."

Does all this mean one can be a Christian and go to heaven but lack real
treasure there if he has devoted his life more to the accumulation of earthly things?
This way of understanding the expression seems obviously misguided. Instead
(even though it may well be true that some Christians have more laid up there than
others), "having treasure in heaven" appears to be essentially equivalent in meaning
to having eternal life, to having heaven for one's final home.[48] To be sure, such an
expression has a *context*: it is especially appropriate whenever (as in these passages)
the concerns are about what one values most. A Christian is one who values eternal,
heavenly things rather than earthly things.

Even so, one cannot be a Christian and at the same time live for the pursuit of
worldly riches. That is, from one perspective, exactly what one must renounce or
leave in order to be a disciple.

People Identified as *Righteous* in the Synoptics

Several persons are pronounced *righteous* or *just* in these three Gospels, thus
demonstrating not so much the direct teaching of Jesus as the evaluation of the Holy
Spirit who inspired the writers to say this. In these instances the word (*dikaios*)—
adjective of the verb often translated "justify" (*dikaioō*)—is the very same as that
which is used by Paul so often in explaining the transaction model outlined in the
previous chapter.

Two of these are Zacharias and Elisabeth (Luke 1:6), soon to be the parents of
the Messianic forerunner, whom Luke describes as "righteous before God, walking
in all the commandments and ordinances of the Lord blameless." Was Luke, in
writing this, thinking specifically of justification in the Pauline sense? More likely, he
meant the godly couple were "upright people"[49] before God—which is not all that
different from having right standing with God (justification). "Before God" is the
key to this understanding, and so it does not *merely* mean practicing right conduct.
Even so, the "walking" phrase further defines and is apparently seen as a way of

understanding (or even as a basis for saying) "righteous before God."[50] In short, it would not be possible to say of them (or anyone else) that they were righteous before God unless they were walking in the commandments and ordinances of God (to be) blameless.[51]

If this is the right understanding, it can also be said of the others so evaluated, like Joseph (Matthew 1:19) or Simeon (Luke 2:25). In neither case is it clearly said what served as the *basis* for this evaluation. That Joseph decided not to expose Mary to a public divorce and that Simeon was consciously awaiting the One whom God would send to console Israel were more likely results or manifestations of their "justness" (or in Simeon's case of his devoutness) than bases.

Regardless, all of these can, I think, be taken as examples of those "who sincerely desired 'to do justly, and to love mercy, and to walk humbly with his God' (Micah 6:8)" and so for whom the Mosaic law "taken in its fullness and in its spirit was undoubtedly a path of righteousness and life."[52]

A Requirement for Forgiveness of Sins

If being forgiven for one's sins means the same thing as or is essential to being saved, then whatever is required for the one is likewise required for the other. We often equate the two—probably rightly, even if an over-simplification. Jesus has some interesting things to say about this.

Consider His words to the paralytic man lowered before Him by four others, found in Luke 5:20 (Mark 2:5; Matthew 9:2): "When he *saw* their faith"—that of all five, apparently—"he said unto him, Man, your sins are forgiven you." Here *faith* "must mean the visible expression of faith."[53]

Consider also that line in the Lord's prayer, in Luke 11:4: "Forgive us our sins; for we also forgive every one that is indebted to us." The version of this in Matthew 6:12-15 is, "Forgive us our debts, as we forgive our debtors," and in that context Jesus adds the stern warning that if we forgive others the Father will forgive us and if we do not do so neither will He.[54]

Mark 11:25-26 represents a different set of circumstances but yields the same truth: "Forgive … that your Father also who is in heaven may forgive you your trespasses. But if you do not forgive, neither will your Father who is in heaven forgive your trespasses." See also Matthew 18:35 for yet another occasion that yielded the same warning.

I confess that it is beyond me to explain why Jesus appears to put our forgiveness of others *before* God's forgiveness of us.[55] On this, Fuller's comments are helpful: "It just may be that the Bible teaches that God's forgiveness is conditioned not only on Christ's dying for our sins, but also on our repentance, which would include forgiving those who have wronged us"; "the reason God will not forgive such people is that an unforgiving heart is an unbelieving heart. Far from being works in which men boast, forgiving another is, in the Scriptural framework, a 'work of faith.'"[56] Regardless, it is very clear that unforgiving people cannot lay claim to forgiveness of their sins—or to being Christians.

What Is Necessary for Eternal Life?

The rich, young ruler (discussed above) was not the only one to ask about the way to eternal life—a way of posing the question we can easily identify with. On one occasion (Luke 10:25-28) a "lawyer" put this very question to Jesus: "What shall I do to inherit eternal life?" Jesus' response was to press the man, knowledgeable in the Mosaic legal system, further (paraphrased): "What do you find written in the law? Is there no answer there?" To which the lawyer replied by citing what Jesus Himself would otherwise state (Matthew 22:36-40) as the two great commandments: Love God with your whole being and love your neighbor as yourself.

Jesus commended the man as having answered correctly, adding: "Do this, and you will live"—surely meaning to live forever.[57] Our almost automatic response to this is to say well, yes, if he could truly have kept these laws, he would have been saved, but we know—wink, wink—he could not and needed to be saved by grace through faith. Such a pity the man did not object that he could not keep the law! Jesus would then surely have given him the gospel.

But can we satisfy Jesus' meaning with such "insider knowledge"? Do we think that had the man recognized his inability to obey God by loving Him and others, and confessed it, Jesus would have gone on and instructed him in justification by faith alone? Perhaps. But, then again, Jesus did not, so far as we know, instruct anyone else in what we may call Pauline soteriology.[58]

Though the situation in Mark 12:28-34 was not the same, the focus on the two great commandments was. There one of the scribes asked Jesus a question the Jewish legal experts argued about: "Which is the first commandment of all?" Jesus replied with the same two the lawyer in Luke 10 stated: whole-hearted love for God and love for one's neighbor as oneself. The scribe was impressed and his affirmation revealed spiritual insight: namely, that for one to do this is more valuable before God than all the Mosaic sacrifices! Jesus' response is telling: "Thou art not far from the kingdom of God." That is, of course, the kingdom He said was "at hand," to be entered by repentance and faith. It seems we must be able, in some sense at least, to equate taking up a life of love for God and others with repentance and faith.

Other Hard Sayings of Jesus

Mark 9:43-48 (Matthew18:8-9) should perhaps be classified with the hardest of Jesus' sayings. He speaks in the extreme about circumstances in which one ought to cut off one's hand or foot or put out one's eye. Better to go maimed into life (vv. 43, 45), into the Kingdom of God (v. 47), than to be cast into the unquenchable fire of hell (*gehenna*)!

Of course, the words do not mean one must perform such literal amputation in order to be saved, but *salvation—entering into life—is the issue*! And the point is that salvation depends on avoiding the offense (literally, a stumbling or fall) that might be otherwise blamed on the body part.

In Luke 13:23-24 a question puts the matter in a way that appeals to us: "Lord," someone asked Him, "are there few who are saved?"[59] Jesus' answer is famous: "Strive to enter in at the narrow gate: for many, I say to you, will seek to enter in, and will not be able." The version of this in Matthew 7:13-14 adds some detail: the way to destruction is wide and broad, and many go that way; but the way to life is strict and narrow, and few find that way. It would be difficult to understand this solely in terms of the transaction model, of justification by faith alone. The "straitness" involved is narrowness, and it refers to what people must put aside if they expect to go through the gate to eternal life.[60]

On Doing the Will of God

There is more than one instance in Jesus' ministry when He appears to have commended doing the will of God as a basis for possessing eternal life. One of these is that occasion when Jesus, who was teaching His disciples at the time, was informed that His mother and brothers were outside, wishing to see Him. In Luke 8:21 His response is that His mother and brothers "are those who hear the word of God, and do it." In Mark 3:35 (similarly in Matthew 12:50) the equivalent words are *doing the will of God.*

The "word of God," in a passage like this, is a general expression for whatever God expresses as His will for our lives. By a justifiable extension, that includes the written Bibles we possess, for they reveal to us the will of God. This is the reason that hearing and acting on the word can be used as another way of describing disciples, recognized by Jesus as His true family,[61] those who will live eternally in His household.

Very similar is Luke 11:27-28 when Jesus, upon hearing someone in the crowd bless the one who gave Him birth and nursed Him, responded by blessing those who "hear the word of God, and keep it." Here *keep* (*phulassō*) means literally to guard, but the result is the same as in Luke 8:15: to keep the word by observing its precepts. Such a person has more claim on Jesus than the one who gave Him natural birth!

Matthew 21:28-32 reports a parable with interesting implications drawn out by Jesus. Two sons are contrasted, one who said he would not obey and did, and another who said he would and did not! Obviously the first one really "did the will of his father," said Jesus, and then applied the lesson: his hearers had refused John the Baptist's call to righteousness and so had not repented in faith. By contrast, despised tax-collectors and harlots had hearkened to John (and thus repented in belief) and were *entering the kingdom of God*, while those who rejected his call remained outside.

The Second-Coming Judgment

The discussion thus far has mentioned the second-coming judgment more than once. Jesus concluded one of His sayings about the demands of discipleship (Mark 8:34-38) by referencing those of whom He will be ashamed when He comes in glory with the angels. In Matthew 10:32-33 (Luke 12:8-9) He spoke of confessing or denying some before the Father. In all such contexts Jesus was anticipating that He will sit in judgment when He returns, and the issue of such judgment will be the eternal salvation or lostness of those who will stand before him.[62] This is at least a part of the point of Luke 12:35-40, where in parabolic fashion Jesus refers to those who are found waiting for their lord when he returns from a wedding. He concludes more directly, "Be ye therefore ready," adding that He is coming "at an hour when you think not." We must be ready because then our final salvation will be at issue in the judgment.[63]

There are at least two other passages where the context and the issue are the same. One is Matthew 13:36-43, where Jesus interprets His parable of the tares of the field. The terms are those of His second-coming judgment, when the Son of man will send His angels to gather out of His kingdom "all things that offend, and those who do iniquity." Probably these two phrases are intended to refer to the same group, and they are of course those who are eternally lost: they will be "cast into a furnace of fire." By contrast, "the righteous" will "shine forth as the sun in the kingdom of their Father." One probably does not stretch this to see in it that the lost are those who do iniquity and the saved are those who are righteous. Nor do we need to fall back on the imputed righteousness of Christ to give this a meaning other than what seems obvious; the Bible is replete with the promise that the righteous will be saved and the wicked perish.

The other is the most dramatic picture of the second-coming judgment that Jesus paints: Matthew 25:31-46, where the scene is set in these similar words:

> Whenever the Son of man comes in his glory, and all the holy
> angels with him, then will he sit upon the throne of his glory: And
> all nations will be gathered before him: and he will separate them
> from one another, as a shepherd divides his sheep from the goats.

This passage has been read in a variety of ways—not necessarily commending the "skill" of interpreters! What seems clear is that (as in Matthew 13:36-43 above) this is at root a final separation between the lost and the saved (although, of course, it may also be more than that). The sheep on the right hand are "the righteous" (v. 37), and the goats on the left are the cursed, destined for everlasting fire (v. 41). The former go into *life eternal*, the latter into *everlasting punishment*. And the only stated basis for that judgment distinction is whether they did or did not give food, drink, lodging, and clothing to Jesus' "least" ones and visit them in prison. This may be spoken of as *faith*, to be sure; but if so, it is a faith whose primary expression is in righteous deeds.

Faith in the Teaching of Jesus

To this point, our gleanings from the Synoptic Gospels speak loudly in one direction, raising an important question: Did Jesus have nothing to say about faith as the requirement for eternal life? We have already seen, in Mark 1:14-15, that His preaching could be summarized as saying *repent and believe the gospel*, by which people could access the Kingdom of God. *Believe* (*pisteuō*) is the verb form of the noun *faith* (*pistis*). If faith is not separated from repentance, neither is repentance from faith. But is this all Jesus had to say about the essential role of faith in order to be a Christian?

On a number of occasions, Jesus credited faith as the basis for physical healing. These include at least three. In Mark 5:34 (Matthew 9:22) Jesus told the woman who had furtively touched Him in the crowd, and thereby was healed from her "issue of blood," that *her faith had made her whole*. Also in Matthew 9:28-29 Jesus restored the sight of two blind men. After asking if they had faith to believe He could do this and receiving a positive answer, He said, "May it be to you according to your faith." Likewise, in Matthew 15:28 the Syrophoenician woman prevailed in faith for the healing of her daughter.

In each of these, faith is the essential requirement, but physical healing is the only thing clearly effected by that. Unless we can confidently affirm that these instances of healing were intended, theologically, to suggest that the same thing applies to spiritual healing—and there are some good reasons for thinking this— the passages do not help us in our search for what Jesus regarded as essential to salvation.

But there is more, in the teaching and actions of Jesus, to call our attention to the importance of faith. There is, for example, Mark 16:15-16, which includes words that refer directly to being saved. Some interpreters will object to including this passage, given its status in the early Greek manuscripts. But whether it was original or not, the words do not finally contradict what Jesus said elsewhere: "The one who believes and is baptized will be saved"—versus those who do not believe and will be eternally condemned. Here Jesus gets very close to saying that salvation is by faith alone, even though in this case the believer is expected to demonstrate that faith by submitting to baptism.[64]

There is also the case of the paralytic brought by four, discussed above (Luke 5:20, Mark 2:5, Matthew 9:2). When Jesus *saw their faith*, He pronounced the man's sins forgiven—and only subsequently healed his paralysis.

In the case of the woman who washed Jesus' feet with her tears in a Pharisee's house (Luke 7:36-50), no physical healing was involved. In the end, Jesus said to the woman, "Your faith has saved you" (v. 50); and the "saving" involved the forgiveness of her sins (v. 48)—and, no doubt, deliverance from her former way of life: the "healing of the whole person brought about by personal trust in Jesus."[65]

I do not think it is inappropriate to observe that in both these latter cases the faith was *visible*. In Luke 5:20, Jesus "*saw* their faith": "Jesus sees it in the actions of the men."[66] The woman's tears were potent expressions of hers.

For yet more we turn to Jesus' explanation of the parable of the sower, seed, and soil. In Luke 8:11-15 (Mark 4:13-20, Matthew 13:8-23) Jesus interprets the first group as meaning that Satan takes away the word from some "lest they should believe and be saved" (v. 12); others believe only temporarily and then fall away (v. 13). This is faith, not works; even so, the antithesis to these failures (the good soil) is expressed in v. 15 as those who "in an honest and good heart, having heard the word, keep it, and bring forth fruit with endurance [perseverance]." Here "keep" (*katechō*) has the idea of taking possession of, in this context implying that one holds fast to, retains. As the opposite of the other three failures, this description appears to indicate that believing and being saved is identical to hearing the word and continuing to make it one's possession: "to continue to believe, with the implication of acting in accordance with such belief."[67] And producing fruit— "ethical in character"[68]—seems essential to this keeping of the word. At the very least, this provides a face that makes genuine faith recognizable.

Perhaps the pronouncement of Jesus in Luke 12:8-9 (Matthew 10:32-33), already discussed above, should also be included here. Jesus affirms that those who confess or deny Him before men will themselves be confessed or denied by Him before the angels of God. Surely, this is confession or acknowledgment of them, at His second-coming judgment, as belonging to Him. And surely, this confession is essential to their admission to heaven. Though faith is not the word here, confession is, and we find it easy to move from one to the other (Romans 10:9-10): perhaps, then, this is one place where Jesus comes near to saying that *the* requirement to be saved is to confess Him in faith as one's Lord and Savior.

The parable of the Pharisee and the tax collector (Luke 18:9-14) belongs in this discussion and appeals to us as speaking specifically about *justification*. At the end (v. 14) Jesus notes it was the latter, who had only beaten his breast and asked God for mercy, who went home justified—in stark contrast to the Pharisee who paraded his self-righteousness before God in prayer. This certainly sounds like justification by faith, and I have no doubt it is. But even then Jesus offers the principle that only those who "humble themselves"—in submission to Him—can likewise expect exaltation to such a standing before God.

The material in this section is not nearly as predominant, in the Synoptic Gospels, as that which I have examined above. Nonetheless, it leads me to a tentative conclusion: namely, Jesus did indeed know about justification by faith; but He did not know of faith that is separated from repentance, of faith that does not heed the demands of discipleship, of faith that does not produce the fruitfulness of hearing and keeping the word of God.

I speak of this as a *tentative* conclusion, however, because there is much more to explore.

What Is a Disciple?

If, indeed, a Christian is a disciple, then discipleship needs to be defined. This can be done relatively briefly at this point, given that the preceding discussion has provided the basic information and context needed. The word *disciple* has already been examined: a disciple is one who has enrolled in the school of Jesus, one who follows and learns from Him. It seems to me that the two ideas—learner and follower—are key to understanding the concept. Rengstorf is surely correct in observing that in the New Testament *following* "is the true mark" of the *disciple*, with *learning* self-evidently included.[69]

During Jesus' public ministry, these were obvious elements, and Jesus' repeated call to *follow* Him underscores how fundamental this was. Here are some of these:

- Matthew 4:19, to Peter and Andrew: *Follow me.*
- Matthew 8:22, to a vacillating disciple: *Follow me.*
- Luke 9:59, to another would-be disciple: *Follow me.*
- Matthew 9:9 (Mark 2:14, Luke 5:27), to tax collector Matthew: *Follow me.*
- Matthew 19:21 (Mark 10:21, Luke 18:22), to the rich, young ruler: *Follow me.*

And these do not include those hard sayings addressed to disciples in general, already examined above. Perhaps those who prefer to identify themselves as "Christ-followers," as I said in the Preface, are on the right track after all—depending on how they define the phrase.

Many of these calls were immediately obeyed, as indicated in Matthew 4:20, for example, when we are told that Peter and Andrew "immediately left their nets and followed him." James and John did likewise, leaving the ship and their father (Matthew 4:22). Matthew "left all, rose up, and followed him (Luke 5:28).[70] Peter (Mark 10:28) could apparently in good conscience avow to Jesus, "We have left all, and have followed you."

Nor was this limited to the twelve apostles. Luke 6:13 makes this clear: "He called to him his *disciples*: and of them he chose twelve, whom also he named *apostles*." The apostles were disciples, to be sure, but there were many more of the latter. Perhaps we get some idea of the size of that following from the scene in the upper room after Jesus' ascension: at least the number of *disciples* present, on that occasion, was a hundred and twenty (Acts 1:15).

As I read the Gospels, my impression is there was a relatively small group of persons worthy of the name *disciple*. Of these the apostles were a sort of inner circle,[71] expected to be with Jesus more or less all of the time—or at least at any time He beckoned.[72] They were disciples, of course, but so were those who made up a larger (but still small) number. They, too, were often with Him. They followed Him about from place to place and from time to time.[73] They took His teachings seriously as meant for them. He was their rabbi and they were His students. They identified themselves as followers of Jesus and practitioners of His teachings.

In addition to these, there was the often fickle populace. Jesus drew gatherings of people whenever He was on the scene. Those who flocked to hear Him (or to observe the miracles) were the "crowds," but by and large they were never *disciples*. To be sure there were those whom we may call "would-be disciples," like those three in Matthew 8:19-22 (Luke 9:57-62), who appear to have evaded Jesus' call with pathetic excuses; even then the issue was whether they would become Jesus' *followers*.[74] And there were some we may call *temporary* disciples, described in John 6:66: "From that time many of his disciples went back, and walked no more with him."[75] That, too, tells us what was expected of a disciple.

What is a disciple, then? One who lays aside every other influence for giving direction to his life and pledges allegiance to Jesus, one who follows where Jesus leads, who enrolls in the school of Jesus and proceeds to learn from Him and put His teachings into practice. No discipleship is less than this. No one really is a Christian who is not such a disciple.

But before we draw this conclusion in too much detail at least one other aspect of this needs discussion. This too, will help shape our concept of what it means to be a disciple of Jesus and therefore to have eternal life. Meanwhile, I am not saying all disciples are at the same place in their walk with Jesus. I am saying, however, that there is a basic threshold requirement without which one is not a disciple at all, and that requirement is what Jesus states in His hard sayings and challenge to the rich, young ruler—not to mention the other passages discussed above.

Discipleship Then and Now

It seems apparent there is some difference between being a disciple during Jesus' public ministry and being one now.

To review what has been said above, "disciples" in Jesus' time *were physically with Him much of the time*, heard Him teaching, and sought to understand His teachings in terms of their lives and ministry with Him. It is immediately obvious that this cannot apply, in its entirety, to a present-day disciple.

After all, the situation changed when Jesus ascended into heaven. One needs only to read from Luke's first volume (the Gospel), and then from his second (Acts), to recognize this. No longer is there any possible confusion between the crowds who gathered in excitement to listen to Jesus or observe His miracles and those who really were disciples. Now the band of disciples is small, though it grows quickly from one hundred twenty to several thousand.[76] And—what is more important— they are not physically with Jesus. They do not travel as an itinerant band. They have homes of their own (Acts 2:46), from which they come and go as daily life demands. They maintain families (Acts 21:5). They are employed in various ways to make a living (Acts 18:3). They meet at appointed times for their own assemblies (Acts 20:7).

In short, their daily lives were at least somewhat like ours, sleeping and waking, going to work, marrying and bearing children, assembling for worship. Clearly for them to *follow* Jesus did not mean the same more or less literal thing that it did when Jesus summoned people to follow Him while He was on earth. Nor does it mean that for us.

So what is it, then, to follow Jesus as a disciple now? Surely, the answer must be found in applying the very same *principles* stated when He called people to follow Him then. These have become clear enough as we have examined the Synoptic Gospels up to this point.

To be a disciple means to repent and believe the gospel and so to enter the Kingdom of God. It means to declare sincerely that one is a follower of Jesus, learning from Him. It means one must renounce all other competing allegiances and values and submit to His Lordship as the one who will teach the will of God. It means applying that teaching to one's own life and so bringing forth "fruit worthy of repentance." It means giving the word of God a favorable hearing and keeping it. In short, this means *leaving*, *following*, and *learning*.

And this is what it means to be a *Christian*.

Questions or Conclusions

At this point I have surveyed both Paul's teaching on justification and Jesus' teaching on discipleship as given in the Synoptic Gospels. There is too much more of the New Testament to be reviewed for us to reach a hasty or final conclusion. There are too many things, yet, to be explored.

One of those things is the rest of the New Testament evidence, and that involves numerous questions. Is the teaching of Jesus *all* on the side of what I have called "the discipleship model," or does He also sound clearly the gospel of justification by faith alone that seems so clear in Paul and that I have outlined in the previous chapter as "the transaction model"? I am quick to say the impressions one receives, about what is required for eternal life, seem (at least at first glance) to be quite different in the Gospel of John as compared to the Synoptic Gospels. There—partly in the inspired writer's observations, partly in the words of Jesus—the fact that one is saved by faith is much more prominent. Indeed, John has been called the Gospel of belief, and there is good reason for that. This must be developed.

Conversely, is the teaching of Paul *all* on the side of "the transaction model"? I think not, but that question must certainly be explored.

And, as I asked to begin with, are these two models of what is required to be saved contradictory or can they be reconciled? It would be premature, at this point, to attempt to answer this, even though any reader may correctly assume that I think there must be a reconciliation. But can we find in the New Testament itself any directions toward this?

Subsequent chapters will attempt to pursue these matters. At this point, however, it seems clear to me that salvation is by faith, even by "faith alone" if those words are properly understood. But it seems equally clear that the faith the New Testament speaks of as required for salvation is a faith that has at its essence repentance and a commitment to discipleship. Further exploration should confirm and clarify—or correct—this.

Meanwhile, we ought not to take lightly the implications of the Great Commission. As recorded in Matthew 28:19-20, it defines—for the disciples of Jesus, and so for His church—our continuing ministry after Jesus' ascension. In this command is one (and only one) imperative verb, with all the rest essential to and explaining it. That is the verb *teach* in "Go ye therefore, and teach all nations." This word is, in fact, *make disciples* (*matheteuō*). That is what we are called to do and the reason we go, and it involves two things, as the rest of the Commission adds:

(1) baptizing them—and so marking their profession of repentance and faith; and (2) teaching (*didaskō*, instruct) them to observe all the commandments of Jesus. Surely, this makes clear there is no discipleship, and so no Christianity or eternal life, apart from the latter.

ENDNOTES

[1] One is tempted to say "genuine Christian" (or something similar). The reader should know when I say *Christian* I mean *disciple*, and my purpose is to validate this.

[2] My Reformation Arminian colleagues might add, "at least as long as a person continues to exercise faith in Christ." I think that even my Calvinist friends would agree that genuine faith is continuing faith.

[3] No doubt, there are other possible ways of identifying this model, but this seems to me to be the most helpful.

[4] Acts uses other expressions for disciples of Jesus, such as "any of this way" (9:2; cf. 19:9, 23; 22:4; 24:14, 22) or "the brethren" (9:30; 15:1, 3, 22, 23). Interestingly, *disciple(s)* occurs in the New Testament only in the Gospels and Acts. It may be, then, that—as implied in the *Theological Dictionary of the New Testament* (hereafter *TDNT*), 10 vols., ed. Gerhard Kittel, trans./ed. Geoffrey W. Bromiley (Grand Rapids: Eerdmans, 1967), IV.459—as a name for Christians the word was especially Palestinian and did not long have common usage in the Gentile church.

[5] I do not mean, by such questions, to appear naïve; I am well aware that some interpreters regard a disciple as more than a mere Christian. I only intend to involve the reader in thinking through the issues with me.

[6] Darrell L. Bock, *Luke: The NIV Application Commentary* (Grand Rapids: Zondervan, 1996), 400-403, apparently thinks that at least at some level *disciple* is the same as *Christian*; he says that "Jesus' remarks come in the context of what conversion may require" (401); "Sometimes discipleship is portrayed as a distinct phase from saving faith, but Jesus rejects such a distinction" (404). But some of his statements about Jesus' requirements seem to soften them, explaining the meaning as "giving God his due and then following him" or "understanding that God has access to all that we are" (402).

[7] Louw and Nida, eds., *Greek-English Lexicon of the New Testament*, 1.328.

[8] See the perceptive discussion of Alan P. Stanley, *Did Jesus Teach Salvation by Works?*, 220-225. When he offers that all (true) believers are disciples, but not all disciples believers (225, n. 37), I think he makes an unhelpful distinction.

[9] And *love* means the opposite: namely, to choose; thus Romans 9:13 refers to Jacob and Esau as the sons of Isaac whom God chose and rejected, respectively. Howard Marshall, *The Gospel of Luke: A Commentary on the Greek Text* (NIGTC: Grand Rapids: 1978), 592, rightly emphasizes *rejection* as the key idea in "hate."

[10] Marshall, *Luke*, 592.

[11] Marshall, *Luke*, 373.

[12] Far from being ignorant of contemporary verbal aspect theory, I am for the most part devoted to it. One will note that I have based my pragmatic explanations of the difference, here, on the use of the tenses *in context* and not simply on their inherent meaning. For a more extensive discussion

of verbal aspect, and of its implications for interpretation, see the discussion of 1 John 3:6, 9, in chapter 4.

[13] Bock, *Luke*, 265.

[14] Marshall, *Luke*, 376: "To refuse Jesus leads to rejection by the Son of man at the judgment."

[15] Bock, *Luke*, 338.

[16] Bock, *Luke*, 467, equates the man's question to "how he can be sure he will be saved when God passes out the gift of life"; his note 3 provides the rich, Jewish background of "to inherit life."

[17] For the ways covenant theologians and dispensationalists approach this passage, see the discussion below, "The Dispensational Framework for Interpreting the Gospels," as well as several of the following footnotes, including note 42.

[18] Bock, *Luke*, 469, adding that Jesus was "asking the man to become a citizen of heaven" (470). Stanley, *Did Jesus Teach?*, 188-211, agrees with much of what I say in discussing the rich, young ruler, although he delves into many details; I think he is right in emphasizing (205) that Jesus' challenge to him was that only by placing his "undivided confidence" in Jesus could he be saved.

[19] Marshall, *Luke*, 685: "'treasure in heaven, i.e. eternal life."

[20] "The disciples are to be seen as those for whom God has made salvation possible." Marshall, *Luke*, 689.

[21] I found it interesting, after writing this, to learn that Stanley, *Did Jesus Teach?*, found a number of these and similar expressions to be equivalent to being saved; see esp. 140-153.

[22] When we read the Bible and encounter "be saved" or "salvation" there, we should not hastily equate the expressions with our developed, theological usage, even though that language is the basis for our usage. The words refer, simply, to being *delivered*, and the nature of that deliverance depends on the context.

[23] All of us provide, in one way or another, for differences in the *form* (not necessarily the *substance*) of God's dealings with His people from one period of revelatory time to another—at least between the Old and New Testaments. The "dispensationalism" I refer to is that which is represented, for example, by Dallas Theological Seminary.

[24] J. N. Darby, *The Collected Writings of J. N. Darby*, 2nd ed., ed. William Kelly, 34 vols. (London: G. M. Morrish, n.d).

[25] C. I. Scofield, *Rightly Dividing the Word of Truth* (Findlay, OH: Fundamental Truth Publishers, 1940); and notes in *The Scofield Reference Bible* (New York: Oxford University Press, 1917).

[26] Lewis Sperry Chafer, "Dispensationalism," *Bibliotheca Sacra* 93 (October 1936), 390-449; "Dispensational Distinctions Challenged," *Bibliotheca Sacra* 100 (July 1943), 337-345; "Dispensational Distinctions Denounced," *Bibliotheca Sacra* 101 (July 1944), 257-260.

[27] Charles C. Ryrie, *Dispensationalism Today* (Chicago: Moody, 1965).

[28] *Holy Bible*, New Scofield Reference Edition, ed. E. Schuyler English (New York: Oxford University Press, 1948).

[29] Daniel P. Fuller, *Gospel and Law: Contrast or Continuum* (Grand Rapids: Eerdmans, 1980).

[30] Marshall, *Luke*, 135.

[31] I am not persuaded by the dispensationalist view of some that what John and Jesus were offering was an earthly kingdom that was subsequently postponed and replaced by the church; and that the "repentance" they preached was different from that required to become a Christian. Charles C. Ryrie, *Dispensationalism Today*, 167, is of the view that this repentance had nothing to do with

42

salvation but required fulfilling the difficult (impossible?) ethical commands of the Sermon on the Mount and thus served as a dispensational test to reveal man's failure to meet God's standard. For a helpful rebuttal, see Fuller, *Gospel and Law*, esp. 150-53.

[32] Stanley, *Did Jesus Teach?*, seems at times to overemphasize that "entering the Kingdom" is a "not yet" eschatological experience awaiting the second-coming judgment, but at one point at least (148-49) he appears to understand that the regenerate have "already" entered the Kingdom in its "already" aspect.

[33] Bock, *Luke*, 366, agrees: "Jesus is really alluding to ultimate judgment and death," for which "repentance now is the only way to survive." Marshall, *Luke*, 554: "All sinners face the judgment of God unless they repent."

[34] Marshall, *Luke*, 639.

[35] Bock, *Luke*, 621. Marshall, *Luke*, 906: "Such repentance leads to forgiveness of sins."

[36] Bock, *Luke*, 109-110, observes that the New Testament usage of *repentance* "has Old Testament roots in the idea of turning to God" and views Luke 3:10-14 as an "exposition of repentance" that defines it "not as an abstract act of the mind, but as something that expresses itself in action."

[37] Marshall, *Luke*, 143: "Such works are the expression of repentance or conversion."

[38] In Matthew 7:15-20 also, Jesus, like John in this passage, contrasts trees that bear good fruit with those that bear corrupt fruit and warns that finally those that do not yield good fruit will be cut down and burned; compare Matthew 12:33-35.

[39] Bock, *Luke*, 483, is probably not helpful in emphasizing that Zacchaeus's desire to make restitution was commended "not as a requirement for the tax collector's salvation, but as an indication that his heart recognized that a wrong needed acknowledging and fixing." But if his action shows that "he is aware of his sin and desires to right the wrongs he has done" (Bock 479), what is that but *repentance*? Marshall, *Luke*, 697, is more on target to characterize Zacchaeus's declaration as "an adequate sign of repentance" and "an example of the sort of change in life that should follow upon the reception of salvation."

[40] What about the thief on the cross (Luke 23:42-43)? Most certainly, he was saved, and that without any life evidence to follow. But the case is exceptional, given he had no further opportunity to demonstrate repentance by a changed life. No problem: God is able to judge perfectly the intentions of a person's heart.

[41] For all their similarity it seems to me that the two passages reflect entirely different occasions. We should not be surprised that Jesus said similar things on many occasions as He moved about teaching in different places.

[42] Dispensationalists contend that these sermons were not for Christians at all but for Jews in the context of an earthly kingdom. Ryrie, *Dispensationalism*, 108, confirms this by asking, "Where can one find a statement of the gospel in the Sermon?" The *New Scofield Bible* editors note, "In this sermon our Lord reaffirms the Mosaic law of the O.T. theocratic kingdom as the governing code of his coming kingdom on earth" (997). That convenient way of dispensing with the Sermon is not open to most of us. Fuller, *Gospel and Law*, 153, appropriately cites Acts 26:20 as evidence that Paul, like John the Baptist, preached to Jews and Gentiles "that they should repent and turn to God, and do works meet for repentance."

[43] Readers will notice that I see "the Kingdom of heaven" and "the Kingdom of God" as essentially interchangeable. Space does not permit a defense of this.

[44] This is one place where the new perspective on Paul might affect what needs to be said, but it would take us too far afield. I assume that those who hold this perspective could well agree with my

understanding of what Jesus required, even if they would reject my final phrase (which begins with "rather than").

[45] I should add that none of this means the Mosaic law itself was to be ignored, as Jesus makes plain up front (vv.17-19). Those who violated the law would be "least in the kingdom of heaven," and those who observe it would be "great in the kingdom"—which seems clearly to mean the first group would not make it in! Even so, mere external observance of the law is not adequate, not even if understood as a sign of the covenant people. Righteousness from the heart is required.

[46] Bock, *Luke*, 191: "To be his child is not only to be brought into a relationship where God has forgiven us; it is the beginning of a process of reflecting God's gracious, merciful, and forgiving character to the world."

[47] Bock, *Luke*, 193. But he goes on to say that fruit may be only a *suggestive*, rather than a *certain* indicator, albeit "regenerated people do bear some sort of fruit" (200; italics mine). This does not sound as sure as Jesus.

[48] Bock, *Luke* 144-145: "Richness towards God means responding to life and blessing in a way that he desires, in a way that honors him—through service and compassion." Marshall, *Luke*, 524, apparently accepts the view of Jeremias that it means "entrusting one's wealth to God." Jesus' remark seems much more pointed and radical than either of these, meaning—at root—that one *has an eternal place with God*. The several references brought together, here, to laying up treasure on earth or in heaven and being rich toward God appear to point in this direction. That one who first *has* "treasure in heaven" can subsequently attend to it in different ways is obvious and secondary, though an important lesson for disciples.

[49] Bock, *Luke*, 50—who does not comment on how this relates to "walking in all the commandments and ordinances of the Lord blameless."

[50] Marshall, *Luke*, 52, is right to say the phrase implies a religious and not simply ethical character, and their obedience to God's commands went "beyond a merely external, legal righteousness."

[51] Nor does this need to mean sinless perfection, I think, but that is a matter for another discussion. E. H. Gifford, *The Epistle of St. Paul to the Romans* (London: John Murray, 1886), 177, appropriately sees their observance of the law as performed in faith and thus leading to true righteousness, in contrast to legalistic Israelites whose efforts toward keeping the law were prompted by pride and to perform works that would merit the favor of God. (Gifford, of course, was not aware of the new perspective!)

[52] Gifford, *Romans*, 184.

[53] Bock, *Luke*, 157.

[54] Marshall, *Luke*, 461 (following Carmignac) appears to think that a forgiving spirit is required for one's prayer for forgiveness to be heard, rather than for forgiveness itself. That seems an artificial distinction that does not fit the several passages brought together here.

[55] Older dispensationalists tended to put this as law for the Jew, as in the *Scofield Bible*, 1002: "This is legal ground. ... Under law forgiveness is conditioned upon a like spirit in us." More recent ones put it as forgiveness for *fellowship* rather than for *salvation*; see *The Ryrie Study Bible*, NASB (Chicago: Moody, 1978), 1454, and the *New Scofield Bible* note on Matthew 6:12. I will discuss in a later chapter this distinction. Bock, *Luke*, 309, observes (without explication) that "it is wrong to ask from God what we are not willing to give to others."

[56] Fuller, *Gospel and Law*, 61-62, 112-113.

[57] Marshall, *Luke*, 440, rightly regards Jesus' answer as one which "expressed his basic agreement with the fundamental teaching of the OT and brought out the continuity between the law, *rightly understood*, and his own teaching." (italics mine)

[58] Charles Hodge, *Systematic Theology* (reprint, 3 vols., Grand Rapids: Eerdmans, n.d.), thinks Jesus' response in such situations was to state the old covenant of works rather than the gospel because the questioners had already rejected the gospel: "If a man will not ... accede to the method of salvation by grace, he is of necessity under law" (2.375)—thus setting God's law and works in stark contrast to grace and faith, which is typical for Calvinistic covenant theology. Lewis Sperry Chafer, "Dispensationalism," *Bibliotheca Sacra* 93 (October 1936), 390-449, disagrees with Hodge and represents Jesus as speaking on such occasions in the terms of the old dispensation, thus offering eternal life to Israelites as an *inheritance* gained by keeping the law. Neither of these positions is appealing: the first means that Jesus' words cannot be taken at face value, while the second espouses two different ways of salvation. To his credit Bock, *Luke*, 299 (although a Dallas professor!), observes that Jesus "is not giving a dispensationally limited commendation, he is asserting the fundamental ethical call of God." But even Bock thinks Jesus' meaning included the implication that "those who love God will hear Jesus, come to him, respond to him, and receive his benefits." As true as this is, one doubts Jesus meant for the man to understand this specific gospel of salvation by faith in Jesus.

[59] Marshall, *Luke*, 564, thinks being "saved" here "refers to the obtaining of eschatological salvation, and is tantamount to entry to the kingdom and the gaining of eternal life." Stanley, *Did Jesus Teach?*, 137, 238, appears to think "saved" in the question "entails both present *and* future salvation," but in the answer has "future salvation" in view. I am more inclined to think of present and future in both verses, but the issue is not essential to my discussion.

[60] Bock, *Luke*, 380-387, focusing on the "door" that is shut in v. 25, appears to think Jesus was thinking primarily about the way people respond to Him. He distinguishes between the application to an individual, for whom the door is shut at death, and Israel, for whom the door was shut at the destruction of Jerusalem in A.D. 70. Marshall, *Luke*, 562, has the more appealing view that "the period of opportunity is limited by the imminence of judgment" and that "entry to the kingdom depends ... above all on turning from evil in repentance." Neither of them gives much attention to the narrowness of the door before it is shut, although Marshall (565) thinks Luke (more so than Jesus) saw in it "the difficulty of repenting and turning from evil"; Marshall inclines to think Jesus had ethical demands in mind, which seems likely but is not all that different from what he thinks was in Luke's mind.

[61] Bock, *Luke*, 233, speaks of "the necessity of hearing and doing the Word," but he does not tell necessary for what. He adds, weakly, "Those to whom [Jesus] feels closest are those who do God's will."

[62] Marshall, *Luke*, 516, regarding Luke 12:9, speaks of "the irrevocable nature of the final rejection of the person in the heavenly court."

[63] This is not to deny that Christians will also be judged in regard to matters that go beyond whether they are saved or lost. Numerous passages speak to this. Even so, salvation is the most fundamental issue at the judgment.

[64] The two—believing and being baptized—go together so closely that the required effect can be stated with the cause, and misunderstanding need not result.

[65] Marshall, *Luke*, 314; he notes that Jesus' command to her to "go in peace" has the "fuller meaning" that is appropriate "in the context of bringing of divine salvation to men in Jesus."

[66] Bock, *Luke*, 157.

[67] Louw and Nida, 1.372.

[68] Marshall, *Luke*, 327.

[69] *TDNT* IV.406. Rengstorf rightly observes that this involves "unconditional commitment" to Jesus (406) and that it "always implies the existence of a personal attachment which shapes the whole life of the one described" (441).

[70] Bock, *Luke*, 159: "Jesus is asking him to become a disciple. ... Levi responds to the invitation, leaving his vocation and financial security behind to follow Jesus." Marshall, *Luke*, 219, appropriately sees this as stressing "his decisive break with his old life."

[71] "At the top of this organized group of disciples stand these twelve men." Bock, *Luke*, 179.

[72] That even the apostles still had their own lives and involvements may be gathered from the fact that Jesus went with Simon Peter to his home, where He healed Peter's mother-in-law (Mark 1:29-31, Matthew 8:14-15, Luke 4:38-39).

[73] Marshall, *Luke*, 219, thinks the call to *follow* Jesus meant "a literal accompanying of Jesus on his travels, although not all disciples were called to do so."

[74] Marshall, *Luke*, 411, thinks the second of these was already a "disciple" whom Jesus was calling "to join his group of closer companions." But this is unlikely, given that (1) the call to follow was fundamentally a call to discipleship and (2) that Jesus bade the man to "go and preach." Bock, *Luke*, 284-285, appears to regard the issue of discipleship as one of salvation: discussing the third excuser he says, "Those who cling to life on earth as it is are not ready for the reformation that salvation brings."

[75] One may argue whether these were ever more than *would-be* disciples, taking the name but not meeting the requirement. If they were disciples for a while, then John appears to imply they ceased to be when they turned back from following Jesus.

[76] The amazing thing is not primarily how many came to identify themselves with Jesus but how many of the Jews did *not*!

Chapter Three

JESUS AND SALVATION IN THE GOSPEL OF JOHN

In the previous chapter, we looked to Jesus as He is presented to us in the Synoptic Gospels. There we hear Him answering the question how one can have eternal life. His response, somewhat oversimplified, is to call us to repentance, to forsake everything, take up a cross, and follow Him in committed discipleship.

We look, now, to the Gospel of John for an answer to the same question. At first reading, at least, we encounter a response that appears to be different from what is found in the Synoptic Gospels.

The Verb *Believe* in John

By far the single most common expression of Jesus (and of the writer of John), on this subject, is the verb *believe*.[1] More than thirty times this verb (*pisteuō*) appears when it refers specifically to faith (the noun does not appear in John) in Jesus.[2] In most of these, if not all, the context is clearly soteriological. There is no room for doubt that this verb often expresses the condition for receiving eternal life. Here are a few of the most telling passages.

- 1:12-13: *Believing* in His name is the condition for becoming children of God and being born of God. Yet this believing apparently has implications for one's way of life.[3] Leon Morris quotes W. Turner, "The sense must be that the believer throws himself upon his Lord in loving, self-abandoning faith and trust," adding that "if one believes God one acts on that belief," and that "when we believe we yield ourselves up to be possessed by Him in whom we believe."[4]

- 3:14-36: At least four times in this chapter (vv. 15, 16, 18, 36) Jesus or John says that anyone believing in Him will have eternal life, adding pointedly that such a one is not going to be condemned, while the one not believing has been condemned already (v. 18).[5] Interestingly, in verse 36, not believing becomes, literally, "not persuaded" or disobeying, which is thus the opposite of faith: "If faith in the Son is the only way to inherit eternal life, and is commanded by God himself, then failure to trust him is as much disobedience as unbelief."[6] "Those who believe do in fact obey the Son."[7]
- 6:40, 47: Jesus affirms that God's will is that every person who is beholding the Son and believing in Him will have eternal life, reiterating that this is the case for the one believing.
- 11:25-26: to Martha Jesus said, "I am the resurrection, and the life: the one believing in me, even if he dies, will live: And everyone who lives and believes in me will never die." "The moment a man puts his trust in Jesus he begins to experience that life of the age to come which cannot be touched by death."[8]
- 20:31: John draws his Gospel toward a conclusion by stating his purpose in writing: namely, that the readers may believe in Jesus Messiah, Son of God, and as a result of believing may have life. While some interpret this as addressed to Christians in behalf of maintaining their faith, others view this as evangelistic.[9] Either way, it is clear that faith is the condition for salvation: "Reading this programmatic purpose statement ought to send the reader back to the preceding narrative in order to ... ponder once more what it means to have faith in Jesus and hence to have life in his name."[10]

Other passages say essentially the same thing, clearly representing spiritual salvation as by faith.[11] Even so, the faith is not *mere* belief. Keener comments, "Throughout the Gospel, many people become initial believers, but their initial faith proves insufficient. ... John's goal is not simply initial faith but persevering faith, *discipleship* (8:30-32; 15:4-7)."[12] I will return to this below. If Keener is right, this has implications for understanding the Synoptic Gospels and the Gospel of John together.

Other Expressions of the Way to Eternal Life in John

Other actions are placed on a par with believing and likewise stand as ways of expressing what one must do to be saved. Interestingly, all of them use verb forms.

1. Twice, *receiving* Jesus is equated with believing in Him. These are in 1:12 and 13:20.[13] Those who *received* Him, according to John, were given the right to become children of God. According to Jesus, to *receive* Him amounts to *receiving* the Father who sent Him. As Carson observes, when faith "yields allegiance to the Word, trusts him completely, acknowledges his claims and confesses him with gratitude," this "is what it means to 'receive' him."[14]

2. In the well-known conversation with Nicodemus (3:1-21), Jesus clearly expressed the requirement that one must be "born again"—or "born from above"[15]—in order to "see" the Kingdom of God (v. 3). Regeneration (as the new birth is expressed in traditional terms) is certainly a requirement for eternal life. But Jesus does not say what Nicodemus, or anyone else, must do in order to be born again.

He *does* say that one must "be born of water and spirit," but it is not clear that this provides any clue as to what requirement a person must meet. There is more than one way to interpret this somewhat enigmatic statement. Some think the water indicates baptism; some think it metaphorically represents the Word of God. I am more inclined to the view that it refers to one's natural birth and thus parallels the contrast, in the following verse, between being born of flesh and of spirit. Regardless, unless it does refer to baptism—which seems unlikely—it does not specify anything a human must do.

Still, it seems significant in this very context[16] that Jesus speaks directly in verses 14-18 about the necessity of *believing* in Him in order to obtain eternal life, as discussed above. Likewise, in 1:12-13 being born of God is the experience of those who *believe* in His name. One is left with the clear implication that faith is required for the new birth.

3. Especially intriguing is the fact that Jesus chose, more than once, to represent the requirement for being saved by the metaphor of *eating* or *drinking*.

The first of these comes in His interaction with the woman at the well just outside the Samaritan city of Sychar. After the preliminary interchanges He says (4:13-14): "Everyone drinking of this water [in the well] will thirst again; but whoever *drinks* of the water that I will give him will by no means thirst forever, but the water that I will give him will become in him a spring of water bubbling up into eternal life."

The second is in 6:53-58, in a lengthy discourse (vv. 22-59) that apparently is part of Jesus' teaching (in Capernaum) about Himself as the bread of life. Among other things, Jesus says: "Unless you *eat* the flesh of the Son of Man and *drink* his blood, you do not have life in yourselves. The one *eating* my flesh and *drinking* my blood has eternal life, and I will raise him at the last day … The one *eating* my flesh and *drinking* my blood will remain in me and I in him … The one *eating* me, even that one will live by me … The one *eating* this bread will live forever."

A third time is in a similar discourse identified as on the final day of a Feast of Tabernacles in Jerusalem,[17] when Jesus said (7:37-38): "If anyone is thirsting, let him *come to me and drink*. The one *believing* in me, as the Scripture said, from his belly will flow rivers of living water." Then John adds an explanatory note (v. 39): "But this he spoke of the Spirit, whom the ones believing in him were going to receive: for the Holy Spirit was not yet given; because Jesus was not yet glorified."

As to the meaning of these metaphorical affirmations, some things seem clear; one being that the same essential meaning is at the root of them all. As one might expect, some interpret them, especially the second (6:53-58), as sacramental, referring to the bread and wine of the Eucharist.[18] That, I think, is to confuse the symbol with the real thing, and Jesus really meant that one must partake of Himself—and of His truth and redemptive work—in order to be saved. The woman in Sychar must imbibe, for the thirst of her soul, what Jesus alone could give her in the truth He spoke and the salvation life He offered. Those in Capernaum must seek not the bread He divided to the 5,000 on the other side of Galilee but the provision He was making for them in His own life and impending death. At the feast in Jerusalem, when the booths would remind the Jews of God's provision for them in the wilderness and the ritual drawing and pouring out of water was highlighted, Jesus pointed them to Himself as the source of the water of life.

For the most part, the commentators have little to say about *how* one thus partakes of Jesus' saving work and life-giving Spirit, perhaps because they focus on other issues. Morris sees in the metaphor in 6:53 "a very graphic way of saying that men must take Christ into their innermost being," adding that the words contain "a cryptic allusion to the atoning death that Christ would die, together with a challenge to enter the closest and most intimate relation with Him."[19] He does not say how this is to be done. Keener, on 6:53-58, thinks Jesus "probably refers ... to embracing his death."[20] We are left to assume that he means by faith.

In fact, the last of the three passages turns the metaphor into the concrete language of *believing* in Jesus. Just so does one "come and drink," and in this way the *how* is defined. "To come to Jesus and drink is to believe."[21] That passage also adds an important dimension to the whole by clarifying that the presence of the Holy Spirit of God with the one believing explains the metaphor of the flowing water of life, no doubt the same as the bubbling spring or fountain in 4:14.[22]

Then none of this changes what was already clear: *believing* in Jesus is what a human being must do to be saved. Tenney observes, "Belief, in turn, is defined as one's coming to Jesus. 'Let him come unto me and drink' and 'he that believeth' are practically synonymous terms."[23] Carson agrees, emphasizing that verses 54 and 40 are parallel: "The conclusion is obvious: the former [eating and drinking Jesus' flesh and blood] is the metaphorical way of referring to the latter [looking to and believing in Jesus]."[24]

4. There are some words of Jesus to the effect that *hearing* His word is essential to eternal life. In 5:24, He says, "The one *hearing* my word, and believing on the one who sent me, has everlasting life, and will not come into condemnation: but has passed from death to life." In Jesus' discourse on the Good Shepherd He avers, "My sheep *hear* my voice, and I know them, and they follow me: And I give to them eternal life" (10:27-28). In 12:47, Jesus characterizes the unbeliever as one who *hears* His words and does not *believe*.

The focus on the necessity for hearing need not complicate the requirement: *hearing* is simply a necessary prelude to *believing*. Two of the three passages explicitly link the two. Indeed, the linkage may be stronger than this. On 5:24, for example, Carson says, "Hearing in this context, as often elsewhere, includes belief and obedience," which reflects his view that the hearing here (as in 8:47) is the *result* of belonging to God.[25] But the way hearing and believing are linked together, and linked to the possession of eternal life in this verse, seems more likely to refer to the *condition* for salvation. Carson's construction comes close to saying that the one who has been given the gift of eternal life hears and believes, and that seems different from what Jesus was saying.[26]

It is true, of course, that in its most pregnant sense hearing approaches believing; this is especially true in 10:27-28, when *hear* has essentially the meaning *hearken to* (in faith): that is, to hearken to Jesus' "summons"[27] to follow Him. At the same time,

12:47 makes clear there can be mere hearing without coming to faith: "without obeying," as Keener appropriately defines it.[28] Carson calls this "superficial faith,"[29] although the words "and believe not" hardly justify calling it faith at all. Indeed, verse 48 makes clear that rejection of Jesus and His words is the same as hearing and not believing.

In each instance, the extent of the hearing must be discerned from the context. Meanwhile, it is clear that a sympathetic hearing leads to faith: "Faith comes by hearing, and hearing by the word of God" (Romans 10:17).

5. Jesus also sometimes represents the requirement for eternal life as *coming to* Him. In 5:40, for example, He says, "You are not willing to come to me, in order that you may have life"—which "stresses the activity of the will."[30] In 6:35, 37: "I am the bread of life: the one coming to me will never hunger; and the one believing in me shall never thirst. ... The one coming to me I will in no wise cast out." In 7:37 (as discussed above): "If anyone thirsts, let him come to me and drink."

Again, this need not confuse us about the condition for eternal life; to come to Jesus is simply another way of expressing what it means to *believe* in Him: "to accept his claims and believe in him."[31] In 6:35 (as in 7:37), coming and believing are parallel.[32] Even so, coming to Him means *truly* believing: "In the whole of John's theology, true 'coming' to Jesus implies more than initial faith, for it demands perseverance."[33] Morris notes (on 6:35) that this "stresses the movement ... into all that association that Christ means, ... '*come* with the whole needy personality.'"[34]

6. On one occasion (10:9) Jesus uses the verb *enter* as a way of expressing the condition of salvation: "I am the door: by me if anyone enters, he will be saved, and will go in and out, and find pasture." But this is explained by the fact that Jesus figuratively represents Himself as the door to the Father's sheepfold. So to *believe* in Him is obviously the means of "entrance."

Whether this refers to our salvation at all is perhaps to be debated, given that it is easy enough to equate "saved," here as "safe" in the fold from the threats of predators, for example. But Keener may be right in suggesting that this is the eschatological salvation God promised His own flock."[35]

7. In the great discourse on the bread of life in John 6, already discussed above, we meet what at first glance may seem to suggest that one *works* for salvation. There, in the context of the metaphor of food, Jesus recalls they had eaten of the miraculous loaves fed to the 5,000 and then admonishes, "*Work* not for the food that perishes but for the food that abides into eternal life, which the Son of Man

will give you" (v. 27). To this, the listeners responded (v. 28), "What are we to do that we may *work* the *works* of God?" Jesus' answer was plain: "This is the *work* of God, that you *believe* in the one whom he sent."[36]

But this is far from teaching salvation by works. In the first place, the verb *work* (*ergazomai*) grows out of the metaphor: Jesus is contrasting the bodily food people *work* for with the eternal life to which they ought to devote their efforts. The hearers pick up on this and ask their question using the same terminology, and Jesus answers in those terms. Then, and most important, He translates the metaphor: they will pursue eternal life by *believing* in Him as the one whom God sent to reveal the way of life. Morris notes that the one *work* that Jesus commends is faith, and Jesus calls it a work because it is "that which God requires of men."[37]

On any reading, this passage does not teach salvation by works: "Faith ... is what God requires, not 'works' in any modern sense of the term, ... making this 'work of God' diametrically opposed to what Paul means by 'the works of the law.'"[38]

8. We saw in our survey of the Synoptic Gospels that to *follow* Jesus was a way of expressing the response of one called to be a disciple. Although not so common in John, that same verb (*akoloutheō*) appears in some of Jesus' summons to eternal life. In 8:12, for example, Jesus says, "I am the light of the world: the one *following* me will by no means walk in the darkness, but will have the light of life." Surely to walk in darkness is a clear (if metaphorical) way of describing the life of the unsaved; and having "the light of life" describes the life of the disciple, now spiritually enlightened and alive. The condition for this is *following* Jesus.

The same verb appears in 10:27-28 (as above): "My sheep hear my voice ... and *follow* me: And I give to them eternal life." The words sound more like a statement about the characteristics of one who is already a believer; but the linking of the gift of eternal life should cause us not to be too hasty in discarding the implication that this is a condition for eternal life.[39]

To some in attendance at the final Passover of His ministry, Jesus said, "If anyone serves me, let him *follow* me; and where I am, there will also my servant be: if anyone serves me, my Father will honor him" (12:26).

These assertions need not cause us to abandon the idea that *believing* in Jesus is *the* condition for receiving eternal life. They may cause us, however, to understand the nature of this faith more clearly, and in a way that harmonizes with the emphasis of the Synoptic Gospels: the faith that saves is a faith that heeds the call to discipleship.

9. A couple of times, in the so-called Upper Room Discourse with the disciples at the Last Supper, Jesus may equate *loving* Him with meeting the condition for eternal life. Thus in 14:15 He says, "If you love me, keep my commandments," expanding on this in verse 21: "The one who has my commandments and keeps them, that is the one who loves me: and the one who loves me will be loved by my Father, and I will love him, and will manifest myself to him." At the end, the promises in this verse seem at least to include the promise of an eternal presence with God.

But to read this in terms of our question—what must one do to have eternal life?—may be stretching. Keener is probably right in saying, "What Jesus describes here is not a formula—it is far too circular for that—but the pattern for a developing relationship."[40]

Even so, it is interesting that loving Jesus is defined as obeying Him, and that Jesus "is revealed only to those who love and obey him" (v. 21).[41] As stated in the previous chapter, to *love*, in the Bible, is to choose the object of one's love over other possibilities. So to love Jesus is to choose His directions for one's life. No doubt, this is believing Him; but believing the directions of the Lord of one's life is to choose to follow those directions. As Carson comments, this linkage of love and obedience "approaches the level of definition."[42]

10. Perhaps we can group together two more verbs Jesus links to His message in a way that at least sometimes appears to speak of the condition for salvation. I have already mentioned, above, *hearing* His words. Now we can add to this the necessity of *remaining* or *abiding* or *continuing* in His word, thus treating a verb (*menō*) frequently highlighted in John. Morris observes, "believing and abiding … clearly mean much the same," and "abiding in Christ which is stressed in the opening verses of ch. 15 is practically equivalent to believing."[43]

In 8:31 (as above), Jesus said to some Jews who "believed" in Him: "If you *continue* in my word, then are you my disciples indeed; and you will know the truth, and the truth will make you free."[44] Here *abiding* or *continuing* in His word may define genuine faith in contrast to the superficial belief reflected in their objection to Jesus' implications. "It is important that they be led to see what real faith means."[45] "Keener insists that belief without perseverance in "true discipleship" is not saving faith.[46]

This same verb is prominent in the well-known parable of the vine and branches (John 15), where Jesus appeals to His disciples to *abide* in Him (vv. 4-7, several times), links with it the condition that His words *abide* in them (v. 7), and urges that they *abide* (or *continue*) in His love.

Does this speak of a condition of eternal life? Probably the general tendency of interpreters is to answer in the negative. Typical is Morris, who observes, "To abide in Christ is the necessary prerequisite of fruitfulness for the Christian."[47] Perhaps some interpreters are unwilling to read any condition of salvation into this simply because they are convinced that individual apostasy from saving faith is not possible. But verse 6 sounds a serious warning to those who do not abide in Christ. Morris takes note of the "strong words," rendering them as being "thrown out," branches that "wither away," "are gathered and burnt"—adding that their fate is "not known" and concluding that this "emphasizes the necessity of remaining in vital contact with Christ if fruitfulness is to continue."[48] I am more inclined to think verse 6 is a broader warning to anyone who does not "abide" in Christ, and so to regard the expression as a condition for eternal life that means the same thing, at root, as a *being-in-union* with Christ by faith.

Köstenberger is not saying the same thing, but I appreciate the implications of his observations on 8:31. "The measure of any disciple is the ability to hold to the master's teaching"; and, "The reference to being 'truly' Jesus' disciples implies that there is in Johannine thought such a thing as false (or temporary) disciples, that is, people who follow a teaching only for a season"[49]—to which he compares the parable of the sower and soils. I would add that these "temporary disciples" in John were never real disciples, so that eternal life is involved in what Jesus is saying here, after all. Carson is on the right track to indicate that this "holding to" Jesus' teachings is "exactly what it is that separates spurious faith from true faith, fickle disciples from genuine disciples. ... In short, perseverance [continuing in Jesus' word] is the mark of true faith."[50]

In 15:10 Jesus adds, "If you keep my commandments, ye will *abide* in my love," which brings us to the verb *keep* (*tereō*).[51] Morris calls keeping Jesus' commandments "simple obedience" and "a means of abiding in His love"[52]—which I assume he can say only if he takes "abiding in His love" to refer to something other than remaining saved, perhaps to what Köstenberger calls "the close-knit relationship that Jesus desires with his disciples."[53] Carson seems to take the text more seriously, acknowledging forthrightly "obedience is the condition of continuously remaining in Jesus' love" after saying (on v. 9) that Jesus expresses His love "as a completed thing, so imminently does the cross stand in view."[54] I would suggest that anyone who is not "abiding" in the redemptive love of Jesus that culminated in the cross does not, in fact, possess eternal life.[55] Keener maintains that love is both the result and condition for abiding in Christ.[56]

The verb appears again in 8:51: "If a man *keeps* my saying (*logos*, word), he will never see death." Here Morris cites Calvin as saying "Christ promises eternal life to His disciples, but demands disciples who will not merely nod their assent like donkeys, or profess with the tongue that they approve His teaching, but who will keep it as a precious treasure"[57]—which seems to recognize more perceptively the soteriological implications. Köstenberger appropriately equates *keeping* Jesus' word, here, with *abiding* in His word (8:31).[58] Carson agrees and paraphrases, "keeps his word, *i.e.* believes it, cleaves to it, obeys and lives by it"; he adds "after all, Jesus has the words of eternal life" and approvingly cites Beasley-Murray to say that the assurance Jesus gives here "relates to life which physical death cannot extinguish."[59] The issue of final salvation is clear.

In 14:23-24 Jesus gives us both sides of this truth in a manner that makes them direct opposites (and so sounds much like 1 John 3:7-8): a person who loves Him *keeps* His sayings (*logous*, words), while one who does not love Him does not do so. Whether focusing on *love* or *keep*, this is obedience; and if this loving obedience is not a condition, it is a *necessary* evidence of salvation and marks the difference between those who have eternal life and those who are forever lost. Carson speaks of Jesus' "frank links" between "personal devotion to Christ that breeds obedience and therefore moral probity" and John's "candid report of Jesus' promise that Christians will *experience* God."[60]

At least some of these sayings with *abide* and *keep* appear to speak about how to obtain eternal life. Do they contradict the condition of *believing* that is so much more prominent in John? Surely, they do not, but they add an important dimension to our understanding of what *believing* in Christ, and in His message, really means. There is no faith to affect a being-in-union with Christ apart from loving observance of His teaching.

Indications in John That Saving Faith Is More Than Mere Belief

We are assured that Jesus, as reported in John, would answer that *believing* is what one must do to have eternal life. Even so, there are some clear indications in this Gospel that the believing that qualifies as saving faith has a fullness of meaning that may well approach the requirement of discipleship He states so forcefully in the Synoptic Gospels.

1. For one thing, even when *believing* is the key word, the context often indicates it is pregnant with implications of commitment and obedience. The comments of the interpreters I have quoted above make this clear; one may review them to underline this point. They need not be repeated here, except to emphasize their conclusions that faith *necessarily* involves obedience, a commitment to a way of life, the abandoning of self, a yielding up of oneself to be possessed by Jesus, the way one thinks, lives, and acts. This is, in other words, true discipleship.

2. There is also the implication of some of the other verbs discussed above, (especially items 8-10): *following* Jesus, *loving* Him, and *abiding in* and *keeping* His word (the condition of being a true disciple, 8:31). These, too, may be read again to see that, while believing really is what one must do to have eternal life, this believing is not some sterile "decision" to trust Christ as one's Savior. These are ways the faith that saves expresses itself and can be distinguished from mere belief.

3. A key to understanding that faith is more than mere belief is the fact that both Jesus and John use *believing* in such a way as to allow us to distinguish mere belief from genuine, saving faith. All the interpreters I read, in one way or another, appear to recognize this distinction.

There are instances in John when the verb *believe* (*pisteuō*) does *not* denote genuine, saving faith. Some possible examples are:

- 2:23: In Jerusalem, at Passover during the first year of Jesus' ministry, "many *believed* in his name, when they saw the miracles which he did." The very next verse adds, "But Jesus did not commit [entrust] himself to them" because He knew them.[61] "Their faith was spurious, and Jesus knew it."[62] Keener observes, on this verse that "signs-faith, unless it progresses to discipleship, is inadequate."[63]

- 4:39: Many Samaritans *believed* in Jesus because of what the woman at the well said, but then they subsequently informed her they no longer believed for that reason (v. 42), perhaps meaning for that reason alone. Keener may be right to view the first as "initial faith" and the latter as "a firsthand faith which characterizes true disciples."[64] At least in the latter case their faith included understanding that Jesus was the Savior of the world.

- 8:30: In response to Jesus' "light of the world" discourse, "many *believed* in him" as He was speaking. John adds that Jesus proceeded to speak to the Jews who "had believed," urging that those who abide in His word are truly His disciples and will know and be set free by the truth. They objected to this. Köstenberger says, appropriately, this faith is "shallow," and "what is required for lasting discipleship is not merely immediate assent, but continued adherence to Jesus' word."[65] This "word" is apparently the call to discipleship and eternal life.
- 10:42: When Jesus spent some time where John first baptized, people resorted to Him, speaking highly of His miracles and recognizing what John had said about Him was true; and many "*believed* in him there." But this "does not necessarily imply lasting success on Jesus' part in eliciting faith."[66]
- 11:45: Many Jews, coming to Mary (at the time of Lazarus' death and resurrection) and seeing the things Jesus did, "*believed* in him." Carson notes, wryly enough: "The caliber of their faith (*cf.* 2:23-24; 8:30-31) is not discussed."[67]

It seems likely that in some of these, at least (and perhaps a few others[68]), the verb means something more akin to taking one's claims seriously, to being convinced that what Jesus said was true and He really did exercise supernatural powers.[69] Leon Morris seems to credit this level of belief more than I would, saying (in commenting on 11:45) that a faith "based on miracles is not the highest faith but it is accepted throughout this Gospel as better than no faith at all."[70] He also says (on 2:23) that such faith is not "profound" and is "no more than a beginning."[71]

4. There is, finally, at least one time in the Gospel of John when Jesus might be interpreted to answer our question—what must one do to have eternal life?—in a way that sounds like salvation by works. In the observations growing out of the healing of the lame man at the pool called Bethesda (5:28-29), He speaks of the universal resurrection to come: "All that are in the graves will hear his voice and come forth; they who have done good, unto the resurrection of life; and they who have done evil, unto the resurrection of damnation."

One might be tempted to object to this saying were it not for the fact it is precisely in accord with so much of what the Bible says: namely, that the righteous will be with God forever and the wicked will be eternally separated from Him in

Hell. We could hardly criticize Jesus—if we dared on other grounds!—for saying what is, in fact, biblically commonplace.

The interpreters do various things with this. Keener, for example, first dulls the edge of what Jesus said by observing, "For John, those who do works in God embrace Christ and those whose works are evil are those who reject his light"—as though the doing of good and evil is not the basis of judgment after all. Then, more on target, he notes the idea that God will judge according to each one's *deeds* "was a commonplace of both early Jewish and Christian teaching, rooted in their common biblical heritage."[72] Carson treats different approaches, first referring to C. K. Barrett's view that these are all *unbelievers* who are divided into doers of good and doers of evil—apparently for different levels of judgment, a view Carson rejects. He also rightly rejects the idea that verses 27-28 were not original with John. His own view is that those who have done good, in the context of John here, "are those who have come to the light so that it may be plainly seen that what they have done they have done through God." He insists, "John is not juxtaposing salvation by works with salvation by faith"[73]—an insistence that none of us could deny. Köstenberger seems more loyal to the text: "The division will take place on the basis of what people have "done." He explains, "Because believing often proves superficial, a person is to be judged by what he or she does, not merely says." Yet he too insists—appropriately, no doubt—that "This does not amount to salvation by works; rather, the life that one lives forms 'the test of the faith they profess.'"[74] Here he is citing Morris, who is equally confident that "Salvation is by grace and it is received through faith. Judgment is based on men's works."[75]

Without disagreeing with Köstenberger or Morris, I feel constrained to say their solution reads just a little more into Jesus' words than is really there. In the first place, this is *not* a judgment of works that is different from whether a person is saved or lost, as though among believers (and likewise among the lost) the judgment of works assigns different recognition. There may well be such a judgment, but Jesus is speaking about the basis for those who are raised to eternal life versus those who are raised to eternal damnation. The issue here is final destiny, Heaven versus Hell.

In the second place, the basis of the difference is *doing good* versus *doing evil*. To be sure, those who do good are believers and those who do evil are unbelievers. But the construction these interpreters place on the words makes Jesus say, in essence, that those who have put faith in Him (and manifested the evidence of it in good works) will be saved, while those who have rejected Him (and manifested that rejection in evil works) will be lost. As true as that is, it is not exactly what Jesus said; He could easily have said that, had it been His focus.

In other words, the problem with this "insider knowledge" approach to interpreting Jesus is that doing good becomes *merely* the result of faith and faith becomes the *real* (though unspoken) basis of the judgment. In this way we avoid taking what Jesus said at face value. In fact, if we take Jesus to mean what He said, it most certainly sounds like those who inherit eternal life are those who have done good things—and this is the grounds of their salvation. As soon as we start down that road we are met hard by the fact that otherwise, pervading this whole Gospel, the focus is on *faith*: people are saved because they *believe* in Jesus.

The solution to this dilemma that makes best sense, and takes *all* Jesus said at face value, is to bring *believing* and *doing good* into a relationship where the one essentially equals the other. This must not mean that faith and good works are *two* conditions for eternal life, else saying the latter just once (in this Gospel), compared to the former more than a score of times, leaves one thinking Jesus often spoke less than the whole truth—an unacceptable idea.

That is the question, then: can we understand the relationship between faith and acts of obedience in such a way they are two ways of viewing what is at root the same thing? If we can, Jesus' words in 5:28-29 will be better interpreted. In subsequent chapters, we will return to this. Meanwhile, this kind of understanding does seem possible, and all the preceding observations I have made point in this direction. After all, faith is a believing response to whatever God says. If God says we should do certain things, then doing those things is the exercise of faith. If I claim belief in Jesus, disobeying Him would put the lie to my claim. Even so, this leaves us with a number of questions, not least of all why that kind of obedience is not the same as the "works" the New Testament—Paul, especially—so clearly denounces as the grounds of our saving relationship with God. That question, with other related ones, remains to be addressed more fully.

For now, it is more than clear that Jesus, as represented accurately in the Gospel of John, assuredly taught that eternal life depends on *believing* in Him. In this much, we may say that Jesus and Paul were agreed, even though neither Jesus nor John drew out the full theological implications we find in Paul. At the same time, this Gospel also includes some pointers in the direction of understanding that faith necessarily expresses itself in actions. These may well make it possible to avoid some sort of bifurcation between the teaching of Jesus in the Synoptic Gospels and what He says about the way of salvation in John.

In other words, salvation is by faith in Jesus (John), and this faith includes a positive response to His call to discipleship (the Synoptics). Jesus is the source of both of those teachings, and they are not finally two different teachings but different words for the same thing. I take Keener's observations to make a similar point: namely, the faith that saves is "the proper response to God's revelation, a faithful embracing of his truth … a conviction of truth on which one stakes one's life and actions, not merely passive assent to a fact."[76] He argues that to read such passages as these as though saving faith is "passive" and does not require active, persevering obedience, is to read them in a "modern" light that is utterly foreign to the context in John. He adds to this, in a note, his approval of a citation to the effect that Johannine faith is "a way of life."[77] Belief that is less than this is apparently not faith and does not save.

ENDNOTES

[1] Merrill C. Tenney entitled his commentary *John: The Gospel of Belief* (Grand Rapids: Eerdmans, 1951).

[2] Craig S. Keener, *The Gospel of John: A Commentary* (2 vols.; Peabody, Mass.: Hendrickson, 2003), 1.326, reports that the verb appears 98 times in John, in comparison to 30 times in the three Synoptics combined and 54 times in Paul's writings.

[3] H. Ridderbos, *The Gospel According to John*, trans. J. Vriend (Grand Rapids: Eerdmans, 1997), 45, observes that in context this means believers who "went against the current, who broke with the general pattern by which the world thinks, lives, and acts."

[4] Leon Morris, *The Gospel According to John* (NICNT; Grand Rapids: Eerdmans, 1971), 99 (n. 75), 100.

[5] In context, faith in v. 15 is, specifically, faith "in the *crucified* Jesus" (Keener, 1.563, italics mine). Morris, 232, notes that the death of Jesus "does not automatically bring salvation. No man is saved unless he believes."

[6] D. A. Carson, *The Gospel According to John* (Pillar NTC; Grand Rapids: Eerdmans, 1991), 214.

[7] Morris, 248.

[8] Morris, 550.

[9] For discussion of this, see Carson, 661-62; Morris, 855-56; Keener 2.1215-16.

[10] Andreas Köstenberger, *John* (ECNT; Grand Rapids: Baker, 2004), 582. Morris, 856: "Faith is fundamental, and John longs to see men believe."

[11] Interesting that in each of these the verb *believe* is in the present tense—which may have some significance in that the constructions are not in the indicative mood and require the speaker to make a choice of tenses rather than falling back on the aorist as the default tense. By choosing the present tense, the author views the action from the perspective of action-in-progress. In the

context of this Gospel (and the entire New Testament), we are probably justified in thinking that such statements imply ongoing faith.

[12] Keener, 2.1216 (italics mine). He adds that "John's purpose is to address believers at a lesser stage of discipleship and to invite them to persevere as true disciples." I take him to mean that the "lesser discipleship" is not real discipleship and does not rest on genuine faith.

[13] Tenney, 69 (on 1:12): "The redundant grammatical construction ... serves to make all the clearer the fact that receiving and believing are equivalent terms."

[14] Carson, 125-26.

[15] The Greek adverb (*anōthen*) can mean either; since both are true, it does not seem crucial to make a certain determination (if that were possible) as to which Jesus intended. See the careful discussion in Keener, 1.537-39.

[16] One finds it difficult to be absolutely sure how far, in this passage, the words of Jesus extend: whether all the way to v. 21 or to some point prior to that, like v. 19 or v. 16. But even if some of the elucidation is directly from John, the inspired author correctly puts these words in the context of the conversation about the new birth.

[17] Whether on the seventh or eighth day need not occupy us here.

[18] For a thorough discussion, see Carson, 296-98.

[19] Morris, 378-79.

[20] Keener, 1.688.

[21] Morris, 423.

[22] Interpreters are divided over whether the one from whose belly the living water flows is Christ or the believer. That need not be pursued here. For discussion see Morris, 423-25; Carson, 323-25.

[23] Tenney, 135.

[24] Carson, 297.

[25] Carson, 256, as also on 10:27 (393).

[26] Carson's view may reflect his Calvinism, but my purpose in this work does not include pursuit of the differences between Calvinism and (Reformation) Arminianism.

[27] Keener, 1.825, uses this word to indicate what the hearing is a response to. Köestenberger, 311, renders "listen to."

[28] Keener, 2.888.

[29] Carson, 452.

[30] Morris, 331.

[31] Köstenberger, 193.

[32] Morris, 366, notes this parallel and says that the coming "indicates another facet of the same essential process." Köstenberger, 210, may draw too precise a line when he defines "coming" and "believing," respectively, as the definition of "eat my flesh" and "drink my blood" in 6:54; but the general parallelism is correct.

[33] Keener, 1.684. See note 77 for further comment about Keener's emphasis on perseverance.

[34] Morris, 366, citing Wright.

[35] Keener, 1.811.

[36] My translation brings out the repetition of the verb and noun for *work*.

[37] Morris, 360. Köstenberger, 208, is right to put Jesus' words in contrast to "people's apparent confidence that they are able to meet the demands of God."

[38] Carson, 285.

[39] Tenney, 167, lists the elements of vv. 27-28 as "the nature of true believers," observing also that these qualities "distinguish believers from unbelievers, and are both the basis and the result of belief."

[40] Keener, 2.972.

[41] Keener, 2.975.

[42] Carson, 498.

[43] Morris, 336.

[44] That there were objections to this probably means that some who "believed" in Him did so without essential understanding. On this verse see above.

[45] Morris, 455. He goes on (456) to say that by this Jesus "is not laying down a condition of discipleship, but telling them in what discipleship consists." He may be right, but the promise to know the truth and thereby be set free (v. 32) may indicate otherwise.

[46] Keener, 1.747.

[47] Morris, 671.

[48] Morris, 671.

[49] Köstenberger, 261.

[50] Carson, 348. He would, of course, make this absolute; but that perseverance in keeping the teachings of Jesus is the mark of true faith does not rule out the possibility of swerving from that faith and obedience. After all, this is the *conditional* part of the sentence. Like Carson, Stanley, *Did Jesus Teach?*, 257, is convinced that only those who persevere to the end were ever truly saved. That this may go beyond the evidence obtained from exegesis of the passages is beyond the scope of my treatment here.

[51] Morris, 468 (n. 102) notes that this verb occurs 18 times in John, 7 in 1 John, and 11 in Revelation, whereas it appears no more than 8 times in any other New Testament book.

[52] Morris, 673.

[53] Köstenberger, 453; he agrees (456) that the disciples must obey Jesus' commands in order to "remain" in His love.

[54] Carson, 520.

[55] Whether such a person has ever been a Christian I will not argue here.

[56] Keener, 2.1002-03. My purpose for this volume does not include serious pursuit of the differences between interpreters who do not believe apostasy from saving faith is possible and those who do. I do not know Keener's position on that issue, but in this statement he appears to show awareness of the fact that continuing faith is required for continuing salvation, and that this faith is marked by continuing obedience.

[57] Morris, 468, n. 102.

[58] Köstenberger, 269-70.

[59] Carson, 355.

[60] Carson, 504-05. (Italics original.)

[61] The verb *commit* is the same (*pisteuō*) as *believe*, thus illustrating the possibility of very different levels of "faith."

[62] Carson, 184.

[63] Keener, 1.531, also 1.277. Köstenberger, 115-16, speaks of this as "dubious belief" that "was not trusted by Jesus," adding that readers are "quickly cautioned" that the inference these are God's children "is not necessarily warranted." John 20:30-31 may contradict Keener in some measure; it at least shows that the faith that responds to signs may indeed be genuine.

[64] Keener, 1.626.

[65] Köstenberger, 261.

[66] Köstenberger, 318.

[67] Carson, 419.

[68] Keener, 1.746, lists 2:23; 7:31; 10:42; 11:45; 12:11, 42 as places where John reports that many "believed" in Jesus, "but at least in many of these cases this faith proves inadequate to persevere for salvation." He notes (1.277) that in 4:50, 53 John "explicitly distinguishes two levels of faith ... though the second only *implies* discipleship." (Italics original.)

[69] Tenney, 85, 146, refers to the "faith" in 2:23 as "superficial," and of that in 8:30 he says its "sincerity and depth ... may be questioned." I find it interesting that in each of these five instances the verb *believe* is aorist tense in Greek, in contrast to the usual present tense of the verb in John. But this may not be significant (and I did not select them for that reason), given that each is a historical report of what happened and the aorist tense is the one used in such contexts without giving any special attention to the aspect or perspective of the action. Carson, 662, observes, "It can easily be shown that John ... can use *either* tense to refer to *both* coming to faith and continuing in the faith." (Italics original.)

[70] Morris, 563.

[71] Morris, 205-06.

[72] Keener, 1.655.

[73] Carson, 258.

[74] Köstenberger, 189-90.

[75] Morris, 322. Stanley, *Did Jesus Teach?*, emphasizes that such passages refer to "salvation" in a specifically futuristic sense, meaning "righteousness that admits anyone into eternity" (197-98) at the judgment. As true as this may be, it is too easy to make this different from what is required for present salvation.

[76] Keener, 1.327.

[77] Keener, 1.570. If he includes in this description the implication that those who are saved will never turn away from following Christ, then that assumes a conclusion I think is not in evidence. But he is right that saving faith, so long as it continues, is a faith that perseveres in the discipleship "way of life."

Chapter Four

DISCIPLESHIP, FAITH, AND SIN IN 1 JOHN

The preceding chapter has explored the Gospel of John for Jesus' (and John's) answer to the question, What must I do to have eternal life? The answer that pervades that Gospel is *believing* in Jesus Christ. Even so, the survey has shown this faith must be understood as having essential implications for one's way of life. Those implications, in a measure of agreement with the Synoptic Gospels, are that saving faith issues in discipleship.

For a full view of John's theology of salvation, however, we must go on to his epistles.[1] First John, in particular, has a way of developing all of this more pointedly, even though the epistle does not primarily address the question what one must do to obtain eternal life. Instead, the apostle focuses on what a true disciple is and on how to tell the difference between those who falsely and those who truthfully claim to be born of God. Even so, in his description of the latter we find an essential relationship between faith and behavior.

The Role and Nature of Faith in 1 John

In this epistle, as in his Gospel, John leaves us in no doubt that *believing* in Jesus is what one must do to have eternal life. Although the major part of the letter is devoted to more practical instruction, by the time he finishes the final chapter this fundamental soteriological truth is clear:

- "Everyone *believing* that Jesus is the Christ has been born of God" (5:1).
- "Who is the one who overcomes the world, if not the one *believing* that Jesus is the Son of God?" (5:5).
- "The one *believing* in the Son of God has the witness in himself" (5:10).

- "These things have I written to you who *believe* in the name of the Son of God; that you may know that you have eternal life, and that you may *believe* on the name of the Son of God" (5:13).

Even so, First John provides some of the strongest reasons for thinking there is more to saving faith than a mere, intellectual belief in Jesus. We do well, then, to explore more carefully what John meant by faith. As in his Gospel, this epistle expresses this condition *verbally*; only in 5:4 does the noun *faith* occur.

Start with three well-known "tests" of the genuineness of Christian character stated in chapters one and two. (I summarize or paraphrase, rather than translate.) One question is whether these are merely evidences of faith or more closely related to faith than that.

- 1:6-7: If we claim to be in fellowship with God but walk in (spiritual) darkness we are lying. But if we walk in the light (of spiritual understanding) we are in fellowship with one another *and the blood of Jesus Christ His Son cleanses us from all sin*. Indeed, this seems a little stronger than simply saying our walk gives evidence we are in fellowship with God. Surely the first clause, *if we walk in the light*, is a condition for the second, *the blood of Jesus cleanses us from sin*.[2]
- 2:3-5: We know that we know God if we keep His commandments. The one claiming to know Him without keeping His commandments is a liar. Whoever keeps His word, truly in this one the love of God has been brought to perfection or completion. The last clause at least *sounds* conditional, which would mean that by the keeping of God's word the love of God is brought to its full, saving efficacy. This reminds us of what we have found in the Gospel of John.
- 2:9-11: The person who claims to be "in the light" but hates his brother is in (spiritual) darkness. The one loving his brother abides in the light. Again, this sounds like abiding in the light is conditioned on loving one's brother.

It is common to deal with these by viewing them as *evidences* of the genuineness of one's faith. We tend to say a person is saved by faith, not by the way he walks, but the way he walks will give evidence of his faith. Consequently, John is giving us some tests by which we can know whether our faith is really saving faith.

I have no quarrel with this approach, but I wonder if it goes far enough. John appears to link these evidences so closely with faith that they are *essential* to faith. They are *required* evidences. Consequently, on the one hand we do not need to jettison the idea that *faith* is the one condition for salvation. On the other hand, we do not need to strip away from this condition the role of works of obedience as essential to genuine faith.

Some of John's other statements seem appropriate for this understanding. Consider 2:15, for example: "If anyone loves the world, the love of the Father is not in him." At the very least, John apparently means that these two are mutually exclusive. Or 2:17: "The one doing the will of God abides forever." This sounds a lot like John 5:28-29, discussed in the previous chapter, and "doing the will of God" sounds exactly like a condition for eternal life. Unless we think there are two conditions for salvation, then faith and doing the will of God may well be two ways of viewing the same thing.

Does John Mean That Christians Are Sinless?

If John means that the one who has faith in Jesus (and is thereby a genuine disciple of His) does the will of God—or else does not really have faith—does he mean this absolutely? In other words, does he mean a Christian *perfectly* does the will of God (2:17), or *perfectly* loves the Father and other believers (2:10, 15), or *perfectly* keeps God's commandments (2:3-4), or *perfectly* walks in the light (1:7)?

This question becomes most acute when we reach chapter 3, verses 6-9, where these strong pronouncements occur: "Whoever abides in him sins not" (v. 6) and "Everyone who has been born of God does not commit sin" (v. 9). To the latter John adds, with emphasis, "He cannot sin, because he has been born of God" (v. 9). The same affirmation appears again in 5:18: "We know that everyone who has been born of God sins not."[3] By themselves, and taken at face value, these statements raise the question of sinlessness: Did the inspired John intend to say those who are born again live without sin?

Furthermore, these statements occur in an epistle that has apparently already made clear that Christians cannot claim sinlessness. In 1:8 John says, "If we say that we have no sin, we deceive ourselves, and the truth is not in us." Almost repetitiously, he adds in 1:10: "If we say that we have not sinned, we make him a liar, and his word is not in us."[4] Apparently, Daniel Akin is correct to say, "Christians, by definition, believe in Christ and confess their sins. This truth rules out the teaching of perfectionism this side of heaven, that is, that Christians can get to a state where they do not sin in this life."[5] Therefore, John provides for forgiveness and cleansing from a three-fold perspective. First, he grounds this in the redemptive work of Jesus, involving the blood of His atonement (1:7), His propitiatory sacrifice (2:2), and His advocacy (2:1). Second, he conditions this on our confession of sin (1:9). Third, he bases assurance of this on God's faithfulness and justice (1:9).

When these earlier affirmations are placed beside those in chapter three, the difficult affirmations of sinlessness are compounded by the question of contradiction. Marianne Meye Thompson summarizes, "Because of their absolute and emphatic nature, these statements [3:6, 9] pose a great challenge to interpretation. ... They seem both overstated and inconsistent with human experience. And to make matters more complicated, 3:4-10 also seems to contradict earlier statements (1:8, 10) that the denial of sin is a sin in itself."[6] Most interpreters take note of this problem.

We who accept the divine inspiration of the biblical text assume there is no *final* contradiction here, but this does not free us from the obligation to grapple with John's several statements about sin and the Christian. Even commentators firmly committed to the authority of the Scriptures recognize the problem and regard it as a matter worthy of serious exploration. Furthermore, it speaks pointedly to one of the fundamental problems of our existence as disciples of Jesus and to one of my primary interests in this particular work: namely, how do we believers deal with sin in our lives?

Approaches to the Problem

Before discussing at greater length what I view as the correct understanding of 1 John 3:6, 9, I will give some relatively brief attention to the various ways interpreters have dealt with the apparent tension between 1 John 1:8-2:2 and 3:6, 9. Assuming the tension, then, how do the commentators address it?[7]

Attempts to make the sin in chapter 3 something more radical than "ordinary" sins

This approach to 1 John 3:6, 9 can take more than one form. Perhaps the most common one, among some contemporary commentators, is to take John as referring, specifically, to the kind of sin that is identified in 3:4: "Sin is *anomia*" (AV: "the transgression of the law"). Colin Kruse, for example, suggests that the Greek noun *anomia* refers to *rebellion*, particularly the rebellion associated with satanic power and opposition to God: "It is impossible for those born of God to have any part in *anomia*."[8]

In other words, the references to *sin* in this passage—but not earlier in the epistle—must take on the character of this more serious sin of *anomia*. Instead of being a definition of sin, the sentence limits John's meaning for *sin* to willful rebellion against God as a child of the devil. That way, when John continues by saying the person who abides in Christ does not "sin," he means a Christian is not guilty of the kind of rebellious disobedience that characterizes the devil (vv. 8, 10) or those under his sway. On the other hand, when he refers earlier to the sins of a Christian, which one must confess for forgiveness, he means "sin" more generally.

The view of Robert Yarbrough is similar.[9] He defines *anomia* as "transgression so weighty that the perpetrator is outside the pale of Christ's followers."[10] He believes "there is probably a close relationship to 'sin' in this sense and the 'fatal sin' spoken of in 5:16.[11] Commenting on verse 9, Yarbrough maintains that John "speaks rather of types or degrees (or both) of sins that are tantamount to defection from God's people."[12]

For various reasons—only some of which I will mention briefly here—I do not think the approach of Kruse and Yarbrough is helpful or convincing. First, it does not work well to read *anomia* (as a singular, specific type or degree of sin that represents willful rebellion against God, rather than a description of all sin) throughout the passage (2:29-3:10) every time *sin* (*hamartia*) appears. Verse 5 clearly militates against this in affirming that Jesus "was manifested to take away our sins." Surely that refers to all types and degrees of sin, including—as 2:2 has plainly indicated—those that Christians commit! Furthermore, the last line in verse 5 adds, "Sin is not in him [Jesus]." It would be strange to limit this to a certain type or degree of sin called *anomia*. Consequently, if in the next verse (after the sentence in verse 4) *sin* cannot be limited to *anomia* as rebellion, there are no grounds for such a limitation in verses 6 and 9.

Second, the doing of *anomia*, in verse 4, like the doing of *hamartia* throughout, stands in contrast only to the doing of *righteousness*—not to the doing of lesser sins by Christians. Five times in the passage, John uses the verb *do* (*poieō*) with a noun to refer to behavior of people in a class, as follows:

- 2:29: everyone *doing* righteousness has been born of him.
- 3:4: everyone *doing* sin also *does anomia*.

- 3:7: the one *doing* righteousness is righteous.
- 3:8: the one *doing* sin is of the devil.

What seems clear is that these two ways are in direct contrast. The difference is not between people who live right and people who live in a serious kind of sin that is tantamount to apostasy and to be distinguished from more ordinary sins. The difference is between those who do right and those who do sin.

There is no need to take verses 6 and 9 to mean *only* the more serious sins that can be committed by apostates or others who have declared independence of God. *All* sin is rebellion against God, even sins committed by Christians. *All* sin participates in the program of Satan and—consciously or not—manifests his paternity, just as do all lies ("white" ones or otherwise): "He is a liar, and the father of it" (John 8:44).

I. Howard Marshall describes (but does not adopt) a different variety of this approach: namely, that 1 John 3 refers to willful and deliberate sin "as opposed to the involuntary sins and errors into which a Christian may fall without intending consciously to sin against God."[13] In discussing this, he cites John Wesley's view that John means "an actual, voluntary transgression of the law ... acknowledged to be such at the time that it is transgressed."[14] There is, of course, a biblical distinction between willful sins and sins of ignorance, but Marshall is right to reject this solution on three grounds. (1) Even Wesley had to admit that saintly people sometimes commit deliberate, gross sins, so that the text is not universally true; (2) "it is notoriously difficult to distinguish between voluntary and involuntary transgressions"; and (3) "there is no indication that John is working with such a limited definition of the term sin. He is talking about all sin."[15]

Indeed, the Wesleyan view is *not* that all Christians are actually perfect, but only that they *can* reach such a state.[16] Stott, responding to the view that John means only that Christians do not commit willful and deliberate sin, approvingly quotes Robert Candlish: "I dare not persuade myself that I never sin voluntarily."[17] Stott is right, I think, but I will save further treatment of this until dealing with the nature of sin in chapter eight.

Saying Christians do not sin cannot be understood by making *sin* something more serious and damning than ordinary sin. Smalley observes that John does not mean to distinguish between kinds of sin but to refer to any sin.[18]

Attempts to read John's affirmations as idealistic or eschatological

Marshall, after mentioning and rejecting three approaches to the tension between 1 John 1:8-10 and 3:6-10, adopts a fourth: namely, "that what John is depicting here [in chapter 3] is the ideal character of the Christian."[19] This approach, too, can take more than one form. Marshall mentions, as an example, Dean Alford's view that John, in chapter three, is speaking "of the ideal reality of the life of God and the life of sin as absolutely excluding one another."[20] He also cites C. H. Dodd, who apparently suggests that John was speaking with "pardonable exaggeration."[21] Furthermore, he notes the possibility of taking John's affirmations as implied imperatives, implicit appeals to Christians to avoid sin, "injunctions to them to approach the ideal. This feature will obviously be present in any attempt to interpret John's teaching as the presentation of an ideal."[22] Any other interpreters will fall in this category, who take John's statements as implicit appeals to avoid sin. Additionally, Marshall notes, it is possible to view John's affirmations as conditional in effect. Where verse 6 says that everyone abiding (*menō*, to live, remain, continue) in Jesus does not sin, what is implied is that *if*, or "so long as a person abides in Christ, he will be free from sin."[23]

Marshall's own tendency is to adopt many of these elements and then to view this idealistic statement about the Christian life from an eschatological perspective. In light of Old Testament promises of a coming age, "characterized by perfection" (Ezekiel 36:27; Jeremiah 31:33-34), "It would not be surprising if the early church concluded that the age of fulfillment had come, and that therefore God's people could now expect to be sinless. The texts under review thus express the eschatological reality brought about by the coming of Jesus."[24] In the end, Marshall sums up the teaching of the entire passage thus:

> John is describing the ideal character of the Christian, ideal in the sense that this is the reality intended by God for him, even if he falls short of it while he still lives in this sinful world. The person who is conscious of the new beginning that God has made in his life will seek to let that divine ideal become more and more of a reality. He knows that he cannot claim sinlessness—for he has already read the first chapter of this Epistle—but at the same time he can claim God's power to enable him not to sin.[25]

Smalley's view is similar, suggesting that in 3:4-9 John is speaking about potential, while in chapters 1 and 2 he is speaking about actual sins. Even so, he thinks that the affirmations in chapter 3 were intended to serve as imperative appeals for right attitudes and living.[26]

The most important reason for rejecting this view of 1 John 3 is that it is not a straightforward reading of the passage. Rather than describing the ideal Christian or saying what we ought to be or will be, John is forthrightly declaring what we are and are not. Throughout the passage, his statements about "everyone who" (pas + the articular participle) use indicative or declarative verbs that certainly appear to be statements of fact:

- 2:29: everyone doing righteousness has been born of God.
- 3:3: everyone having this hope in Him purifies himself.
- 3:4: everyone doing sin also does anomia.
- 3:6: everyone abiding in Him does not sin.
- 3:6: everyone sinning has not seen or come to know Him.
- 3:9: everyone having been born of God does not do sin (compare 5:18).
- 3:10: everyone not doing righteousness is not of God.

Add the simple statements without "everyone" (articular participles without pas), which are essentially equivalent in meaning:

- 3:7: the one doing righteousness is righteous.
- 3:8: the one doing sin is of the devil.
- 3:10: the one not loving his brother is not of God.

What seems clear is that all of these, in such a tightly packed context, ought to be read in the same way, and some of them simply cannot be read as expressions of yet unreached ideals, or as implicitly imperative, or as implicitly conditional. In 2:29, for example, "has been born of God" is a present reality, not an ideal. All the statements about sinners are unqualified: they are guilty of anomia (3:4), they have not come to know God (3:6); they are of the devil (3:8) and not of God (3:10).

What is clear is that John is contrasting two ways of life, not two ideals. The list of statements just given does this in convincing manner and John's conclusion in verse 10 says this specifically: "In this are manifested the children of God and the children of the devil." Most interpreters make the point that John shows us how to distinguish the two, which must be a pragmatic test of any view we consider. What a Christian is *ideally*, or what one will be *eventually*, does not suffice for this test. One must be able to distinguish them now.

To add to this, even if one should read the declaration in verse 6 as "conditional," as Marshall does, it is not possible to read the equally strong declaration in verse 9 in the same way: "everyone who has been born of God does not do sin." Marshall acknowledges this,[27] but it does not keep him from proceeding to make use of the conditional reading of verse 6 in his concluding summary, cited above.

Attempts to read John's affirmations as citations of his opponents' claims

I mention the approach of Harry Swadling only briefly.[28] None of the commentaries I have consulted adopts it. His view is that 3:6 and 3:9 are in fact quotations of heretical secessionist claims, "using their own words with scorn and horror."[29] That a Christian does not sin was the *false* claim of "proto-Gnostics" who said the Christian's spirit is divinely begotten by a divine seed and is unaffected by his physical behavior: "his magical divine birth granted him immunity from the effects of his actions."[30]

It is true that the inspired biblical writers sometimes quote what others have said without necessarily agreeing with them. Even so, there are two things to be said about this way of reading 1 John 3:6, 9. One is there appears to be no hint in the text that John is citing what others had said and then correcting or qualifying it. In both verses, he seems to be saying Christians do not sin, and in both cases he lets the words stand.

The other thing is that all the "everyone who" statements ought to be taken in the same way. I will not list them again, given that they appear not far above. They all carry the same semantic force, and the rest of them most certainly cannot be taken as quotations John does not agree with. That seems especially obvious for 5:18, prefaced as it is with "We know," words hardly appropriate to introduce an opponent's claim.[31] Swadling apparently feels the effect of this and travels a somewhat tortured path to try to negate the impact of 5:18. He raises the question whether 5:14-21 may be a later addition to 1 John, suggesting that a later editor— not understanding that 3:6, 9 were quotations from the heretics—might at least have amended it (and adjusted 3:9!). He offers this reading of 5:18: "We know that no child of God is a (habitual) sinner"[32]—a reading that would have "solved" 3:6, 9 equally well. He even notes that the author of 1 John "never loses sight of the basic Christian tension between the ideal and the reality."[33]

Finally, Kruse observes that in Swadling's view "the reason that the author introduced these slogans was to immediately refute them by urging his readers to assess the claims involved by using the criterion that those who do right are righteous and those who do evil are of the devil."[34] That would hardly seem to refute those who claimed Christians do not sin; indeed, John's "correction" would appear to say the same thing!

Attempts to "divide" the Christian in such a way that he both can and cannot sin

Recent interpreters apparently do not find this view appealing, but I mention it briefly since Smalley introduces it into the discussion. He attributes the view to Alfred Plummer, who suggested John was making a distinction between the Christian's two natures. Thus (as Smalley summarizes Plummer), John meant that while the old nature may continue to sin, the new nature cannot do so.[35] Only in the latter sense is it impossible for the believer to commit sin.

This interpretation builds on the famous discussion in Romans 7:14-25 (cf. Galatians 5:17) where—if the passage is expressive of a *Christian's* experience— Paul describes an unending struggle within believers.[36] Plummer, indeed, thinks John is saying the same thing as Paul in Romans 7:20: "If what I would not, that I do, it is no more I that do it, but sin which dwells in me." He observes, "By these apparently contradictory statements [1:8-10; 2:27; 3:6] … John expresses that internal contradiction of which every one who is endeavouring to do right is conscious."[37] On verse 10, he says the statement is "literally true of the Divine nature imparted to the believer. That does not sin and cannot sin."[38]

As true as any of this may be, a person cannot be divided in such a way as to say that *he* does things *he* does not (or cannot) do. As Galatians 5:17 makes clear, while the two natures have different desires and pull the believer in two different directions,[39] the *person* (not one or the other of his natures), acts. It will not do to blame my sins on my sinful nature and then exonerate myself. John Stott answers Plummer well. He points out that (1) this would play into the hands of the heretics John was opposing, in their separation between spirit and flesh; (2) there is no biblical warrant for isolating a person's "natures" from himself; (3) in Romans 7 Paul's purpose was "to explain why his behaviour conflicts with his will"; and (4) verse 9 means that the *person* (not his spiritual nature) has been born of God and cannot sin."[40]

For that matter, Plummer's view is probably more complex than this. He also observes, in commenting on the second half of verse 6, "S. John does not say this of every one who commits a sin, but of the habitual sinner (present participle). Although the believer sometimes sins, yet not sin, but opposition to sin, is the ruling principle of his life," while for "the habitual sinner," "sin is his ruling principle."[41] This sounds very much like the approach I will treat next at greater length.

Attempts to interpret the sinning John says is not possible for a Christian as habitual sin, in contrast to occasional sins, and to ground this in the meaning of the Greek tenses

This has probably been the most common approach to the tension between 1 John 1 and 1 John 3. Kruse calls it the "traditional way of resolving the tension."[42] Marshall says it is "the most popular understanding of the passage among British commentators."[43] In most instances, where this "solution" is preferred, the interpreter grounds the view in the meaning of the Greek tenses. In particular, the tense that John uses in chapter 3 is the present tense, traditionally viewed as a *linear* tense that describes actions as ongoing or repetitive.

The New International Version (NIV) translators have apparently intended to express this view with their rendering of the present tense verbs. Verse 6 reads thus, "No one who lives in him *keeps on sinning*. No one who *continues to sin* has either seen him or known him." Verse 9 reads, "No one who is born of God *will continue to sin*, because God's seed remains in him; he cannot *go on sinning*." The italicized verbal forms all translate either the simple verb *hamartanō* ("sin") or the verb *poieō* ("do") with the noun for *sin* as its object—all in the Greek present tense.

That translation only serves to support what a number of interpreters have said. Gary Burge, for example, commends the NIV rendering as helpful, explaining: "In Greek a present tense (in certain forms) indicates continuous, repeated activity." He concludes: "John may well be emphasizing that ongoing, habitual sin should find no place in the believer's life."[44]

Akin, for another example, observes that the "most reasonable" approach "still seems to center on John's use of the present tense verb."[45] He explains: "John is not suggesting that the child of God will not commit a single act of sin. Instead, John is describing a way of life, a character, a prevailing lifestyle. Here the present tense verb contextually depicts linear, continual action. In other words, the believer will not live a life characterized by sin."[46]

Any number of interpreters could be cited to show how common this view is. David Smith writes:

> The Apostle's meaning appears when account is taken of the terms he employs with accurate precision. In the earlier passage he says that there is indwelling sin in the believer. The sinful principle remains, and it manifests its presence by lapses from holiness— occasional sins, definite, isolated acts of sin. This is the force of the aorists ... in 2:1. Here he uses the present ... with the implication of *continuance in sin*. ... The believer may fall into sin but he will not walk in it.[47]

Robert L. Thomas also focuses on the present tense verbs but states his view a little differently. He takes the verbs to be progressive presents and interprets John to mean a Christian does not go on sinning in an unbroken continuity with the past.[48] In the end, I do not think this view is significantly different, since it also finally has to rely on a definition that sin, after the break with the past that occurs in conversion, is not "still characteristic of his life."[49]

This approach cannot be helpfully evaluated apart from some technical discussion of the meaning of the Greek tenses. Until recently, the statements quoted above could be affirmed without much fear of contradiction. That is no longer true. The advent of contemporary *verbal aspect theory*, if nothing else, has served to make informed interpreters leery of this approach to John's affirmations of Christian sinlessness. Thus Burdick, writing in 1985, could say the solution to the problem of John's meaning "lies in the present tense verbs in 3:6 and 9." He stated, "The normal function of the present tense" is "to express continuing action," which involves "valid distinctions based on recognized differences between the kinds of actions expressed" by the tenses. The present tense expresses "some degree of linear action or continuing state," and this last point "is recognized in all grammars."[50] He would not be able to say this now.

There is no need to delve deeply into aspect theory here.[51] What is important, in this view of the tenses, is they do *not* mean "kind of action" (*Aktionsart*), as was traditionally thought. The aorist does not mean punctiliar ("point") action and the present does not mean linear action. Instead, the tenses indicate simply the way the user chose to view or perceive the action. The aorist (as the "default" tense) simply sees an action as a whole without indicating any particular perspective beyond that. The present views the action from within, viewing it *as it is occurring.*

The clearest implication of this is that one must not say the present tense (which John uses in 3:6, 9) *means* "linear" or ongoing action. The present tense cannot be *defined* as habitual or continuing action. An action stated in the aorist or present tense might actually be ongoing, or it might not. All we can tell from the tense alone is that John viewed the action from the inside, as one who looks at it (so to speak) in its progress, while it is taking place.

Whether because of verbal aspect theory or for other reasons, a number of recent interpreters make statements like this one by Kruse: "The habitual/occasional distinction fails because the meaning of the present tense in Greek does not support this distinction as those who advocate this view claim."[52] Yarbrough rejects the NIV, saying, "The present tense cannot bear the weight that the translation 'keeps on sinning' places on it in 3:6, 9."[53] Marshall agrees with the criticism of Kubo: "We must, therefore, wonder whether an important point of interpretation can be made to rest on what has been called a grammatical subtlety."[54] Whether they thought this was so because of verbal aspect theory is not clear, but some interpreters, even before the advent of verbal aspect theory, also dismissed the view that John's claims can be explained on the basis of the Greek present tense. Smalley gives three reasons for discounting this approach to the tension. (1) It stresses the tense meaning in a way that is not natural; (2) it does not hold good in 1 John 5:16, which refers to specific acts of sin that can be committed by Christians; and (3) it raises the question why God can keep the believer from habitual sin and not from occasional sin.[55] (I will touch on these objections below.)

What shall we say about the view that the solution lies in the tenses? It seems probable that the tenses alone cannot explain John's meaning or reconcile His statements about sin in chapter one with those in chapter three.[56] This means the present tense, as such—that is, the inherent *meaning* of the tense—cannot be said to express action that in its original occurrence was continuing, repetitive, or habitual. An action viewed while in progress might have been habitual, for example, but the tense does not say so.[57] All such notions arise entirely from *context*. What the current theory means is that one cannot make an immediate leap from tense to conclusions about kind of action; there might be any number of reasons a writer viewed an action from a certain perspective. If one is to discuss the nature of an action as it actually was, then one must carefully weigh the whole construction: the lexical meaning of the verb (and other words used), the tense, and the context. In addition, when doing so, one must express his conclusions about the nature of the action as *interpretation*, not as though the tense proved the point.

At the same time, this understanding of the present tense need not eliminate from consideration the view that John's affirmations in chapter 3 mean a Christian does not practice sin. That view, which seems most likely on its own merit, can be based on broader considerations, and I turn now to that.

Understanding John to Mean Sin as Practice

As just indicated, contemporary verbal aspect theory—for those who follow it—means the present tense verbs in 1 John cannot be taken, *simply because they are present tense*, to indicate action that occurs habitually or continuously. However, this does *not* mean a given verb cannot be used, pragmatically, to express an ongoing action. For that matter, even an aorist verb might do so.[58] A present-tense verb, while it does not inherently *mean* ongoing action, may well be *used* for such an action.

If we are to decide this is the case, in any given instance, more than the present tense alone will be required to serve as grounds for doing so. At least two other closely related things must be considered: other elements in the *context* and what makes the best sense—*coherence*, in other words. This calls for judgment, a requirement the *interpreter* of the text (any text, for that matter) can never get away from.

I would submit, while the present tense does not inherently mean that an action in the real world is ongoing, it can be used for such an action. In other words, it does not necessarily rule in the idea of continuance or habit or repetition, but it does not rule it out, either! Indeed, when we consider that the perspective of the present tense is to view the action from within, while it is in progress, then it lends itself well to statements about ongoing action. Perhaps we should not hastily abandon the idea that the tense plays *some* role in bringing us to understand that John is speaking of lifestyle rather than occasional acts.[59] At least Chrys Caragounis must think so. He tells about reading both 1 John 2:1 and 3:9 to an unschooled Greek woman and asking her whether the writer was contradicting himself. She responded she did not think so. In 2:1, John was speaking of something "instantaneous," while in 3:9 he spoke of "something that goes on or is repeated again and again ... which would imply that the believer lives in sin."[60]

Even so, context and coherence are required to confirm such a reading. Then is there anything else in the context that may support reading John as having ongoing action in mind? Kerry Inman has offered an appealing suggestion: John's *vocabulary* points to habitual sinning.[61] The fact is "to do sin" (*poiein hamartian*) and "to do righteousness" (*poiein dikaiosunēn*), used generally, are especially Johannine expressions and appear—both in themselves and in context—to indicate continuing practice, a way of life. "Do righteousness" occurs in 1 John 2:29; 3:7, 10, as also in Revelation 22:11. "Do sin" occurs in 1 John 3:4a, 8, 9, as also in John 8:34. To the former we may add John 3:21 and 1 John 1:6, where "doing the truth" is similarly characteristic of a way of life. To the latter we may add 1 John 3:4b, where doing sin is equated to "doing *anomia*" (as discussed above). Indeed, *practice* appears as one of the lexical meanings of *poieō*, especially appropriate in such expressions as these.[62] Stott appears to support this understanding when he says, "It is not the isolated act of sin which is envisaged, but the settled habit of it, indicated by the verb *poiein*, to do or to practice, which is used of 'doing' sin in 4a, 8 and 9, of 'doing' lawlessness in 4b, and of 'doing' righteousness in ii. 29, iii. 7 and 10a."[63] The New American Standard Bible (NASB) renders, appropriately enough, "No one who is born of God *practices* sin."[64]

Indeed, the statement of Jesus in John 8:34-35 is enlightening on this score: "Everyone doing sin is a slave of sin. And the slave does not abide in the household forever, the son abides forever." As Inman observes, "Thus one is a slave to sin, which is a continuing state, because he continues to sin."[65]

Furthermore, there is the matter of context. Both in chapter three and in the larger context of 1 John we are dealing with a number of expressions that contrast the way of life of Christians to the way of life of those who cannot be said to be Christians. All of them can be viewed in essentially the same way, as descriptions of a lifestyle. In 2:3, for example, we know we have come to know God (or Jesus) "if we are keeping his commands," whereas the one who is *not* keeping His commands, but claims to have come to know God, is a liar. In 2:29, the same point is made with different terms: "Everyone doing righteousness has been born of him." Standing opposite to this is "everyone doing sin" (3:4). Marshall observes (on 3:4-10), "The world is divided into the children of God and the children of the devil, characterized by righteousness and sin respectively."[66] (One wonders why this did not seem to him a sufficient explanation of John's intent.) As Thompson says, somewhat naively,

"What is meant, then, by the statement *no one who lives in him keeps on sinning* is quite simple: sin is not the identifying characteristic of those who live *in him*."[67]

Kotzé, although he opted to explain the tension as that which exists between the "already" and the "not yet" in Christian experience, finds "plausible" the distinction between habitual sin and sins of the moment. He quotes J. P. Louw to the effect that the Greek present "may be used if the *context* suggests linear or habitual occurrence" and adds: "The context of 1 John 3:9 has durative meaning and on the strength of this it can be said that ["is not able to sin"] means: one cannot live in sin."[68]

Must we say 2:3 is an absolute statement that brooks no exceptions, that it means *perfectly* keeping His commands? Or 2:29 means *perfectly* practicing righteousness? Both 1 John 1:8-10 and our empirical judgments tell us this is not what John means. Why must we understand 3:6, 9—which are in the same vein—to mean *perfectly* committing no sin? If the positive statements allow exceptions to what is generally true as a lifestyle description, why not the negative ones also? The manner of life of a Christian is to keep His commands, to practice doing right, to avoid sin, while the manner of life of a non-Christian is the opposite. While neither the Christian nor the non-Christian *absolutely* or *perfectly* fits these descriptions, their lifestyles are characteristically different. As Akin expresses the point of 2:29, "This specific righteousness is a distinct characteristic of the one who has been born of God. Likewise, it is a continual, life-characterizing righteousness that comes from having a personal, saving knowledge of him who is absolutely righteous."[69] Thompson observes, commenting on 1:5: "To walk *in the light* means to shape one's whole being, all one's actions, decisions, thoughts and beliefs by the standard of the God who is light. … It does not mean to be perfect."[70] Again (on 2:3-6), "'Obeying God's commands' points to the shape of the Christian life as a whole, to the consistency of our discipleship, and not to individual acts taken in isolation."[71] And again (on 2:29): "'To do righteousness' means to 'practice it as a pattern of life which comes from one's very nature.'"[72] Such observations serve well for *all* John's statements about Christian behavior.

Saying this, therefore, does not depend solely (not even primarily) on the fact that the verbs are in the Greek present tense, even if the Greek present may "oil the hinges" on the door to this understanding. Deciding this is the correct understanding depends even more on the immediate context and the larger context of the entire epistle.

There is also the larger context of the New Testament. The previous chapters in this volume tend to show that to be a Christian is the same thing as being a disciple. Being a disciple means to answer Jesus' call to turn from our sins in repentance, to renounce anything or anyone else as having first claim on us, to put our trust in Him, and follow where He leads, observing all the things He has commanded (Matthew 28:20). Then it *has* to be true that those who know God (those who have been born of God, those who are children of God, those who abide in Him—to pick up some of John's equal expressions) do in fact walk in the light (keep His commands, avoid sin). This is absolutely true, even if it does not describe absolute sinlessness. As Thompson appropriately notes, we are "prodded to reflect on what we say and do, how we think, pray, spend our time and money, raise our children, treat our coworkers, spouses, and neighbors. Our aim is to live for one master, God alone."[73]

This "solution" to the problem of tension in 1 John, I think, makes best sense (coherence) of all the data. It has the advantage of making sense of both passages in the epistle. If, as seems likely, in chapter 1 John was responding to some who denied they were sinful or committed sin, then John has made clear that such a claim is not just unrealistic but wicked. Then if, as seems likely, in chapter 3 he was responding to some who claimed sin does not matter, who practiced sin with no sense of guilt, then John has made clear sin is not the way of a Christian. Indeed, it is possible both claims arose from the same basic error: nothing done in their flesh was sinful, after all, since in their spirits they were sinless.

This solution also answers three objections raised by Marshall.[74] (1) As noted above, he doubts the tense can bear such a weight of interpretation and accuses the NIV translators of "stressing the present continuous form of the verb in a way which they do not do elsewhere in the New Testament." But the solution I have offered does not rest on the tense alone. And, for that matter, while the NIV translators have probably gone too far in their translation of the present tense in 1 John 3:6, 9, there may well be many places in the New Testament where at least a "progressive" translation of the present tense is very appropriate. (2) Marshall notes that in 1 John 5:16 the present tense is also used to refer to a Christian's *sinning* (a sin not to death), and that if it *has* to mean ongoing, characteristic committing of sin it would contradict 3:6, 9. But the solution I have offered rests as much on context and coherence as on tense, and the context in 5:16 is very different. (3) Marshall observes, since 3:9 says the Christian cannot sin "because he has been born of God" and "His seed remains in him," it is "hard to see why God preserves him from some sins [a characteristic practice], but not from all sins [occasional ones]." But he seems not to notice that this objection would apply to almost *any* view of the Christian life. In fact, it makes very good sense to read John as saying that because of the presence of the regenerating activity of God in a Christian,[75] the Christian cannot live a lifestyle characterized by sinful disobedience. Thus Marshall himself observes, appropriately, that this divine birth "is the explanation of the moral character of a child of God"—a moral character in the *real* world, we may add, and one that is not *perfectly* moral. Why the new birth, the indwelling Spirit, the implanted Word do not produce absolutely sinless Christians we will have to leave to the wisdom and knowledge of God for the moment.

The view outlined above seems clearly superior to other attempts to explain John's affirmations about Christian sinlessness and how those affirmations cohere with his provision for a believer who sins. John means disciples of Jesus do not practice sin, they do not "live in sin," and sin is not the habit and character of their lives. This is an understanding not based on the Greek tense alone, but on a coherent view that incorporates tense possibilities, plus vocabulary, plus context—including the immediate context, the larger context of the entire epistle, and ultimately the context of the New Testament. Furthermore, this view has the advantage of fitting what almost all commentators eventually conclude about the Christian lifestyle according to John, regardless how they exegete the specific verses.

Conclusions: Implications and Application

What must I do to possess eternal life?

The conclusions reached in this chapter have implications for this issue, one of the main concerns I intend for this book to address. At one level, 1 John 3 tells us as readers *how we may recognize* the children of God and how they are different from unbelievers. We may safely classify these statements as expressing *evidences* of faith rather than *conditions* for salvation—at least not as conditions to be distinguished from faith.

When 3:6-10 is combined with what we have discussed in the previous chapters, however, the passage expresses something more than merely how a person on the sidelines can tell the difference by observing the lives of believers. It expresses *what is essential to the nature of Christians as Christians.*

In other words, once we have acknowledged John is not laying down conditions by which one may receive eternal life and instead is describing the evidence of regeneration; and once we have acknowledged he does not mean sinless perfection but a general character of life that distinguishes the Christian from the unbeliever, we still have something very important left. This way of life *is indeed characteristic of those who possess eternal life.*

John is not describing options but *essential* things. A person whose actions are characteristically sinful (3:6-10), who does not love fellow-believers (2:9-11), who does not keep Christ's commandments (2:3-5), who walks in the darkness and not in the light (1:6-7), who loves the world (2:15), who does not do the will of God (2:17)—any of these things—*is not a disciple of Jesus.* To put this positively, *it is the very nature of a disciple* to do the will of God, to love the Father and fellow-believers rather than the world, to walk in the light of the commandments of God, and so to avoid sin.

As sure as it is that a Christian *believes* in Jesus Christ, so sure is it that a Christian avoids sin. To express this differently, it is sure (as John says) that "whoever believes that Jesus is the Christ has been born of God" (5:1). But it would be just as accurate to say (*with the very same relationship between the words*): "whoever loves fellow-believers has been born of God," and "whoever keeps the commandments of Christ has been born of God," and "whoever does the will of God has been born of God," and "whoever does righteousness has been born of God."

If this sounds like eternal life requires something more than faith, it is not meant to. But it is meant to demonstrate—just as became clear in the study of John in the previous chapter—that faith means something more than *mere* intellectual belief. For John, a person is saved by a faith that necessarily expresses itself in obedience.

Must one be sinless to be a disciple?

This question, which relates to one focus of this book on sin in the Christian life, grows out of the means John provides for distinguishing between true Christians and non-Christians. That this is one of the main points of his discussion is clear from 3:10: "In this the children of God are manifest, and the children of the devil: whoever does not righteousness is not of God." A similar point, if less directly stated, has already been made in 2:3-4, where the difference is between keeping and not keeping God's commandments, or in 2:10-11, between loving and hating one's brother. (See also 3:6 and indeed the epistle as a whole.) Kruse is right to emphasize that any explanation of 1 John 3:6, 9 must fit with the fact that John says we can distinguish "the children of God from the children of the devil on the grounds of not sinning and sinning respectively."[76]

That is one of the reasons the solution I have offered seems preferable to others: we can distinguish saints and sinners by their lifestyle, by their practice. Those who possess eternal life practice righteousness, they do not practice sin. Non-Christians practice sin, not righteousness. Even so, this answer immediately raises a question: can we, in fact, tell the difference between those who have been regenerated and those who have not by the character of their lives? Does this work in practice?

The answer is at once yes and no. Speaking generally, yes, disciples of Jesus practice righteousness and avoid sin, while unbelievers do neither of those things. But when one must be specific, it is wise not to be glib. Some people who are avowed unbelievers approach the morality of many who at least profess to know Christ. Indeed, it has become increasingly difficult in our culture to tell the difference between those who populate the church and those who never occupy a pew.

What can be said with confidence is that, while John's affirmation provides a sure way of *defining* the difference between the children of God and the children of the devil, that affirmation is not quite so easy to apply in *recognizing* the one and the other. At the same time, it may well be that the greater part of our practical problem lies in the fact that many professing Christians are not Christians at all. John's teaching has clear implications for that.

A closely related practical problem is how we define *practice*. If John means a disciple practices righteousness and does not practice sin, sin is not the habit and character of his life, then the question arises almost uninvited: how much sin can a disciple commit without falling into the practice of sin?[77] The commentators do not raise this question; perhaps to raise it is considered bad taste. Even those who explain that John is distinguishing between habitual and occasional sin say little if anything about how to tell the difference between the two—for ourselves or for others we minister to.

Perhaps the question cannot be answered. Sometimes, however, even unanswerable questions must be raised. We are too much surrounded, in Christian circles, with professing Christians who seem entirely sincere and show some evidence of the work of God in their lives who stumble into sin, not just once but repeatedly. To put this in the crassest of specific terms, we want to know how often the "Christian" who used to be a drunkard can go on a binge and still be regarded as a Christian. Once a year? Once a week? Never? We have to admit, when we are laboring with some in our churches, we do not always know how to use John's criterion, that we cannot always know whether the persons we minister to are disciples or not.

Can we have assurance of salvation?

This problem arises immediately out of the preceding: What are the implications of John's affirmation for assurance of salvation—for ourselves, or for those we bring to Christ? Unlike the preceding, at least some of the commentators are aware of this issue. Marshall, for example, observes, "For those who wish to be God's children the lesson [of 1 John 3:10] is obvious. They must examine themselves to see whether they do what is right." He adds, "This could be hard advice for a believer who is all too conscious of his own sins and is lacking in confidence; he could well be tempted to doubt his own status as a child of God."[78]

Marshall thinks this is the reason some interpreters have "watered down" John's words so they refer only "to the believer's freedom from habitual sin."[79] I, however, have not found this understanding to be all that reassuring, given that I am confronted with the question how often I can sin without it being "practice." Meanwhile, I do not find Marshall's view to provide assurance: namely, that "John is describing the ideal character of the Christian, ideal in the sense that this is the reality intended by God for him, even if he falls short of it while he still lives in this sinful world."[80] Any professing believer, regardless how wicked, could lay claim to that! Nor do I think that this discussion justifies Marshall's concluding words on the subject, as correct as they may be. "To maintain the balance between warning believers of the seriousness of their falling into sin and consoling those who are overwhelmed by their sins is not easy; John's attention moves from the one to the other, and we must allow both types of statement to have their full effect."[81] Having "full effect" is, of course, the issue.

Akin touches on the matter of assurance:

> This particular order [speaking first about doing what is right, in 2:29], therefore, offers assurance to the child of God. For the child of God, faith precedes behavior, but right behavior is the natural result of proper belief. As Stott affirms, 'A person's righteousness is thus the evidence of his new birth, not the cause or condition

of it'. Hence, believers can be assured of their acceptable status before God if their lives are marked by a godly righteousness. ... Righteous living is a confirmation ... of an already existing relationship with God.[82]

Akin is apparently correct on both counts. First, John never says practicing righteousness (positive) or not practicing sin (negative) is the *cause* or *condition* of being born of God. That is always faith, and the practice of righteousness and avoidance of sin are *evidences* of faith and regeneration—albeit *essential* evidences. To say this as I have said it elsewhere in this book, obedience is the form in which faith expresses itself. Second, to witness the fruit of righteousness in one's life is indeed a source of assurance. Akin says nothing about the possibility that John's insistence, that one born of God does not practice sin, may raise doubts about one's status as a child of God.

Burge seems most acutely aware of the potential for a problem here. He says: "Taking a passage such as this [2:3-11] at face value comes with significant risk. Above all it demands that the measure of saving faith can be seen in some tangible outworking of grace and goodness in a person's life. The timeless theological problem is here, however: How do we preach such a theme without destroying Christian assurance or making obedience a criterion for salvation?"[83] Subsequently, at the end of his discussion of 2:28-3:11, he raises this issue again, admitting: "In the Reformed tradition the emphasis on God's grace and love has made many of us uncomfortable with bold calls to holiness."[84] Then, in a discussion of righteousness and assurance, he notes, "At the risk of taking away the assurance that I have so carefully protected in the preceding paragraph, I cannot help but feel troubled by verses such as 3:6, 8, and 10. John seems to sound a warning here, a final and terrible warning, that lives characterized by sin, lives willfully disobedient and unrighteous, cannot be lives that are born of God."[85] This comes after his acknowledgement that "Sadly, there are many in our churches for whom habitual sin is nothing of real consequence,"[86] an observation few of us would challenge.

For Burge, it is the *practice* of sin (not isolated acts of sin) that raises the question of assurance, and he is true to John's teaching in expressing that. However, this does not give us a certain answer to the question of what is practice and what is not.

Once again, we are brought to the issue that dominates this book. My purpose in this concluding section has been only to bring the discussion back to that.

Meanwhile, 1 John has taught us something important about being a disciple of Jesus and about sin. A disciple keeps the commandments of God (or Christ) and avoids sin. If a person claims to have *faith* in Christ, and so to be born of God, without such a lifestyle to match, that person is a deceived deceiver. At the same time, this refers to *practice* and does not rule out specific lapses that require confession and forgiveness.

This part of what 1 John teaches us, however, does not answer every question about the sins of Christians. It remains for the rest of the book to resolve these issues, if that is possible. Meanwhile, the question of assurance remains: How can I, conscious of my continuing sinfulness, face John's pronouncement that everyone who has been born of God does not practice sin (3:9) and confidently say I am a Christian? Already, this much suggests itself to me: I can have assurance only so long as I am convinced sin is an exception, rather than the rule, in my life, that it contradicts rather than manifests my character. That is a *principle*, however, that calls for further discussion about how to apply it. I will return to it in a subsequent chapter.

ENDNOTES

[1] I leave it to others, or to another time and place, to explore the linking between John's Gospel and his epistles. I assume them to be by the same author, the Apostle John. There are very many commonalities between them (commonalities not shared with other New Testament writings) to support this view.

[2] This is a true conditional sentence in the original, expressed by *ean* with the subjunctive. The construction is the same as in v. 9, where confession of one's sins is stated as a condition for forgiveness and cleansing.

[3] To avoid repetition, I will not often make reference to 5:18, but the reader should understand that it is included by implication in what I say about 3:6, 9.

[4] The difference between v. 8 ("have no sin") and v. 10 ("have not sinned") is debatable. Some interpreters think they are synonymous, some that the first means the sin principle or guilt and the second means acts of sin. That difference need not occupy us here.

[5] Daniel L. Akin, *The New American Commentary: 1, 2, 3 John* (Nashville: Broadman & Holman, 2001), 87.

[6] Marianne Meye Thompson, *1-3 John* (IVPNTC; Downers Grove: InterVarsity, 1992), 91. Donald W. Burdick, *The Letters of John the Apostle: an In-depth Commentary* (Chicago: Moody, 1985), 244, expresses the matter similarly: "John makes it clear that there is not a single regenerated person who commits sin. This assertion, however, does not agree with reality or with other statements that the apostle has already made."

[7] For surveys of proposed solutions, see Raymond E. Brown, *The Epistles of John* (AB 30; New York et al.: Doubleday, 1982), 411-16; Stephen S. Smalley, *1, 2, 3 John* (WBC 51; Waco: Word Books,

1984); Burdick, 244-247 (who lists and answers nine views). Perhaps the most thorough treatment of different approaches, giving numerous arguments for and against twelve views, is found in the relatively less available work by Robert L. Thomas, *Exegetical Digest of I John* (Robert L. Thomas, 1984), 253-261. The book is available from Grace Books International (1-800-GRACE15 or www.gbibooks.com).

[8] Colin G. Kruse, *The Letters of John* (PNTC; Grand Rapids: Eerdmans, 2000), 35.

[9] Robert W. Yarbrough, *1-3 John* (BECNT; Grand Rapids: Baker, 2008), 181-89.

[10] Yarbrough, 182.

[11] Yarbrough, 182.

[12] Yarbrough, 195.

[13] I. Howard Marshall, *The Epistles of John* (NICNT; Grand Rapids: Eerdmans, 1978), 178.

[14] Marshall, 179.

[15] Marshall, 179.

[16] In fact, the Wesleyan view provides that even those who have reached a state of perfection can fall from that state! I will give some attention to the Wesleyan view of sanctification in chapter seven.

[17] John Stott, *The Epistles of John: An Introduction and Commentary* (Tyndale NTC; Grand Rapids: Eerdmans, 1964, 1969 reprint), 134-35. He is referencing Robert S. Candlish, *The First Epistle of John Expounded in a Series of Lectures* (A. & C. Black, 1877).

[18] Smalley, 160.

[19] Marshall, 180.

[20] Marshall, 180, citing H. Alford, *The Greek Testament*, 2nd ed., vol. IV (London: 1862), 465.

[21] Marshall, 181.

[22] Marshall, 181. Georg Strecker, *The Johannine Letters* (Hermeneia; Minneapolis: Fortress, 1996), 96, similarly, says the indicative verb in verse 6 ("does not sin") "is not the statement of an objectively discernible fact, but rather ... a warning to the community. ... It is more proper to interpret this expression as the prelude to the admonition not to sin. ... Anyone who is born of God is subject to the demand to refrain from sinning."

[23] Marshall, 181.

[24] Marshall, 182.

[25] Marshall, 187.

[26] Smalley, 164. P. P. A. Kotzé, "The Meaning of 1 John 3:9 with Reference to 1 John 1:8 and 10," *Neotestamentica* 13 (1979), 81, holds a somewhat similar view, at least insofar as the tension between the "already" and the "not yet" is concerned: "With respect to life one can say that the believer already has it but in a sense he does 'not yet' have it. In a negative sense the same must also be true with respect to sin." What he means by this in practical terms is not clear.

[27] Marshall, 181. Smalley, 161, also raises this objection.

[28] Harry C. Swadling, "Sin and Sinlessness in I John," *Scottish Journal of Theology* 35 (1982), 205-11.

[29] Swadling, 208.

[30] Swadling, 211.

[31] A comparison with other instances of "we know" in 1 John puts this beyond doubt; see 2:3; 3:2, 14, 19, 24; 4:6, 13; 5:2, 15, 19, 20.

[32] Swadling, 210.

[33] Swadling, 211.

[34] Kruse, 131.

[35] Smalley, 160.

[36] Whether the passage applies to saints or sinners is an ongoing debate among interpreters. I do not think it important enough for the present discussion to enter the debate.

[37] Alfred Plummer, *The Cambridge Bible for Schools and Colleges: The Epistles of John* (Cambridge: University Press, 1883, 1954 reprint), 124.

[38] Plummer, 127.

[39] I will discuss this passage in more detail in chapter seven.

[40] Stott, 131-32.

[41] Plummer, 125.

[42] Kruse, 129.

[43] Marshall, 180. He need not have limited it to British writers.

[44] Gary M. Burge, *The NIV Application Commentary: Letters of John* (Grand Rapids: Zondervan, 1996), 150. To match John, he should have said, "will find" instead of "should find." Burge goes on to observe that a number of interpreters have outlined problems with this view, but he does not reflect objections offered in the name of verbal aspect theory (discussed below). In his preparation for a 1996 publication, he might not have been aware of verbal aspect theory.

[45] Akin, 143.

[46] Akin, 143.

[47] David Smith, "The Epistles of John," *The Expositor's Greek Testament*, vol. 5 (Grand Rapids: Eerdmans, 1951), 184.

[48] Thomas, 260-61.

[49] Thomas, 260.

[50] Burdick, 246.

[51] For an introduction, which includes a survey of the sources of this theory, see Robert E. Picirilli, "The Meaning of the Tenses in New Testament Greek: Where Are We?" *Journal of the Evangelical Theological Society* 48:3 (2005), 533-55.

[52] Kruse, 131. His denial is both blunted and confusing in light of several statements he makes in his commentary like this one (on 3:9): "The author uses a present tense form of the verb 'to sin' ... indicating that it is sinning as an ongoing action that he has in mind here as impossible for those born of God" (124). See also 64 (on 1:7), 68 (on 1:9), 79 (on 2:4), and 120 (on 3:6). One wonders, therefore, just what Kruse meant when he said the force of the present tense does not sustain the habitual versus occasional distinction.

[53] Yarbrough, 183.

[54] Marshall, 180, reflecting the criticism of Sakae Kubo, "I John 3:9: Absolute or Habitual," *Andrews University Seminary Studies* 7 (1969), 47-56. (This article is summarized in *New Testament Abstracts* 14 [1969], § 290.)

[55] Smalley, 159-160.

[56] I understand the meaning of the Greek tenses in terms of verbal aspect or point of view, although I prefer the term *perspective* (over *aspect*) as the definition of tense.

[57] In this Kruse, 129, is correct in saying, "The use of the present tense says nothing about the habitual or nonhabitual character of the sinning."

[58] In John 2:20, for example, an aorist verb names an action that had taken 46 years to bring to its present state!

[59] Indeed, this tense is characteristic of such descriptive statements often in this epistle (when verbs are used to express conditions of practice, both righteous and wicked). Those occurring up to this point are: *walk* (1:6-7; 2:6); *confess* (1:9); *keep* (2:3-4); *hate* (2:9, 11; 3:15); *love* (2:10, 15; 3:10, 14, 18); *do/commit* (2:29; 3:4, 7, 8, 10); *abide* (3:6); *sin* (3:6, 9).

[60] Chrys C. Caragounis, *The Development of Greek and the New Testament* (Grand Rapids: Baker, 2006), 90. Caragounis, 326, does not follow the verbal aspect theory of Porter. It remains to be seen whose views of tense will prevail.

[61] V. Kerry Inman, "Distinctive Johannine Vocabulary and the Interpretation of I John 3:9," *Westminster Theological Journal* 40 (1977-78), 136-44.

[62] See *A Greek-English Lexicon of the New Testament and Other Early Christian Literature,* by Walter Bauer, William F. Arndt, and F. Wilbur Gingrich (Chicago: University of Chicago Press, 1957), under *poieō*. See also Johannes P. Louw and Eugene A. Nida, eds., *Greek-English Lexicon of the New Testament Based on Semantic Domains,* 2nd ed. (New York: United Bible Societies, 1988, 1989), 1:804.

[63] Stott, 126. Stott also notes that the present tense indicates "a settled character" or "sin habitually."

[64] My colleague Leroy Forlines, in conversation, suggests that the verb *do* in these contexts suggests deliberate or willful actions. That is worth pursuing, I think, but it would not necessarily change the point I am making here.

[65] Inman, 141.

[66] Marshall, 175.

[67] Thompson, 95 (italics hers). Thompson's view is not entirely clear. Some of her statements appear to incline to the idealistic/eschatological perspective: "The power that is at work in the children of God in the present is the same power that shall transform them at the return of Christ. ... In the present they are exhorted to live in anticipation of that promise since the same transforming power is at work in them" (91); "If John's statement seems hyperbolic, it is because of his eager anticipation of the blessings of the future age" (99).

[68] Kotzé, 79. He is citing Johannes P. Louw, "Verbal aspect in the first letter of John," *Essays on the General Epistles of the New Testament* (Pretoria: NTSSA, 1975), 102.

[69] Akin, 131.

[70] Thompson, 43.

[71] Thompson, 53.

[72] Thompson, 87, quoting R. A. Culpepper, *1 John, 2 John, 3 John* (Knox Preaching Guides; Atlanta: John Knox), 56.

[73] Thompson, 57.

[74] Marshall, 180.

[75] I am aware of the differences of opinion as to the meaning of "his seed remains in him," but do not think it helpful to delve into that here.

[76] Kruse, 132.

[77] I find it hard to resist the temptation to express this in the terms of the old woodchuck conundrum: "How much sin can a Christian sin if a Christian can't do sin?" I apologize for my irreverence!

[78] Marshall, 187.

[79] Marshall, 187.

[80] Marshall, 187.

[81] Marshall, 188.

[82] Akin, 132.

[83] Burge, 107.

[84] Burge, 156.

[85] Burge, 157.

[86] Burge, 156.

Chapter Five

PAUL AND THE DISCIPLESHIP MODEL

The question before us in this chapter is, Does Paul know anything other than the "transaction model" that so firmly rests on his exposition of the gospel, summarized in chapter one? He is the New Testament theologian of salvation *par excellence*, and he has insistently taught us that eternal life is by faith alone (*sola fidei*, as we have expressed it since the Reformation) and not by works. By Paul's direction, we seek the righteousness of Christ accounted to us in response to faith. We do not stand righteous before God because of good works. We have nothing of merit to offer Him.

In our examination of the teaching of Jesus in the Synoptic Gospels, however, we have encountered a somewhat different expression of what one must do to obtain eternal life. In the Gospel of John we have been prodded to think faith implies a certain lifestyle. In concord with this, 1 John has taught us that faith manifests itself in some *essential* actions. Is Paul ignorant of this "discipleship model"? To answer this we focus on Paul again, surveying his epistles. In this, we are not seeking so much to explicate his theology of salvation—that seems already clear—as to discover whether he shows any awareness of what we seem to have found in the Gospels and 1 John.

Romans 2:6-10

This passage bears scrutiny. In the broader context (Romans 1-3) Paul is making a case that all the world—Gentile or Jew—is lost and needs God's provision for righteousness in Christ by faith. In this chapter, he appears to be showing that a Jew[1] is not an exception to this universal sinfulness and need. All alike stand under "the righteous judgment of God" (v. 5), which Paul proceeds to describe thus (in summary): God will render to all persons in accord with their *deeds* (*erga*): eternal life "to those who by perseverance in doing good seek for glory and honor and immortality" (NASB), but (eternal) wrath to those who disobey Him (vv. 6-8). Those who "do evil"—Jew or Gentile—will experience tribulation and anguish. Those who "work good"—Jew or Gentile—will experience glory, honor, and peace (vv. 9-10). Verse 13 adds that the *doers* of the law, as opposed to hearers who do not obey, are the ones who will be justified before God.[2]

Here is where our "insider knowledge" may take over to prevent us from taking Paul at face value. Paul is answering his critical, Jewish readers on their own terms we can say. They have assumed the possibility that eternal life will depend on whether people have observed the law of God. Paul wants them to understand that by such a standard what counts is *keeping* the law, not simply *knowing* it; and by that standard, eternal life is awarded to those who keep the law. All the same, Paul knows—but keeps it to himself for the time being—no one really can keep the law and therefore the issue of eternal life must finally be decided on some other basis: namely, the redemptive work of Christ and whether a person has responded to that in faith.

While such an approach appears more often at the popular level, even Robert Mounce can say, "In the immediate context Paul adopted for the moment the perspective of Judaism. What needs to be added is that no one could ever keep the law so perfectly as to be considered righteous before God."[3] I am not sure how far Mounce would press this, but what he says earlier is better: "It is beside the point to interpret the verses to mean that if a person did persist in good deeds God would grant eternal life because no one can live a perfect life. It is better to assume that only those who have placed their trust in God through Jesus Christ are capable of, or even want to, seek godliness. Paul was clear that 'no one seeks God' (Romans 3:11)."[4] Mounce also observes, "God judges faith by the difference it makes in how a person actually lives."[5] This is appealing.

It is interesting how much Paul's words sound like what Jesus said in John 5:28-29, which I have treated in chapter three: specifically, those who have "done good" will experience the resurrection of life and those who have "done evil" the resurrection of condemnation. As I said there, surely we are not surprised that Jesus—or Paul, now—would say something that so much sounds like the general tenor of Scripture! For that matter, Paul may be quoting Psalm 62:12. Indeed, Leon Morris is correct in saying Paul "gives attention first of all to the general principle, setting forth the position uniformly taken up in the New Testament that judgment is on the basis of works."[6]

Morris recognizes the potential for tension between this and the fact Paul has already "put considerable emphasis on the truth that salvation is God's free gift," asking, "But if people are saved by grace through faith, why should they be judged by their works?"[7] He briefly surveys five ways interpreters have grappled with this. (1) Paul is contradicting himself and reconciliation of the two ideas is not possible. (2) In verses 7, 10, and 13, Paul is speaking hypothetically, of the way things would be without the redemption that is in Christ. (3) Paul is "expounding the law, not the gospel"—which is essentially the same thing as the preceding. (4) Justification by faith applies to *becoming* a Christian but not to the judgment. (5) Justification is a work of power that makes the believer a new creation. In the end, he does not decide between the last two interpretations, and the implications he sees in them are not entirely clear.[8]

Osborne similarly summarizes the views of several interpreters. He adds to these five that Paul refers to the period before Christ, or to people who never hear the gospel, or (when he promises eternal life) to Christians only, or he means faith as the "good work," or the offer would be valid if anyone could actually perform the required works.[9] He concludes, with some uncertainty, "the saint could be the subject of verses 7 and 10 and the sinner the subject of verses 8 and 9"[10]—a view that unnecessarily divides the passage in a way readers are not likely to catch. Osborne has already observed, "Paul is describing all people, Christian and non-Christian alike, in verses 6-11."[11] Leroy Forlines lists three views and then suggests Paul is speaking of those to whom the perfect righteousness of Christ is imputed, so they are "doers of the law" (verse 13) as a result of justification. He cites the old Reformed Baptist theologian, John Gill, in support.[12] It seems more likely that Paul is referring to a person's actual deeds than to the imputation of the active obedience of Christ.

Moo's outline of various approaches, with extensive notes indicating who supports them, is perhaps the most helpful. He concludes "that vv. 7 and 10 set forth what is called in traditional theological (especially Lutheran) language 'the law.' Paul sets forth the biblical conditions for attaining eternal life apart from Christ. ... The promise can, in fact, never become operative because the condition for its fulfillment—consistent, earnest seeking after good—can never be realized."[13] This view—he prefers to call it a *theoretical*, rather than a *hypothetical* provision—

is disappointing; he goes on, more helpfully, to assert that "the initial declaration of the believer's acquittal before the bar of heaven at the time of one's justification is infallibly confirmed by the judgment according to works at the last assize."[14]

Schreiner also mentions various ways of dealing with this tension, calling "attractive" the view that Paul is speaking hypothetically but finally concluding what Paul says cannot be dismissed as hypothetical. He maintains that Paul is referring (vv. 7, 10) to Christians who keep the law by the power of the Holy Spirit and that Paul "shared in common" with James the conviction that good works are essential for participation in the coming age.[15]

It is valid, of course, to distinguish between faith as the condition for salvation and works as the basis for judgment, even for Christians (2 Corinthians 5:10).[16] But the judgment of Christians' works, commonly called "the judgment seat of Christ," is not for their eternal salvation but for their "rewards"—whatever that may entail.[17] That fact, however, will not explain what Paul says here in Romans: he is speaking not of rewards for the saved but of people's very salvation itself, as shown by the reference to "eternal life" in verse 7 and to being "justified" in verse 13, verses at the heart of the passage. Even verse 10, in this context, must refer to the blessings of eternal life as received by all the saved. Osborne, referring to the three things sought in verse 7, says, "These three define the meaning of eternal life for the faithful."[18]

What we need is a way of taking Paul to mean what he says every time. On the one hand, he says, "by the deeds of the law there shall no flesh be justified in his sight" (3:20). On the other hand, he says, "the doers of the law shall be justified" (2:13). He says both that "a man is justified by faith without the deeds of the law" (3:28) and that God will grant the blessing of eternal life "to every man that worketh good" (2:10). If both of these are taken at face value, that would appear to mean that both are, at least in some sense, saying the same thing. Perhaps F. Godet's observation points in the right direction: "God demands, from … the recipient of grace, the fruits of grace."[19] The words of C. K. Barrett may also be helpful: "The reward of eternal life, then, is promised to those who do not regard their good works as an end in themselves, but see them as marks not of human achievement but of hope in God. Their trust is not in their good works, but in God."[20] This is, after all, obedience as the form in which faith expresses itself, to which I will return in chapter six. Moo's comment is helpful, to the effect that perseverance in good works represents "a persistent lifestyle of godliness."[21]

This understanding is seen best in Schreiner's treatment, already anticipated above. When he reaches discussion of 2:25-29, he insists Paul is referring to Gentiles who, as believers, obey the moral norms of the law of God as a result of having received the Holy Spirit and thereby having been circumcised in heart where God's law is now written. In that light, the promise of eternal life (in 2:6-11) to those who "work good" is to all who by faith, and through the operation of the Holy Spirit, obey God. This represents such good works done as "*obedience* that has its source in faith," obedience enabled by "the dynamic power of the Spirit." These are works "necessary to be saved."[22]

As Schreiner has suggested, the discussion of James, in the following chapter, will develop this at greater length.

Romans 6

This chapter is part of a section (chapters 5-8), that translates justification into life, focusing on the results of justification and how it affects experience. There is not space here for a full exegetical treatment of the chapter, but a survey of its main argument seems necessary for my purpose.

Leading up to this Paul has said, "Where sin abounded, grace did much more abound" (5:20). Since that could theoretically lead into what we have come to call antinomianism, Paul hastens to clarify that this does not mean we are thereby free to continue in sin. He grounds this denial in the following closely related truths.[23]

(1) Christians are "dead to sin" (v. 2, literally "we died to sin"), a point that is generously reinforced from verse 2 to verse 11, at least. Our baptism testifies to our having died with Christ (vv. 3-4). We were "planted" with Him in the likeness of His death (v. 5). The persons we used to be ("our old man") were crucified with Him (v. 6). We are "dead" (v. 7), "dead with Christ" (v. 8). We must count ourselves "dead indeed unto sin" (v. 11). The obvious implication of this, explicitly stated by Paul (in the form of a rhetorical question with an unambiguous answer), is we do not any longer live in sin (v. 2). We have been made free from sin (v. 7) and are no longer servants of sin (v. 6). "It is quite impossible for anyone who understands what baptism means to acquiesce cheerfully in a sinful life. The baptized have died to all that. ... Being united [by faith to all that is Christ] in living out the life is not an option but a necessary part of being saved in Christ. ... An old way of life passes away completely."[24]

(2) Correlatively, Christians have been raised to a new way of life (v. 4), likewise reinforced in verses 5, 8, 10, and 11. These first two truths serve as the foundation for a distinction that appears elsewhere in Paul, between the "old man" and the "new man" (Ephesians 4:22, 24; Colossians 3:9-10)—to which I will return in chapter seven. These do *not* refer to the sinful nature (flesh) versus the spiritual nature—a different contrast that is also frequent in Paul (as in Galatians 5:17). The old man and new man refer instead, more simply but fundamentally, to the persons we were before conversion versus the persons we are after the new birth: the pre-regeneration self versus the post-regeneration self.[25] Moo correctly affirms that to refer these expressions to a person's two natures "is incorrect"; he goes on to cite John Stott favorably: "What was crucified with Christ was not a part of me called my old nature, but the whole of me as I was before I was converted."[26] Paul is saying, here in Romans, that the persons we used to be died and we were restored to life as new persons. The obvious implication, again explicitly stated, is that new persons live new and different lives (v. 4). We live to God (v. 11). As Mounce expresses this (commenting on 6:4), "The lives of believers are to be as different from their preconversion days as life is from death."[27]

Another way of saying this is that all persons who are justified are also regenerated and sanctified. The words can be distinguished for discussion, but (regardless of differences of opinion about the *ordo salutis*[28]) they are all true of every converted person. Regeneration is but the beginning of the work of sanctification. (I will discuss sanctification at greater length in chapter seven.)

(3) This means one of two slightly different things, crucial to my discussion: either we *ought* not, or we *do* not, allow sin to dictate the course of our lives. As Moo expresses this, "Is 'living in sin' a possibility to be avoided, or an impossibility to be recognized?"[29] Before deciding which one Paul means, we must observe that he is apparently depicting two possible ways of life. First, he sees the possibility of a way of life that will not match that of the truly regenerate person. He represents this as "serving" sin (vv. 6, 16, 20, etc.), as "obeying" it or allowing it to "reign" in one's life (v. 12), as "yielding one's members as instruments of unrighteousness" (v. 13), as allowing sin to "have dominion" (v. 14). Standing in sharp contrast to that way of life is another, represented as "yielding" to God so that one's members serve righteousness (v. 13) and practice "obedience unto righteousness" (v. 16) as "servants of righteousness," with holiness as the fruit (vv. 18-19).

The question is whether Paul is saying the regenerate *ought* not to live according to the first of these two—implying all the while that though they *should* not, they *can*. Or does he mean, in warning against the first way, the regenerate *do* not live that way? This is not an easy question to answer, and the discussion must begin with an acknowledgement that Paul approaches this, in the middle of this chapter, as *exhortation* rather than as *affirmation*. Using imperative verbs he *appeals* to his readers—taking for granted they are Christians—to count themselves dead to sin and alive to God (v. 11), to refuse to allow sin to reign in their lives (v. 12), to yield themselves to serve righteousness rather than sin (v. 13), and so on.

At first glance, at least, this seems to raise the possibility that they might not hearken to Paul's appeal and might pursue a lifestyle inimical with the second way—and still be children of God at that! Perhaps they, although disciples of Jesus, were already living in the service of sin and this was what led Paul to make such an appeal? If this is the implication of Paul's instruction, it paints an incongruous picture: a regenerate person, saved by faith (the "transaction model," apparently), but living in the service of sin (v. 6), allowing sin to reign in his life and have dominion over him (vv. 12, 14), obeying sin (v. 12), and yielding his members as instruments of unrighteousness (v. 13). This is so appalling a picture that one is forced to take a second look at the passage.

In fact, although Paul speaks exhortation he also speaks affirmation, both in the beginning and before he is finished. As already observed, he has begun by affirming that regenerate persons are dead to sin. His connection of this to Christian baptism (vv. 3-4), along with his way of stating the truth, makes clear this *is* true of all those who have been born again and not simply something that *ought* to be true.[30] Moreover, after the appeals of verses 11-13, Paul returns to affirmation. In verse 17, he expresses thanks to God that his readers had been the servants of sin but have in fact obeyed the teaching that stood in contrast to that. Verse 18 affirms that they did indeed become servants of righteousness. In verse 22, Paul affirms again that they have been made free from sin and have become servants to God, with fruit for holiness. Schreiner confirms that Paul is not "exhorting" but "proclaiming" that believers have died to sin.[31]

We should also note that in this affirming section Paul indicates the final "end" (*telos*) of each of the two ways of life he has presented. The service of sin, with its (shameful) fruit, has as its end death (vv. 20-21). The service of God, with its fruit (holiness), has as its end everlasting life (v. 22). Verse 23 reiterates. What seems clear is these two ways are precisely the same as have been referred to throughout the chapter. In that case, the first way (as defined above) is *not* a way that is possible for a regenerate person. It is, instead, the way of the unbeliever, and eternal death is its consequence. The second way is the way of all disciples and eternal life is its consequence.

Why, then, does Paul *appeal* to his believing readers to avoid the service of sin? Why does he not just say they *will* live in the service of God? Or say nothing at all since they—inevitably?—will do so? The answer to that question is also hard, but it must be something like the following. Paul is dealing with *professing* Christians, as in fact are we all. Only God knows for sure the genuine and the impostor; He sees the heart. The professing Christian Paul assumes is a genuine one (with apparently a lifestyle that does not clearly contradict the profession). He reminds this Christian that as such he is dead to sin and will not live in the service of sin. "Such habitual sin, 'remaining in sin' (v. 1), 'living in sin' (v. 2), is not possible, as a constant situation for the one who has truly experienced the transfer out from under the domain, or tyranny, of sin. Sin's power is broken for the believer and this *must* be evident in practice (see also James 2:14-26; and perhaps 1 John 3:6, 9)."[32] That is the difference between those who possess eternal life and the unregenerate: the latter live in the service of sin. Since that is the difference, he appeals to the Christian not to allow the lifestyle of the unregenerate to become his.

This is, in fact, the same exhortation that appears often in Paul: you *are*, now *be*. The person you were (the "old man") died, was crucified, with Christ, so "put off" the deeds of that person. You were restored to life as a new person (the "new man") in Christ, so "put on" the deeds of the new way of life (Ephesians 4:20-32, Colossians 3:1-15, etc.). "The imperative challenges us to become what we are."[33] As Schreiner observes in connection with this, "Believers will never obtain eschatological salvation if obedience does not characterize their lives."[34]

A few observations appear to be in order. First, appeals to the regenerate to avoid sin do seem to open the door to the possibility of sin. How that fits into our view of the nature of true Christianity needs further discussion and that is a major purpose of this entire work. Meanwhile, we are justified to say Paul's admonitions seem to acknowledge the possibility that Christians may sin as individual acts; but they do not seem to allow for the possibility of a sinful lifestyle. "To come to Christ means the complete end of a whole way of life. There may be slips, but they are uncharacteristic."[35] Again, "The sin of the unbeliever is the natural consequence of the fact that he is a slave to sin, whereas the sin of the believer is quite out of character."[36]

This leads to a second observation. This discussion may well have wound up in the same place as our earlier discussion regarding the teaching of 1 John 3 (chapter four). In other words, Paul's affirmations, like John's, indicate that Christians do not live in sin. His appeals, like John's provision in 1 John 2:1, indicate the need for warnings against particular sins. Osborne's suggestion about the possibility of sin in the life of the believer seems to suggest a fruitful approach: "While sin has lost its ability to overpower, it has not lost its ability to deceive."[37] Schreiner makes a helpful addition to the effect that Paul is speaking of sin's dominion being broken instead of perfect sinlessness."[38]

As for our pursuit of the New Testament teaching on what is required for eternal life, Romans 6 may not offer much help. Even so, we should note that verses 22-23 finally appear to provide grounds for saying eternal life is both the "end" of a life lived in the service of God and the gracious gift of God. But this is not as pointed as Romans 2. Once we take at full face value the affirmations of Romans 2:6-10, we can with relative ease fit these verses in with that.

Romans 7:14-25

This passage is also (like chapter 6) part of that larger context which focuses on the experience of justification. But interpreters have not yet solved the problem whether this passage refers to the experience and self-consciousness of an unbeliever or of a regenerate person. Many interpreters believe Paul is recalling his spiritual state before he was saved. Others (I with them) believe he is reflecting his state at the time he wrote the letter, and thus the situation of a child of God. Given this difference, I will touch on this passage only briefly. For that matter, it does not speak to what one must do to have eternal life.

What is clear is that Paul is reflecting a struggle between doing right and doing wrong. If this is the struggle of a person who has been instructed in the law but is not regenerate, as some think, then it has little if any bearing on the problem of sin in the believer's life, one of the issues to which this work is devoted. On the other hand, if it is the struggle of a regenerate person, then here is a true Christian who experiences the conflict between his sinful nature and his spiritual mind, apparently the same as that referenced in Galatians 5:17, which I will discuss in chapter seven. In that case Paul indicates a regenerate person can commit sin ("the evil which I would not, that I do," v. 19) and still be a child of God ("it is no more I that do it," v. 20; "I delight in the law of God after the inward man," v. 22).

Even if the latter could be established to gain general agreement, there would still be questions. Is this the *necessary* experience of one who has been born again and thus true for all who have eternal life? Or is it the experience of the so-called "defeated Christian" as opposed to other believers who reach a level of victory intended by God?[39] Does this represent the struggle with the sinful nature one longs to be rid of, or is it a struggle with habitual sin? I have opinions about all such questions, but in the end I think exploring them will not change any verdict about what is required for salvation. I will, however, give some attention to the matter of habitual sin later in this work.

Romans 8

Something must be said about this chapter, however, especially about verses 1-13. The passage provides an interesting contrast between two ways of life. On the one hand are those who "walk after" the flesh, or "are after" the flesh, or are "carnally minded," or "are in the flesh," or "live after the flesh." Such phrases stand over against those who "walk after" the Spirit, or "are after" the Spirit, or are "spiritually minded," or are "in the Spirit," or "through the Spirit put to death the deeds of the body."

Interpreters who want to think there are two essentially different levels of Christian living—"average" or "defeated" Christians versus "victorious" or "crucified" Christians—sometimes seek confirmation of that in this passage. I will deal with this again in chapter seven, devoted to the matter of sanctification. Anticipating the results of that discussion, I need only insist that here the two ways being described are those of the unregenerate and of the regenerate. The unregenerate walk after the flesh, and their end is eternal, spiritual death (vv. 6, 13). The regenerate are those in whom the Holy Spirit dwells (v. 9). "The believer walks *according to the Spirit*."[40] They are "in the Spirit" and the destiny of all in that group—provided, of course, they do not forfeit that Spirit—is to live forever (v. 13).

Verse 14, then, does not refer to *some* disciples who are "led by the Spirit of God," but to *all* disciples: "These, and only these, are sons of God."[41] Moo, I think, has it mostly right when he lists the four expressions in verses 5-9—"being according to" the flesh or the Spirit, "thinking the things of" the flesh or the Spirit, having "the mind of" the flesh or the Spirit, and "being in" the flesh or the Spirit—as "a contrast between non-Christian and Christian."[42] But then he posits a measure of difference between these four and "walking according to" the flesh or the Spirit in that the previous expressions are "positional" while this one is "behavioral." But that is a secondary difference. In Paul's discussion, this last expression is as descriptive as the first four, defining all who are regenerate. Moo apparently realizes this when he goes on to observe, "Paul's interest here is descriptive rather than hortatory," he "is contrasting two groups of people: the converted and the unconverted," and "life, eschatological life, is conferred only on those who 'walk according to the Spirit' (cf. v. 4b)."[43]

Closely related, I find disappointing the comments of some that make it sound as though Paul's discussion is only or primarily hortatory. Thus, Osborne says, "The message of the section is that we can experience progressive sanctification in the Spirit, that is, grow in righteous living. This can only occur when we live not *according to the flesh but according to the Spirit*."[44] As true as this is, it misses Paul's point: *all* the regenerate experience progressive sanctification and live according to the Spirit. Of course, there are implications of this that should motivate believers to right conduct, but Paul is defining all those who possess eternal life by these standards and contrasting their lifestyle and destiny to that of unbelievers. As Forlines insists, "If we are justified, we are also sanctified. ... While [the two] are distinct, they cannot be separated."[45] Osborne goes on to say "there are two choices—to live by the flesh or the world's standards or to live in obedience to the Spirit's leading."[46] If he means the believer has such choices *as a child of God*, he is wrong. The two ways Paul is describing are those of the believer and the unbeliever. A regenerate person could only choose to "live according to the flesh" in connection with apostasy.

Schreiner is more on track, introducing this section of Romans, when he observes, "Verses 5-11 do not constitute an exhortation to live according to the Spirit or to fulfill the law. Rather, they describe what is necessarily the case for one who has the Spirit or is still in the flesh.[47]

Interpreters who are aware of textual differences in the New Testament manuscripts are fond of pointing out that the words "who walk not after the flesh, but after the Spirit" belong only in verse 4 and not in verse 1—as though this matters in some important way. It would matter *only* if one takes verse 1 (if the words are included) to mean a person is free from condemnation *because* he walks after the

Spirit and not after the flesh. That would sound like justification by lifestyle. In fact, however, if that is a problem it will apply just as much to verse 4 (where the words indisputably belong)—if one takes the words to mean the righteousness of the law is fulfilled in us *because* we walk after the Spirit and not after the flesh. In the end, this textual issue has no bearing on the understanding of the passage. Even if Paul did not write the phrase in verse 1, the meaning is no more misconstrued by reading it there than by its inclusion in verse 4. Schreiner writes that this is "descriptive" and conveys the "inevitable result of the work of Christ on the cross."[48]

According to the way we typically understand Paul's theology of salvation—the transaction model, as I have called it—one is free from condemnation only because the righteousness of Christ is imputed to him by faith. Paul is saying clearly that freedom from condemnation (v. 1), standing righteous in terms of the requirements of God's law (v. 4), life and peace (v. 6), the promise of resurrection by the power of the Spirit (v. 11), and the promise of eternal life (v. 13), are things that belong to those who do not live under the dominion of the flesh! We would have expected him to say, instead, that these belong to those who are justified by faith—and no doubt he could easily have said that.

To be sure, what he says does not quite equate to saying these things are ours *because* we live under the dominion of the Spirit. It will require further discussion before we can say exactly how the defined lifestyle and the promise of life go together.

1 Corinthians 6:9-10

This epistle, devoted as it is to specific problems and questions among the original readers, does not give detailed attention to what a person must do to possess eternal life. There is consequently not much treatment of either the transaction model or the discipleship model. Even so, this passage seems important for the purpose of this chapter.

Transitioning from discussion of the Corinthians' lawsuits in pagan courts to discussion of the importance of moral purity, Paul inserts this forceful warning: "Do you not know that unrighteous persons will not inherit the kingdom of God? Do not be deceived: neither fornicators, nor idolaters, nor adulterers, nor homosexuals, nor men who have sex with men, nor thieves, nor covetous, nor drunkards, nor revilers, nor extortioners, will inherit the kingdom of God." The kingdom, here, is obviously "the future kingdom in all its glory."[49]

We quickly tell ourselves that, although this is obviously true, the opposite is not necessarily so. In other words, one could not with equal accuracy say those who avoid such wickedness *will* inherit the kingdom of God. Even if that were said, we would put our theological "spin" on its meaning: only those who are justified by faith and become new creatures in Christ are able, in fact, to avoid such wickedness. It is their faith, however, not their avoidance of wickedness that will give them entrance into the kingdom of heaven, now and forever.

But we must not forget Romans 2:7-11, where (unlike here in 1 Corinthians) Paul states all the implications of this on both sides: those who do evil perish, while those who do good have the promise of eternal life. In that case, we need not shy away from reading this passage, too, to mean that one's way of life, whether wicked or good, at least *results* in eternal death or a place in the kingdom of God. Fee discerns a warning, here, that "the whole community, ... if they persist in the same evils as 'the wicked' ... are in the same danger of not inheriting the kingdom."[50] Whether such a warning is implied, here, can be debated,[51] as can whether the possibility of apostasy from saving faith is involved in the warning. Regardless, Fee is right to focus on the direct connection between lifestyle and destiny. That is a fundamental biblical concept—and it works both ways! Marion Soards is right to say "Wickedness has no future with God, and so those who are devoting themselves to ungodly behaviors are forming lifestyles that ... will not be given a place in God's kingdom. ... Some things do not belong in God's kingdom."[52] And some things do, including all the good works that express faith.

Galatians 5:16-21

As in 1 Corinthians 6, Paul identifies those who will "not inherit the kingdom of God" (v. 21) as adulterers, idolaters, murderers, and the like. Essentially the same things can be said about this as about the passage just discussed. Even so, a few additional observations should be helpful. For one thing, Paul speaks again of two ways of life, reminding us of Romans 6 and 8 (above) and including here both the negative and the positive sides of the truth. Those whose lives are characterized in verses 19-21 are doing "the works of the flesh," and these are in contrast to those who manifest "the fruit of the Spirit" as described in verses 22-23. (I will discuss this passage more fully in chapter seven.)

The latter are those who "live" in the Spirit (v. 25) and whom Paul urges to "walk" in the Spirit (vv. 16, 25). One's "walk" is, of course, his way of living, his lifestyle as defined by his behavior. Walter Hansen is right to insist we must *not* "think that the contrast between *acts* [vv. 19-21] and *fruit* [vv. 22-23] is a contrast between active and passive, our effort and supernaturally produced growth. ... Life in the Spirit is both active (walking) and passive (being led)"[53]—as is life in the flesh!

Once again, we have the clear implication: those who live as described in verses 22-23 *will*, unlike those who live as described in verses 19-21, inherit the kingdom of God. To be sure, this is not quite the same as saying they will inherit the kingdom of God *because* they manifest the fruit of the Spirit. But it at least makes it difficult, if not impossible, to separate faith from character and works.[54] They are apparently closely related enough that one is justified to say a person who avoids wickedness and practices goodness will inherit eternal life. That may not tell everything there is to know about salvation, but what it says is precisely true—even without further qualification, as often stated in the Bible.

In confirmation of this understanding, a few verses later Paul says the person who "sows" to the flesh will reap eternal corruption and the one who "sows" to the Spirit will reap everlasting life (6:8). As Hansen observes, this "sowing" is in the form of our deeds: "If sowing to the sinful nature [flesh] means selfish indulgence, then sowing to the Spirit means selfless service. The harvest of sowing to the Spirit is *eternal life*."[55]

There could hardly be a clearer statement of the eternal results of two ways of life. Timothy George correctly links 6:8 to the "terms of his earlier antithesis [5:19-23] between flesh and Spirit" and then describes verse 8 as drawing out "on a canvas of eternity a scenario of the end results of the two catalogs of virtues and vices" enumerated there.[56] He continues: "If the works of the flesh issue in corruption and death, the fruit of the Spirit yields the harvest of eternal life."[57] Saying this neither draws out nor cancels the truth that salvation is by faith. Apparently, it simply fleshes out the meaning and implications of genuine, saving faith. Surely, Paul's example in stating this truth is one we can emulate without fear of misleading those who hear us.

Ephesians 5:5-7

This passage is much like the preceding two: once again, Paul warns about those who do not have "any inheritance in the kingdom of Christ and of God." And, once again, they are not said to be those who have rejected Christ in unbelief—

although that is of course true—but those whose lives are marked by wicked deeds. Indeed, Paul adds, it is *because* of these things, because of their disobedience, that the eternal wrath of God comes on them. (Essentially the same thing is said in Colossians 3:5-7, which I will not comment on separately.) Then surely, it is once again appropriate to say those who do not live in such disobedience *will* inherit eternal life in the kingdom of God. At the very least, Paul is warning that such wicked deeds contradict the profession of faith: "Those whose lives are characterized by immorality, impurity, and greed, even though they may claim to be Christians, are not included in the kingdom of God."[58]

In this light, as in the passages treated in the preceding paragraphs, Paul urges his readers how to "walk"—how to live and behave, in other words. They are to live in love (v. 2) and in light (v. 8). As elsewhere in Ephesians (4:22-24) and Colossians (3:8-14), Paul again sounds his "you are, therefore be" appeal, as discussed above.[59] The true disciple of Christ is unwilling to "participate" with those who have no place in the kingdom of God, neither in their conduct now nor in the destiny that awaits them (Ephesians 5:7).[60] Hoehner observes, correctly, I think, that—unlike those described in verses 5-6, who are "sons of disobedience"—believers are "sons of obedience or faith."[61] He may not mean to equate obedience and faith, but they are at least two perspectives on the same saving grace. Similarly, O'Brien views Paul as warning his readers "to make sure that they do not share with disobedient Gentiles in their immorality and *thus escape the judgment that rightly falls with it* (cf. 2 Cor. 6:14-7:1)."[62]

What all this appears to make clear is that Paul is indeed aware of the discipleship model of soteriology. To be sure, he focuses often on the transaction model, emphasizing that salvation is by grace through faith and not by works (Ephesians 2:8-9), as we have seen in chapter one. But he also insists this does *not* mean a regenerate person continues to live a sinful lifestyle; instead the child of God practices righteousness. And he states this so firmly it is clear he means this to be *essential* to true Christianity—so essential that persons not living righteously cannot rightly be regarded as Christians. That this does not require sinless perfection has been indicated in chapter four, but the permission to be less than sinless does not amount to permission to live unrighteously.

This understanding is most clearly seen in the important section, Romans 6-8, and in the passages where Paul delineates the differences between those who do not and those who do "inherit the kingdom of God" (1 Corinthians 6:9-10;

Galatians 5:16-21; Ephesians 5:5-7). These passages appear to justify the following conclusion: just as it is eminently proper to say those who have faith in Jesus Christ as their sole claim to salvation will inherit eternal life, so it is likewise proper to say those who live righteously will do so. Although Paul most often emphasizes the first, his words also justify the second. In essence, the two statements ultimately reduce to the same single meaning. Some may respond to this by raising the question whether those who are morally upright, but do not believe in Jesus will have eternal life. The answer, of course, is they will not: their righteousness, such as it is, is not the obedience of faith.

Why, then, does he most often emphasize the first—in comparison, for example, to Jesus (in the Synoptic Gospels) or John (in 1 John) who emphasize the second? Perhaps part of the answer to this is Paul was often in conflict with Judaizers who thought even Gentile converts to Christ ought to live under the Mosaic law.[63] In that case, it may be when Paul contrasts faith and works that the "works" are to be understood as "the works of the law" (Galatians 2:16; 3:2, 5, 10) or "the deeds of the law" (Romans 3:20, 28). If so, he is combating one particular view of "works": the keeping of the law of God (especially the Mosaic law) in an effort to merit salvation by doing so.

This may not be the whole answer to our question. Perhaps another part of the answer lies in the fact the transaction model exposes what is more basic, what one must begin with, while the discipleship model exposes what must follow. The following chapters, I hope, will make this clearer.

ENDNOTES

[1] A number of interpreters think that the direct challenge to the Jew does not begin until v. 17, and that until that point Paul is speaking to anyone who makes moral judgments of others, perhaps based on some knowledge of the revealed law of God. But there are other interpreters who think the Jew is in view throughout the chapter. I see no need to pursue this difference here.

[2] For the chiastic structure of vv. 6-11, see Thomas R. Schreiner, *Romans* (ECNT; Grand Rapids: Baker, 1998), 111-12; Grant R. Osborne, *Romans* (IVP New Testament Commentary; Downers Grove: InterVarsity, 2004), 63; Douglas J. Moo, *The Epistle to the Romans* (NICNT; Grand Rapids: Eerdmans, 1996), 135:

    A. God renders to each equally according to works (v. 6)
        B. Eternal life to those who seek it by persevering in good works (v. 7)
            C. Eternal wrath to those whose works represent refusal of the truth (v. 8)
            C'. The distresses of eternal wrath to all who practice evil, Jew or Gentile (v. 9)
        B'. The blessings of eternal life to those who practice good, Jew or Gentile (v. 10)
    A'. God is impartial (v. 11)

[3] Robert H. Mounce, *The New American Commentary: Romans*, vol. 27 (Nashville: Broadman & Holman, 1995), 94.

[4] Mounce, 92.

[5] Mounce, 91.

[6] Leon Morris, *The Epistle to the Romans* (Pillar New Testament Commentary; Grand Rapids: Eerdmans, 1988), 147. He lists Matthew 7:21; 16:27; 25:31-46; John 5:28-29; 2 Corinthians 5:10; 11:15; Galatians 6:7-9; 2 Timothy 4:14; 1 Peter 1:17; Revelation 2:23; 22:12, etc. as evidence.

[7] Morris, 148.

[8] Morris, 148-49.

[9] Osborne, 64-66.

[10] Osborne, 67.

[11] Osborne, 65-66.

[12] F. Leroy Forlines, *The Randall House Bible Commentary: Romans* (Nashville: Randall House, 1987), 54-55.

[13] Moo, 142; also 211.

[14] Moo, 143.

[15] Schreiner, 115. He also notes, in the same discussion, that Paul in passages like 1 Corinthians 6:9-11; 2 Corinthians 5:10; and Galatians 5:21, regards works as "necessary to enter the kingdom of God."

[16] As does Osborne, 64: "We are saved by grace but judged by works."

[17] It is beyond my purpose to explore this. Whatever else may be involved, it is enough that each one will have the praise or recognition of God that his works deserve (1 Corinthians 4:5).

[18] Osborne, 65.

[19] F. Godet, *Commentary on St. Paul's Epistle to the Romans*, 2 vols. (Edinburgh: T. & T. Clark, 1895), I:196. Cited by Morris, 148.

[20] C. K. Barrett, *A Commentary on the Epistle to the Romans* (London, 1957), cited by Morris, 116.

[21] Moo, 137.

[22] Schreiner, 140-145.

[23] Antinomianism—the teaching that Christians do not have to obey any laws of ethics or morality.

[24] Morris, 247-48.

[25] See Forlines, 153: "'The old man' is the pre-salvation self or person. ... When one becomes a Christian, he is a new person." It is fairly common for interpreters to represent the "old man" as ourselves in union with Adam, and the "new man" as ourselves in union with Christ. See Morris, 252; Schreiner, 307, 315—who views this in an especially *corporate* sense. But this seems an unnecessary refinement that ultimately means the same thing as I have said, given that the pre-regeneration self is still "in Adam" and the post-regeneration self "in Christ." I tend to doubt that the first Adam-second Adam Christology was as frequent in the New Testament as some interpreters think, but that need not occupy us here. Moo, 374-75, may be right in indicating that the two phrases "denote the solidarity of people with the 'heads' of the two contrasting ages of salvation history," but I am not persuaded Paul was thinking along these lines in this passage.

[26] Moo, 373-74, citing John R. W. Stott, *Men Made New: An Exposition of Romans 5-8* (London: Inter-Varsity, 1966), 45.

110

[27] Mounce, 150.

[28] The logical order of different aspects of the salvation experience, like regeneration, justification, conversion, etc.

[29] Moo, 358.

[30] This is the reason statements about verses 1-10 that appear to interpret Paul to mean *only* that we *ought* to live as new persons are disappointing. Thus Osborne, 152, says: "Our daily lives should be characterized by the new realm Christ has brought about. ... We are to live in the Spirit rather than the flesh (Rom 8)." As true as this is, Paul is more accurately represented as saying our lives *are* characterized as new persons, and we *do* live in the Spirit rather than the flesh. The discussion in chapter 8 will reemphasize this.

[31] Schreiner, 305.

[32] Moo, 358; he goes on in this discussion to observe that even though living in sin is impossible "as a constant condition, it remains a real threat. It is this threat that Paul warns us about in v. 2." I agree that the threat is real; I do not agree it is primarily in mind in v. 2.

[33] Mounce, 153. Osborne, 156 (citing also Moo, 338, and Schreiner, 321), puts a little different twist on this: "Become what you are in process of becoming." Although this is not untrue, I tend to doubt it catches Paul's meaning quite as well.

[34] Schreiner, 321.

[35] Morris, 251.

[36] Morris, 256.

[37] Osborne, 154.

[38] Schreiner, 317.

[39] In this case, one's view of sanctification comes into play. See chapter 7.

[40] Morris, 304 (italics his). He goes on to emphasize the "sharp contrast," in this passage, between "the fleshly minded," and "believers," 307.

[41] Mounce, 181.

[42] Moo, 486.

[43] Moo, 486-87.

[44] Osborne, 197.

[45] Forlines, 204. He quotes Charles Hodge, *Commentary on the Epistle to the Romans* (Grand Rapids: Eerdmans, 1983 reprint), 255, as saying that "The benefits of Christ's death are experienced only by those who walk not after the flesh."

[46] Osborne, 197. Subsequently Osborne, 198, acknowledges that the contrast, at least in vv. 5-8, is between the converted and the unconverted. The same applies to the entire passage.

[47] Schreiner, 409.

[48] Schreiner, 405-06. He proceeds in this discussion, 407, to emphasize that verse 4 does not simply mean the righteousness of the law is fulfilled *forensically* in believers, but "those who have the Spirit actually keep the law." This seems to be correct.

[49] F. W. Grosheide, *The First Epistle to the Corinthians* (NICNT; Grand Rapids: Eerdmans, 1953), 140.

[50] Gordon D. Fee, *The First Epistle to the Corinthians* (NICNT; Grand Rapids: Eerdmans, 1987), 242. Grosheide, 140, agrees: "The Corinthians might by their trespasses place themselves in that same line of sinners."

[51] Marion L. Soards, *New International Biblical Commentary: 1 Corinthians* (Peabody, MA: Hendrickson, 1999), 124, is more inclined to think that "Paul's true concern is to remind the Corinthians of their pre-Christian pasts, as becomes clear in the following lines."

[52] Soards, 124.

[53] G. Walter Hansen, *Galatians* (IVPNTC; Downers Grove: InterVarsity, 1994), 174.

[54] Hansen, 177, notes that this is, indeed, judgment by works: "Those who practice the works of the flesh are denied entrance to the kingdom of God." Whether he would say those who practice the fruit of the Spirit will obtain entrance into the kingdom of God, I do not know; but I will say it—and insist that Paul's words clearly imply this. He does say (177) "Sanctification is not the basis of justification but the *inevitable* result of justification" (emphasis mine), which means the same thing.

[55] Hansen, 195.

[56] Timothy George, *The New American Commentary: Galatians* (Nashville: Broadman & Holman, 1994), 423.

[57] George, 424.

[58] Harold W. Hoehner, *Ephesians: An Exegetical Commentary* (Grand Rapids: Baker Academic, 2002), 662. So also Peter T. O'Brien, *The Letter to the Ephesians* (PNTC; Grand Rapids: Eerdmans, 1999), 363.

[59] See also my discussion in chapter seven.

[60] Hoehner, 668: "In the light of the coming judgment (v. 6), believers should not be deceived into thinking that it is harmless to become participants with unbelievers."

[61] Hoehner, 665.

[62] O'Brien, 365-66. I assume he means that by not sharing in wickedness the readers would escape God's wrath.

[63] I am aware when I say this that I may be judged as uninformed about the "new perspective" on Paul. It would be more correct to say I am unconvinced by that perspective. One of its problems, as I see it, is it must discount a good bit of the historical information in the book of Acts. But I need not pursue this here.

Chapter Six

FAITH AND WORKS IN JAMES AND HEBREWS

So far, we have pursued the question, what one must do to have eternal life, in the Gospels, Paul, and 1 John. What we have found there is enough to cause us to mind how we say a person is saved by faith alone. That is obviously the truth, but it is a truth that needs to be biblically understood. For one thing, saving faith is not mere belief; it involves a commitment to discipleship. It remains, in this chapter, to pursue this survey of the New Testament one step more.

Primarily, I want to consider what bearing James, especially, may have on these issues. His short epistle is sometimes set in contrast (if not contradiction) to Paul on the subject of justification. Perhaps, then, James will show us the way to understand both faith and works together, both the transaction model and the discipleship model of what one must do to be saved. And we need to explore, as well, whether the book of Hebrews can contribute anything to this.

Numerous interpreters have concluded—rightly, I suppose—that James and Paul are in some degree of tension. Paul emphasizes faith *without* works (Romans 3:28), James advocates faith expressed *in* works (James 2:22). Perhaps it was for that reason the great reformer, Martin Luther, viewed the latter as a "right strawy epistle."[1] But this seems too drastic a way to handle the inspired word of God. If the two prophetic voices are in tension, "It is a healthy tension, one that is reflected within Paul's epistles themselves. James here echoes the teaching of Jesus in the Gospels."[2]

James 2:14-26 and the Nature of Faith

In the context of a very practical epistle, one often compared to Old Testament wisdom literature, we encounter what Douglas Moo calls "the most theologically significant, as well as the most controversial" passage in James.[3] James asks a twofold, rhetorical question: "What does it profit, my brothers, if someone says he has faith and does not have works? Can the faith save him?" (v. 14). The rest of the passage is devoted to answering that question, although the simple answer has already been signaled: "Can the faith save him?" (there is a definite article with *faith* in the original) is written to expect a negative answer.[4] It could just as correctly be translated, "The faith [meaning the faith referred to in the previous question, faith without works] cannot save him, can it?"

James begins to develop his answer with an illustration from practical Christian living (vv. 15-16). He pictures someone in serious need of clothing or food. A Christian says to that person—in faith (clearly implied)—"Relax, go your way, everything's going to be OK, God will supply your needs." But the person expressing this confidence does not *do* anything. That sort of "faith" will profit the needy person not at all.

The lesson to be drawn from this is in verse 17: in the same way, faith that does not issue in works (*erga*) is *dead*. "A faith which does not rule the life, is exactly like such charity."[5] This is obviously an important point: James states it three times (vv. 17, 20, 26) to underline it. Nor do we need to be in doubt as to the meaning: such so-called faith is unavailing, ineffective; it has no life. *It is not faith.*

James does not leave us to figure this out for ourselves. He proceeds to make sure we understand the point, and does so in several ways. First, in verse 18, he indicates that faith can only be viewed in the works that issue from it. There are differences of opinion about the identity of "a man" whom James quotes and just how much of the verse makes up the quotation. It is beyond my purpose to deal with this in detail,[6] except to say the "man" in verse 18 must surely be the same as the "vain man" in verse 20. Regardless, James appears to cite an opponent who would attempt to separate faith and works as though either can stand alone. James responds by emphasizing "It is, of course, impossible to show anyone faith, for it is invisible … . The only way for one to know of its presence is by manifestation of it through good works."[7] "James, in a sense, proposes for us … a 'test' by which we determine the genuineness of faith: deeds of obedience to the will of God."[8] "Faith and works—neither is authentic without the other."[9]

Verse 19 follows immediately: the inefficacy of "believing" something, as an intellectual persuasion that is not accompanied by a change of heart and life (faith inadequately conceived, in other words), is pointedly illustrated by demons who believe God is one, and even tremble as a result. And yet they are undoubtedly damned! To James this proves his argument and leads to his first restatement of the truth to be underlined: faith without works is dead, and it is vain (*kenos*)—empty, foolish, without truth, false—to think otherwise.

At this point James provides us with two well-known illustrations from the Old Testament: Abraham (vv. 21-24) and Rahab (v. 25). The case of Abraham rests on the fact that when God asked him to sacrifice Isaac, the promised son, he did so. And in doing so his faith and works were active together and the works made the faith complete. Verse 22 can be literally read, "You see (or Do you see?) that the faith worked together with his works and out of (or by) the works the faith was made complete (or perfected)." In other words, Abraham's act of obedience made his faith fully what faith is supposed to be. As Richardson expresses this, "Faith requires deeds to be whole or complete faith."[10]

Furthermore, James is not speaking merely of general faith but of justifying faith, and in verses 23-24 he proceeds to state this firmly: "You see that out of (or by) works a man is justified and not out of (or by) faith alone." Obviously, the "faith alone" refers back to the faith that does not issue in works, which has been under discussion since verse 14. Not to be outdone by Paul (as though that could even be considered!), he cites Paul's favorite verse on justification, Genesis 15:6: "Abraham believed God, and it was imputed to him for righteousness."[11]

Rahab's works made the same point, although James does not take the time to draw out the implications again. Hebrews 11:31 has already informed us that Rahab's deliverance from the fate of the rest of Jericho was by faith. James makes sure we see that her shielding of the Israelite spies, like Abraham's obedience with Isaac, made her faith complete as what faith really is. And again James makes clear this was not merely a matter of her deliverance from the fate of the city. Her *justification* was included.[12]

So James states the point for a third time: faith without works is dead (v. 26). And in order to make sure we "get" this he offers a comparison: faith that does not issue in works is as dead—lifeless, ineffective, inert, without meaning, impotent—as a body without a spirit! Anyone who has ever gazed on an open casket in a funeral home understands just how powerful this comparison is and just how unworthy of the name is a so-called faith not completed by works.

I do not think it helpful, here, to get deeply involved in what may be called the reconciliation of James and Paul on the subject of justification; but I suppose I must give it summary attention since it seems so important to interpreters. Moo makes two suggestions toward harmonizing James (2:24) with Paul (Romans 3:28). (1) He suggests that "justify" for Paul means God's *initial* declaration of a person's right-standing with Himself, based on faith, while for James it means the final vindication of a person's right-standing with God *at the judgment*—and yet he agrees that in 2:24 the verb has its usual "forensic" meaning. (2) He offers that James's use of "faith alone" (2:24) means the bogus faith introduced in 2:17, and that Paul would have agreed that such professed "faith" cannot be the basis of salvation.[13] I find the second suggestion to be more helpful than the first.

Kent Hughes appears to think the difference between Paul and James is at root a difference in *focus*, with Paul focusing "on the time *before* conversion" and James on the time "*after* conversion."[14]

A number of interpreters rely on taking Paul and James to use *justification* in somewhat different senses. Perhaps the most common view is that while Paul means the basic acquittal verdict of God, James means one is *shown* to be righteous "in a moral sense"[15] by justification. Calvin laid the groundwork for this view, saying that "you must give the word *justify*, as used by [James], a different meaning from what it has with Paul. ... He is speaking of the *manifestation* ... of righteousness, as if he had said, Those who are justified by true faith prove their justification by obedience and good works." Even so, he added, helpfully, "James will not allow any to be regarded as justified who are destitute of good works."[16] Richardson gives justification, in James, an even more "narrow" sense, suggesting one's *claim* to be a believer is "justified" by his works.[17]

My own conviction is that the concept of faith that I define below, faith that *necessarily* expresses itself in works of obedience, removes all alleged contradiction with Paul. There is finally no need to view *save, justify, faith,* or *works* as having different meanings in Paul and James—except Paul, by *works*, may mean the keeping of the Mosaic law as obedience that has merit, while James means "moral deeds flowing naturally from genuine faith,"[18] deeds Paul himself would require in the same way as expressions of faith. James "simply saw faith and works as inseparable."[19]

One final point in analyzing the passage: James is *not* talking about the "works" of one who is doing what he does because of the requirements of the Law of Moses. If Paul, as I have suggested in the preceding chapter, at least often means this when he sets works against faith as the basis of justification, James does not. All his illustrations point in a different direction. The person who responds to someone in need (vv. 15-16), Abraham's offering of Isaac on Moriah (vv. 21-24), Rahab's protection of the spies (v. 25): these are the kinds of works James means, and they are not matters of legalism.

So what does James teach us? Here are some of the things that seem clear.

(1) He is aware of the teaching of justification by faith, or else he would not express things as he does, especially in v. 24: "You see then that a man is justified by works and not by faith only." He is not obviously disagreeing with that teaching insomuch as he is making sure it is correctly understood, and comes from having a right understanding of the nature of faith. We learn, then, there are times when it is important to bring works into our discussion of forensic justification.

(2) James is convinced that a so-called "faith" that does not issue in works is not saving faith. It may be the kind of belief demons have, but it is not faith. Given that it is dead, it cannot be effectual for salvation. Moo quotes from Martin Luther's preface to *Romans*, showing Luther's understanding of faith as "a living, busy active mighty thing, this faith. It is impossible for it not to be doing good things."[20] Moo represents James as teaching that "genuine faith ... always and inevitably produces evidence of its existence in a life of righteous living. *Biblical* faith cannot exist apart from acts of obedience to God."[21] As Stulac puts this, "It is the very nature of genuine faith to express itself in works."[22] We learn, it is important to view faith as a "working faith," to borrow and adapt a Pauline expression (1 Thessalonians 1:3).

(3) James most certainly appears to view works as *essential* to faith: that is, as an effect so necessary to faith as to be properly counted a part of it. That insight may very well be the primary key to understanding the dilemma we face in the transaction model versus the discipleship model. It leads me to the following observations about the relationship between faith and works.

Faith and Its Relationship to Obedience

I begin with a brief discussion of what faith is. It is indeed multi-faceted and can be examined from more than one perspective. It is, at root, *belief*, but it is not *mere* intellectual persuasion that something is true. Faith involves a personal appropriation of truth, an acceptance of what is true for oneself. And in that appropriation faith turns to reliance or trust or confidence. To put faith in God is to commit oneself to Him as one's own God, with all that the very idea of *God* entails. And so faith immediately and necessarily wears the face of submission.[23] Then—and this is the important thing for understanding both James and the rest of the New Testament—the exercise of faith finally incorporates everything that manifests this believing trust and commitment.

Long ago I decided (entirely apart from the present discussion) to define faith as *a believing response to whatever God says*. That is not an exhaustive definition, of course, but it is a correct description of faith and it applies to both promises and commands. When God speaks a promise, faith embraces the promise. And when God speaks a command, faith obeys.

This description leads to an important understanding: *obedience* is an evidence of faith. I suppose no one will directly dispute that. The numerous quotations from interpreters given above would clearly support this. What some might—or might not?—dispute, however, is to add a word I intend to be included: obedience is a *necessary* evidence of faith. Without obedience, there is no faith. To repeat James, faith without works is dead. (I realize the reader may immediately ask how much obedience? For the purposes of this discussion, that question is out of order. I will deal with it later, but for now, I regard the observation I have made about obedience and faith as absolutely true. Here, at least, it does not need qualification.)

Then I think it is justified to say this even more forcibly: obedience is the exercise of faith, and faith expresses itself in obedience. To say this another way, *obedience is the form which the substance of faith takes when confronted with a commanding God.*[24] "I will show you my faith by my works," says James. There is no other sure way to demonstrate it. In the terms of James's illustration (and paraphrasing Johnstone[25]), we may say one who seeks to determine whether Abraham had faith must search his *works*, and one who evaluates his works finds *faith* there.

How could this be otherwise? I may believe in, or trust, a *friend* without necessarily obeying every direction or appeal he makes. But how can I trust *God*, believing Him to be everything meant by the word *God*, without doing so? Disobedience of Him, given who He is, is by definition distrust or unbelief. Disobedience and faith are incompatible; they do not grow on the same plant.

The final question, then, is whether this contributes to resolving any possible tensions that may exist between the transaction model and the discipleship model of a saving relationship with God through Christ. I think so.

Is salvation by grace through faith (the transaction model)? Most certainly, only the faith (whether one regards faith as entirely a divine gift, as in the Calvinist system, or as a human response to God's initiative of enabling grace, as in the Reformation Arminian system) is a faith that necessarily expresses itself in works of obedience—although not as one bound by the Mosaic law or in an attempt to merit what is nothing other than God's gracious *gift* of eternal life.

Is salvation by works of obedience, particularly the call of Jesus to follow Him in abandonment to discipleship? Indeed it is, but only when that obedience is itself an expression of faith in God and faith in His Son, Jesus Christ, as one's Savior and the Divine Lord who calls to discipleship. To repeat: obedience is the form faith takes when confronted by a divine demand; obedience is the exercise of faith.

Herein, I think, is the resolution of the apparent tension both between James and Paul and between the transaction model and the discipleship model of salvation. The old Presbyterian divine, Robert Johnstone, expressed this well, suggesting that Paul (in his contest with Judaizers) emphasized a person is justified solely by faith as a work of grace, while James (in his contest with antinomianism) emphasized that faith works by love, producing a life devoted to the service of God. "In the writings both of Paul and James there is evidence that each of them held and taught the whole of this doctrine in its integrity." To those who need to know the way to heaven, Paul says "Believe on the Lord Jesus Christ." To professed believers James says, "If ye have not the works of faith, then ye are not justified."[26]

Faith and Obedience

There is considerable New Testament evidence that we must count faith itself, even when viewed narrowly as the acceptance of Christ as one's Savior, as the exercise of "obedience"—although the same New Testament will not allow us to equate "faith" with "works" (Romans 4:5, for example). Start with Romans 16:26, where Paul speaks of "the obedience of faith" as the aim of the gospel he preached for all nations. The very same phrase appears also in Romans 1:5,[27] with the very same point that this is the aim of the gospel Paul preached for all nations.[28]

The interpreters discuss the exact relationship between *obedience* and *faith* in this phrase. Many seem inclined to view the noun *faith* (genitive in Greek) as the source of the obedience, although it is possible to read the words to mean, "the obedience that *is* faith" (appositional genitive). Commenting on 16:26, Grant Osborne renders as "the obedience that comes from faith" (genitive of source), but on 1:5 he seems inclined to think James Dunn is "probably" right in suggesting that *both* aspects of the genitive are included.[29] Thomas Schreiner (commenting on 16:26) also renders as "the obedience that flows from faith."[30] Douglas Moo (on 1:5), although he quibbles about the specific nature of the genitive in the construction, appears to be in full agreement:

> Paul saw his task as calling men and women to submission to the lordship of Christ, ... a submission that began with conversion but which was to continue in a deepening, lifelong commitment. This obedience to Christ as Lord is always closely related to faith. ... In light of this, we understand the words 'obedience' and 'faith' to be mutually interpreting: obedience always involves faith, and faith always involves obedience. ... Paul called men and women to a faith that was always inseparable from obedience.[31]

The comments of other interpreters are along the same line: "To believe on Christ is to live for him, to obey him."[32] "Obedience is the natural result of a faith relationship with Christ, and faith always produces obedience. They are interchangeable aspects of a proper relationship with Christ."[33]

So far, so good. Still, it remains possible Paul means "the obedience that *is* (by another name) faith" (appositional genitive). This might mean, more simply, that when one accepts the truth of the gospel call to salvation in Jesus Christ, that itself is *obedience*. Even on this narrow reading of obedience, then, *faith is obedience to the gospel.* And that is not all: the very idea of obedience, here, is *submission*,[34] and one can hardly submit to Christ as one's Savior without submitting to the demands He makes, as who He is, for one who trusts Him. Can anything less than that be *submission?* In other words, even if a continuing obedience that follows initial faith is not *explicitly* stated in these two verses, it is impossible to rule it out of the clear *implications* of the words. This, I think, is the reason the interpreters do not hesitate to conclude that "the obedience of faith" is more than the initial trusting of Christ as one's Savior.

Thus, Schreiner agrees, "acceptance of the gospel in faith can be described as an act of obedience" (citing Romans 10:16). But he continues by insisting that this is not "a single act of obedience," instead, it is belief that "is validated as one continues to believe and obey."[35]

In this light, then, we move on to Romans 15:18, where Paul echoes this: the very purpose of his ministry was "to make the Gentiles obedient" to the gospel of Christ he preached (v. 19).[36] Faith is, in fact, obedience to God's directive (an invitation that is a command), "Call on me and be saved," "Believe on the Lord Jesus

Christ and you will be saved." In accord with the spirit of the discussion of 1:5 and 16:26, furthermore, Moo insists that obedience, here, denotes "comprehensively the believers' response to the Lord Jesus Christ, including, but not limited to, faith." He refers back to his comments on 1:5, quoted above.[37] One can hardly disagree. Even so, faith is *always* involved when evangelical obedience occurs; I say again, to obey is to exercise faith.[38]

Likewise, the contrast Paul draws in Romans 6:16-17 is especially interesting: on the one hand are those who obey sin and the end is death, while on the other are those who obey righteousness and live (v. 16). These are the lost and the saved, respectively, and Paul is grateful his readers "have obeyed from the heart that form of doctrine which was delivered" to them (v. 17). That "form of doctrine (or teaching)" was surely the gospel, and Paul's readers "obeyed" it when they heeded its call to believe in Christ. At the same time, the context, especially the closely linked verse 16, makes clear the gospel they "obeyed" was also a call to righteous living.[39] One cannot obey one without the other! Moo views these words as focusing "on the initial conversion of the Roman Christians to Christ as Lord," but adds, "Paul uses 'obey' because he wants to underscore the aspect of submission to Christ as Lord of life that is part of becoming a Christian."[40] Comparable to this is Romans 2:8, where Paul contrasts the saved and the lost as those who "obey the truth" and those who obey unrighteousness, even though the word for obedience is different in the original. (It seems significant that these two chapters—Romans 2 and 6—are the very ones that drew our attention in chapter five when treating the question whether Paul knew anything of the discipleship model.)

Acts 6:7, therefore, is right on target, reporting that, in response to the increased effects of the word of God and numbers of disciples in Jerusalem, "a great company of the priests were obedient to the faith"—using the very same vocabulary as that of Paul, above. The meaning of this expression may include more than this, but it at least includes the idea that they obeyed the call to put faith in Christ. Except for discussing the question what "priests" are meant,[41] most of the commentators simply refer to Romans 1:5, as discussed above. J. A. Alexander comments that the phrase means, "submitted to the Gospel, as a system of belief and practice"[42]—a sentiment that corresponds well to the observations above.

Consider also 2 Thessalonians 1:8, where those who do not know God are identified as the ones who "obey not the gospel of our Lord Jesus Christ."[43] As Leon Morris notes, "The gospel is a message of good news, but it is also an invitation from the King of kings. Rejection of the gospel accordingly is disobedience to a royal invitation."[44] Likewise in Romans 10:16 after intoning how beautiful are the feet of those who preach the gospel, Paul sadly acknowledges "they have not all obeyed the gospel." To back this up, he quotes Isaiah 53:1: "Lord, who has believed our report?" Clearly, to Paul, obeying the gospel is synonymous with believing the report: "two sides of the same coin."[45] If we reduce the gospel to its most fundamental terms— Jesus died for your sins and you must accept His atoning work as your eternal salvation—obeying that means to put faith in Him as one's Savior. Schreiner interprets "have not obeyed the gospel" as "have not submitted to the gospel."[46] If nothing else, faith is obedience in that sense; and this discussion has shown that a great deal more may well be implied.

A number of other references can be cited, now that this has been established. There is Hebrews 5:9, for example, where the writer speaks of Jesus as the author or reason (*aitios*) of eternal salvation "unto all them that obey him." Whatever else may be included, this must at least mean obey Him when He calls to eternal life by His own redemptive work. And that obedience is the exercise of faith.[47]

1 Peter 3:1 identifies the unbelieving husbands of Christian wives as those who "obey not the word"—surely the word of the gospel: "Rejection of the gospel message is, therefore, a responsible act of the will, disobedience."[48] This understanding is confirmed by Peter's similar expression in 1 Peter 4:17 (compare 2:8), where he defines the lost (over against those in the house of God) as "them that obey not the gospel of God," which apparently means "those who reject the gospel."[49] And in 1:22 Peter regards his saved readers as "having purified" their souls "in (or by) obeying the truth";[50] "they responded to God by obeying the truth of the gospel."[51]

This survey of New Testament teaching makes clear one thing: obedience is the exercise of faith in response to the gospel call offering salvation to all who will put their trust in Christ. This is variously represented as obeying the faith, the truth, the word, the gospel, but all share the same core meaning. And once we understand that the gospel is more than a call to be justified by faith—that it is inherently a call to repentance and righteousness of life as a disciple of Christ—faith is likewise expressed in obedience to that call. They are the same thing, not two things that can be distinguished in order to choose one over the other.

This makes it easier—yes, desirable—to see obedience as the exercise of faith. Consequently, if our study of the various ways in which the New Testament presents what one must do to have eternal life—Paul, the Synoptics, John, and James—has shown that the discipleship model is as accurate and biblical as the transaction model, then it becomes not just easier but essential to understand faith as expressed in obedience to the call of Jesus to lay down everything else and follow Him as a disciple.

The Contribution of Hebrews to This Understanding

It seems to me the inspired writer of Hebrews—whoever he was, God alone knows![52]—enables us to take this a small step farther. Not only is obeying the gospel another way of saying believing the gospel, so that faith includes obedience to the command to repent and believe the gospel. More than that, faith includes, in an important way, obedience to the Lord's other commands for His people.

This arises in Hebrews 3, in a book where the writer makes clear he understands salvation is by *faith*. In this context, in 3:12, for example, when warning against apostasy, he defines it as "an evil heart of unbelief, in departing from the living God." Morris must be right in saying the unbelief of Israel, which is the ground of this warning, "involved disloyalty as well as the passive failure to believe."[53] And in verse 18, again using the Israelites who came out of Egypt as his illustration, the writer says those whom God judged and who did not make it through to Canaan were, by definition, "those who *believed* not"—literally, those who disobeyed.[54] The conclusion is, "They could not enter in because of unbelief" (v. 19). And yet, leading up to this, the writer defines the circumstances in verse 17: "With whom was he grieved forty years? Was it not with those who had sinned, whose carcasses fell in the wilderness?" In other words, they fell because they sinned, and they fell because of unbelief, and the two reasons express the same basic truth even if from two perspectives.[55] Disobedience is an expression of unbelief, obedience is the exercise of faith: "Unbelief and disobedience are virtually synonymous for our author."[56]

Hebrews 4 matches this, applying it to our salvation needs. In verses 2 and 6 the writer repeats that the ancient Israelites fell because of unbelief.[57] Then, in verse 11, he urges his readers: "Let us labor therefore to enter into that rest, lest anyone fall after the same example of unbelief."[58] What is that example or pattern? It is unbelief as manifested in disobedience to the commandments of God. To turn this around, then, faith is manifested in obedience.

Hebrews 11 makes perfect sense in this light, adding confirmation to this understanding. This "roll call of the heroes of faith" (as it is sometimes called) says repeatedly that persons acted *by faith*:

- Verse 4: *By faith* Abel offered to God the acceptable sacrifice (by which act he obtained witness that he was righteous!)[59];
- Verse 7: *By faith* Noah ... prepared an ark (by which he became heir of the righteousness that is by faith!);
- Verse 8: *By faith* Abraham ... obeyed (that word, again);
- Verse 17: *By faith* Abraham ... offered up Isaac (as James has said!);
- Verses 24-27: *By faith* Moses ... refused ... and chose ... and forsook.

These are part of a familiar pattern throughout the chapter: *By faith people acted in obedience to God.* Surely, that is essential to faith. "Their faith consisted simply in taking God at His word and directing their lives accordingly."[60] And without faith, without the obedience that necessarily expresses faith, it is impossible to please God (v. 6). Ellingworth notes that this principle, in verse 6, is "the basis for the statement that Abel was 'righteous.' ... For Hebrews, unlike Paul though falling short of contradiction, Abel's sacrifice is the expression of his faith."[61]

This is, of course, exactly what James has said. Surely Witherington is correct, then, to say the author of Hebrews, when discussing faith in this chapter, "is talking about that most basic form of trust in God—the faithful living and obedience of believers that should grow out of that trust."[62]

What we have seen in this chapter not only meshes well with the preceding chapters, it does more than that. It helps bring the strands of truth together and gives definition to the larger truth. Biblical faith, the faith required for eternal life, is not mere intellectual persuasion that Jesus is who He claimed to be and provided redemption for us in His death and resurrection. Faith is not that sterile. Faith is the response of loving trust to the word of God, to the call of the Savior to repent, to put confidence in His redemptive work, to renounce allegiance to any other lord, and to follow Him. Faith is always *expressed* in obedience. Faith is *visible* only in obedience. If faith is not exercised in obedience, it is not faith.

I conclude this chapter with two telling quotations from interpreters of James or Hebrews. "Genuine faith, faith that does result in salvation, must acknowledge the lordship of Christ and so respond to Christ's word with actions of obedience. ... Christ is both Savior and Lord; he cannot be separated into two persons. Genuine, saving faith necessarily includes both a trusting of Christ as Savior and a following of Christ as Lord."[63] "If the deeds of faith are absent from the life of the believer, one can only determine that his or her faith itself is not genuine. This at least is what the evidence of their lives demonstrates."[64]

ENDNOTES

[1] In his 1522 edition—but only in that edition—of the New Testament.

[2] Kurt A. Richardson, *The New American Commentary: James* (vol. 36; Nashville: Broadman & Holman, 1997), 44.

[3] Douglas Moo, *The Letter of James* (Pillar New Testament Commentary; Grand Rapids: Eerdmans, 2000), 118.

[4] This is apparently what is called the "anaphoric" use of the article. The NASB appropriately renders, "Can that faith save him?"

[5] Robert Johnstone, *A Commentary on James* (Geneva Commentaries; Edinburgh: Banner of Truth Trust, 1871, 1983 reprint), 187.

[6] See the discussion of this passage by Paul V. Harrison, "Commentary on the Book of James," in *The Randall House Bible Commentary: James, 1, 2 Peter, and Jude* (Nashville: Randall House, 1992). Moo, 127-30, discusses and evaluates three major views, with varieties.

[7] Harrison, 38.

[8] Moo, 120.

[9] R. Kent Hughes, *James: Faith That Works* (Preaching the Word Series; Wheaton: Crossway, 1991), 111.

[10] Richardson, 43.

[11] As Moo, 133, notes, James's use of Abraham is very similar to 1 Maccabees 2:51-52, perhaps indicating James was drawing on an established Jewish tradition. I do not mean to suggest James was familiar with Paul's presentation of the gospel and consciously resisting or clarifying it. It is probably presumptuous to think we can know how much of Paul James knew at a time when none of Paul's written works existed.

[12] Moo, 123, refers to a very small number of interpreters (like Zane Hodges, *The Gospel under Siege* [Dallas: Redención Viva, 1981], 26-27) who take "save" (v. 14) to mean something other than spiritual salvation, such as being rescued from some sort of danger or trial. As Moo shows, attention to the use of the verb for save, *sōzō*, in James and the other New Testament epistles easily exposes the fallacy of that attempt to deny what Hodges mocks as "Lordship salvation." Hodges believes faith without works can save. James's use of justification also disproves Hodges' view of "save."

[13] Moo, 134-141.

[14] Hughes, 108.

[15] George M. Stulac, *James* (IVP New Testament Commentary; Downers Grove: InterVarsity, 1993), 21.

[16] John Calvin, *Institutes of the Christian Religion*, trans. Henry Beveridge (one vol.; Grand Rapids: Eerdmans, 1989), 3.17.12 (p. 115).

[17] Richardson, 44, 129.

[18] Stulac, 21.

[19] Hughes, 120.

[20] Moo, 144.

[21] Moo, 38 (italics his).

[22] Stulac, 111.

[23] Stulac, 113, defines genuine, Christian faith as "believing in Christ with trust and obedience."

[24] I owe this use of *form* and *substance* to my friend and colleague F. Leroy Forlines who developed the concept long ago.

[25] Johnstone, 201.

[26] Johnstone, 197.

[27] The AV translation, here, is "obedience to the faith," but in the original the wording is identical to 16:26 and it would be just as correctly rendered "the obedience of faith."

[28] Interesting, then, that this idea serves like an *inclusio* to open and close this epistle.

[29] Grant R. Osborne, *Romans* (IVPNTC; Downers Grove: InterVarsity, 2004), 419, 33.

[30] Thomas R. Schreiner, *Romans* (ECNT; Grand Rapids: Baker Books, 1998), 815.

[31] Douglas Moo, *The Epistle to the Romans* (NICNT; Grand Rapids: Eerdmans, 1996), 52.

[32] Osborne, 419.

[33] Osborne, 33.

[34] This is implied in the Greek word *hupakouō*.

[35] Schreiner, 35.

[36] Schreiner, 768, thinks this "is nothing less than the conversion of the Gentiles," but he is quick to refer the reader to his comments on 1:5 and 16:26, which indicate the fuller implications of this obedience. Osborne, 390, says the obedience mentioned here "refers not only to their conversion but also to a lifetime of following Christ, the 'obedience that comes from faith.' … Paul centered not just on evangelism but discipleship; when people came to Christ, he wanted to ensure that they surrendered their lives fully to him."

[37] Moo, 892.

[38] This does not rule out the possibility that some unbelievers "obey" some of God's commands, but unbelieving obedience is not full obedience. It is the very nature of God's commandments to require actions that are expressions of loving submission and trust, and that involves faith.

[39] Here Osborne, 162, notes their obeying God means "submitting to his salvific work, obviously in terms of their faith commitment to Christ."

[40] Moo, 400-01.

[41] An issue that need not be discussed here.

[42] Joseph Addison Alexander, *Commentary on the Acts of the Apostles*, two vols. in one (Grand Rapids: Zondervan, 1875, reprint 1956), 248.

[43] We need not explore, here, the argument as to whether one or two groups or unbelievers are meant. F. F. Bruce, *Word Biblical Commentary: 1 & 2 Thessalonians* (Waco, TX: Word, 1982), 151, refers this to persons who have rejected the gospel.

[44] Leon Morris, *The First and Second Epistles to the Thessalonians* (NICNT; Grand Rapids: Eerdmans, 1991), 204. G. K. Beale, *1-2 Thessalonians* (IVPNTC; Downers Grove: InterVarsity, 2003), is content to comment, on this expression: "They do not believe in Christ's redemptive work, nor do they follow his precepts."

[45] Moo, 665. Osborne, 276, comments that "obedience is synonymous with belief."

[46] Schreiner, 569.

[47] Paul Ellingworth, *The Epistle to the Hebrews* (NIGTC; Grand Rapids: Eerdmans, 1993), says that *obey* "denotes a positive response to a spoken call" and compares Hebrews 11:8 where the essential connection between faith and this obedience is clearly indicated. F. F. Bruce, *Commentary on the Epistle to the Hebrews* (NICNT; Grand Rapids: Eerdmans, 1964), 105, appears to think this is "the obedience of the redeemed" that follows their conversion, which does not appear to fit the context as well.

[48] Leonhard Goppelt, *A Commentary on 1 Peter*, ed. Ferdinand Hahn, trans. John E. Alsup (Grand Rapids: Eerdmans, 1933), 147.

[49] Karen H. Jobes, *1 Peter* (ECNT; Grand Rapids: Baker Academic, 2005), 293.

[50] In the first two of these, Peter uses the same verb for obedience (*apeitheō*) that Paul uses in Romans 2:8; in the last one, the same word (*hupakouō*) as in the rest of the passages cited.

[51] Scot McKnight, *1 Peter: The NIV Application Commentary* (Grand Rapids: Zondervan, 1996), 90. Goppelt, 125, agrees that to obey the truth is the same as to obey the gospel, but points (n. 22) to his comments on 1:2, 14, where (74) he says that 1:22 declares obedience (*hupako*) is "acknowledgement of the truth, i.e., faith that gives shape to conduct corresponding to reality. Election takes place, accordingly, as the summons to faith as obedience." On 1:14 (110) he says, "baptism delivers one into 'obedience,' into the life of faith." Jobes, 123, equates "obeying the truth" to "coming to faith in Jesus Christ."

[52] My apologies to Origen!

[53] Leon Morris, *Commentary on the Epistle to the Hebrews* (Grand Rapids: Eerdmans, 1964), 66 (n. 60).

[54] The verb is *apeitheō*, literally to be unpersuaded and thus to disobey. Louw and Nida, 1.468: "unwillingness or refusal to comply with the demands of some authority–'to disobey.'"

[55] Ellingworth, 235-36, notes the close connection between sin (v. 17), disobedience/unbelief (v. 18), and unbelief (v. 19). So too Morris, 69 (n. 74).

[56] Ben Witherington III, *Letters and Homilies for Jewish Christians: A Socio-Rhetorical Commentary on Hebrews, James and Jude* (Downers Grove: IVP Academic, 2007), 175; the entire section (172-76) should be read to appreciate fully the grounds for this assertion. Among other things, Witherington says (172) "Faithlessness involves not simply passive disbelief, but active resistance to the will of God" (quoting Harold W. Attridge, *The Epistle to the Hebrews* [Hermeneia; Philadelphia: Fortress, 1989], 116); and (176) that "disbelief and disobedience ... work hand and hand. By the same token, so do real trust and real obedience to God."

[57] On v. 2 Morris, 73, notes the *reason* the message did not do the ancient Israelites good is that "they did not obey His voice." On v. 6 he, 75, says "It was disobedience ... that kept the generation of the Exodus out of God's promised rest."

[58] In vv. 6, 11, *unbelief* is again *apeitheia*, disobedience. Ellingworth, 244, observes that in this context faith is "related closely ... with obedience (3:18)."

[59] Interpreters have long debated just why Cain's offering was rejected and Abel's accepted. Is it possible Cain's "obedience" was not in loving trust (faith) of God but in begrudging legalism?

[60] Morris, 277.

[61] Ellingworth, 571.

[62] Witherington, 293.

[63] Stulac, 113. I recommend also the understanding of faith affirmed by Stanley, *Did Jesus Teach?*, when he says it means "to submit to Jesus' authority" (231), that it "cannot exist where there is trust in something else" (236); he provides a helpful summary of what Paul meant by faith (205).

[64] Richardson, 143. He goes on to say the "reality" (in contrast to the evidence) may sometimes be otherwise, indicating a believer is "double-minded," mixing deeds of faith with deeds arising from evil desires. That sort of failure, usually only temporary, will be touched on in chapter eight.

Chapter Seven

DISCIPLESHIP AND SANCTIFICATION

At this point, I have completed my survey of the New Testament perspectives on what one must do to have eternal life. All the lines traced finally point in the same direction: one must put faith in Christ, a faith that includes a repentant commitment to Him as one's master, taking up one's cross and following Him in obedience. This is discipleship, in other words.

If one must be a disciple, the question is whether one must be a *perfect* disciple—perfect in the sense of sinless. Then, leading directly from that is the question what implications this carries for sanctification. One of the persistent problems for Christian theology, both theoretical and practical, involves what happens when a Christian sins. The purpose of this chapter, and of the following one, is to deal with these matters—with sanctification and sin, in other words. Ultimately, these chapters will make an important contribution to the conclusions to be drawn in the final chapter.

There are various concepts of the Christian life, and how sin fits in with it, in the market place of Bible-believing teaching. Those who are "Holiness" in doctrine believe one can experience a sanctifying work that for all practical purposes enables a "sanctified" Christian to live without sin.[1] Those who are "Keswick" in their approach tend to suggest that while many, or most, Christians continue to live on a plane of defeat by sin, one can lay claim by faith to the "victorious life."

Most of us who are neither Holiness nor Keswick are not exactly sure just how sanctification and sin go together in our lives, though we are fairly sure they do. Before discussing this, however, I believe it is important to give some attention to these other two ways of viewing Christian experience.

The "Keswick" Concept of the Christian Life

I begin with a summary of the views of those who share a "Keswick" understanding of the nature of the Christian life, also sometimes called the "Deeper (or Higher) Life Movement."[2] The name *Keswick*[3] comes from a place in northern England that has hosted a famous Bible conference each year since 1875. Bible conferences with similar emphases have sprung up at various sites in the Christian world.

Keswick thinking comes in many varieties, and any summary runs the risk of saying what some who are devoted to that position may deny is their view of Christian experience. Still, there are some common threads, and I will attempt to provide an overall picture of the view as I understand it—and as I will evaluate it.[4]

In general, the "Deeper Life Movement" holds that among various Christians some are living on one plane of experience and some on another. Typically, they observe that most—or at least many—Christians are living in defeat, "uncrucified," far too often overcome by sin, struggling without confidence against "the flesh," one's sinful, depraved nature. What they need, and what the Keswick teacher urges on them, is to lay claim, by faith, to the victorious life. In the same way that justification (forgiveness for one's sins) is gained by an act of faith, so one may by an act of faith receive the victorious Christian life as an enabling and supernatural gift of God in Christ. Once a Christian believes he has the victory in Christ, he does! Just as forgiveness for sins is provided for by the atonement of the Savior, so victorious Christian living is likewise provided for in the cross and can be gained in a crisis of faith.

It lies outside my purpose to treat the Keswick movement in detail or to discuss the many healthy emphases associated with it. Among these are the tragic effects of sin in the life of a professing Christian, the fact that a true believer in Christ has been set free from slavery to sin, the importance of completely abandoning oneself to the lordship of Christ, the need to yield complete control over one's life to the Holy Spirit, and the importance of consecrated service to the Lord. Indeed, the typical Keswick conference programs these very five emphases in five successive days of focused teaching.[5] I have nothing but respect for their emphasis on the sins of the spirit, for their call to serious consecration and holy living, and for their challenge to Spirit-filled service.[6]

My purpose, instead, is to focus on that one main point: that victorious Christian living can be gained in a crisis of faith, that a defeated Christian can be transferred to the plane of victory by laying claim to it in Christ and His cross. I hasten to acknowledge Keswick teachers do not call this anything like "entire sanctification," even though in Keswick literature there is frequent mention of a second blessing.[7] They do not typically teach, with some of our Holiness brethren, that the sinful nature can be eradicated in a second definite work of grace.[8] They do not expect, and do not lead others to expect, that Christians will or can live without sin. Much of their preaching, on the broad variety of subjects suggested above, will be very similar to mine. But in the end I find their view of how the Christian obtains victory in the Christian life to be misdirected.

My fundamental criticism of the Keswick view of sanctification is that its construction of the situation prevailing among Christians lacks a sound, biblical basis. By this I refer primarily to their concept that there are two levels of Christian experience I am calling (as they often do) defeated and victorious. Different proponents of this view have used various terms to describe these two levels. J. Robertson McQuilkin, for example, speaks of them as "normal" and "average" Christians. By the former, he means those victorious Christians characterized by "New Testament norms for the Christian life," while the latter fall far short of that.[9]

McQuilkin's description of these two categories is interesting. The *normal* (victorious) Christian is characterized by love, joy, and peace, overcomes temptation, consistently obeys God, grows in the fruit of the Spirit, "authentically reflects the attitudes and behavior of Jesus," gives God first place in his life, gives precedence to the welfare of others over personal desires, and has power for godly living and effective service in the church. *Average* (defeated) Christians, on the other hand, are not very different from well-behaved unbelievers, act in ways that reflect entirely their heredity, environment, and circumstances rather than any supernatural quality, "yield to temptation more often than not"—as manifested in lust and covetousness, and are characterized by self-interest rather than by love for God or others.[10] This two-fold distinction and the descriptions of each are typical of Keswick analyses of the state of things among Christians. Barabas expresses the matter thus: "Christians live in either a carnal or spiritual state, depending upon whether the flesh or the Spirit is in control in their lives"; in the carnal state, "sin and failure are still master" and "it is impossible to receive spiritual truth."[11]

When I say this construction lacks a sound, biblical basis, I mean at least three closely-related things. (1) There are no New Testament descriptions of this difference between defeated and victorious Christians. (2) The New Testament description of *all* the regenerate is very much unlike the Keswick characterization of the so-called defeated Christian. (3) It is difficult, if not impossible, to find New Testament invitations to Christians to come to a new level of sanctification or holiness.[12]

When contrasting ways of life, the New Testament frequently treats the difference between the saved (or righteous) and the lost (or wicked), but not between two levels of Christian living. Indeed, in making this contrast between regenerate persons and non-Christians, the New Testament at times speaks of it as the difference between walking[13] after or in the Spirit and walking after or in the flesh.

If memory serves me well, I have heard Keswick speakers use the phrase "walking after the flesh" as synonymous with the defeated Christian. It certainly is common for them to speak of "carnal Christians" in that light—and that gets close to saying the same thing.[14] The point, however, is whenever the New Testament characterizes people as walking after the flesh *it is describing the unsaved*. (That is also true, most of the time, when the word "carnal" is used; more about this below.)

Romans 8:1-9 is a case in point. The passage involves a sharp contrast between two groups. One group is characterized by several sets of words:

(1) they "walk according to the flesh" (vv. 1, 4);[15]
(2) they are living under the governance of "the law of sin and death" (v. 2);
(3) they "live according to the flesh" (v. 5);
(4) they "set their minds on the things of the flesh" (v. 5);
(5) they are "carnally minded" (v. 6);
(6) they are in a state of "enmity against God" (v. 7);
(7) they are "in the flesh" (v. 8);
(8) they "cannot please God" (v. 8); and
(9) they do not "have the Spirit of Christ" (v. 9).

Over against this group is another, likewise characterized by several sets of words:

(1) they "walk according to the Spirit" (vv. 1, 4);
(2) they live under the governance of "the law of the Spirit of life" (v. 2);
(3) they live "according to the Spirit" (v. 5);
(4) they "set their minds on the things of the Spirit" (v. 5);

(5) they are "spiritually minded" (v. 6);

(6) they are "subject to the law of God" (v. 7);

(7) they are "in the Spirit" (v. 9); and

(8) they are indwelled by (have) "the Spirit of God" (or of Christ, v. 9).

The very activity of listing these word-groups together in this way serves as its own best argument that *the contrast here is not between two kinds of Christians but between the unregenerate and the regenerate.* As John Stott puts it, "Here are two categories of people (the unregenerate who are 'in the flesh' and the regenerate who are 'in the Spirit'), who have two perspectives or mindsets … which lead to two patterns of conduct … and result in two spiritual states."[16] This seems so obvious that one does not need to defend it; perhaps no Keswick teacher would dispute it.[17] Even so, the passage helps us understand two things: first, what walking in accord with the flesh (and the carnal mind) and walking in accord with the Spirit (and being spiritually minded) really mean; second, *all* the regenerate are in the latter category.

If it should be asked how it can be said, of our often less than triumphant Christian lives, that we are walking according to the Spirit and not according to the flesh, I may respond by saying, first, I cannot always give a confident answer. Even so, some of the other passages discussed, in the rest of this book and in the following paragraphs, may help answer this question. Meanwhile, I am confident, exegetically, that *every* child of God can be described—and is so described in Romans 8 and elsewhere in the New Testament—as not only possessing the Holy Spirit but also walking and living according to the Spirit, being spiritually minded, and living in such a way as to please God. The regenerate are no longer (as they once were) in the flesh, living and walking according to the flesh, carnally minded, and at enmity with God.

Does the adjective *carnal* ever describe Christians in the New Testament? Yes, in 1 Corinthians 3:1-4,[18] but this must be carefully evaluated. That these are regenerate persons is clear: Paul calls them "brethren," they are "in Christ," and they are partaking of a "milk" that offers spiritual nourishment, even if for infants. "Paul does not doubt that the addressees have received the Spirit because without the Spirit they could not be [in Christ]."[19]

In what sense, then, are they "carnal"?[20] First, in the sense they are "babes in Christ"—spiritually immature. Second, in the sense they are making evaluations and judgments according to the standards of a human, fleshly judgment as opposed to doing so with spiritual discernment: "The Corinthians are continuing to judge and act in accordance with the standards of 'this age.'"[21] This has led them to think of ministers like Paul and Apollos as though they are competitors between whom they can choose their favorites. They are carnal and need to learn to use God's wisdom rather than natural wisdom; but this is a far cry from what the New Testament typically means by "walking after the flesh" and from the "carnal mind" of Romans 8. "Christians can be carnal in their behavior, they are never carnal by nature."[22]

Galatians 5:16-25 is another case in point, and it helps us on two fronts. First, once again, in the passage as a whole, "flesh" and "Spirit" stand in sharp contrast to one another, depicting the same contrast between unbelievers and believers that appears in Romans 8. The passage also contains an expression that results in frequent references to "the crucified life" (v. 24; compare 2:20) or some similar phrase one often hears on the lips of Keswick teachers.

The basic contrast here is between those who live and walk according to the Spirit and those who live and walk according to the flesh. Those in one group "walk in the Spirit" (v. 16), are "led by the Spirit" (v. 18), and have produced in their lives the fruit of the Spirit (vv. 22-23). They "are Christ's" (v. 24) and "live in the Spirit" (v. 25). In contrast are those who are "under the law" (v. 18) and perform "the works of the flesh" (v. 19). Those whose lives are characterized in this fashion "will not inherit the kingdom of God" (v. 21).

On the second front, verse 17 introduces an element not present in Romans 8: even the Christian experiences a conflict between the flesh and the Spirit: a "conflict that confronts every Christian."[23] The strong desires of the flesh and the strong desires of the Spirit pull at the believer in two directions, with the result that the regenerate person no longer does the (wicked) things otherwise desired. It is possible, of course, to interpret this last clause to mean either the conflict sometimes prevents the Christian from doing the *good* things desired, or it enables him to avoid the *wicked* things desired.[24] I am confident the latter is correct (which can be argued for because of v. 16), but the essential picture of the Christian life is the same either way. (Those who think, as I do, that Romans 7:14-25 describes a Christian find there the same picture in greater detail.)

What seems clear from this passage, as well as from other New Testament passages, is this. Before a person is regenerated, he has only the sinful nature and is therefore dominated by it and unable to overcome its rule. He is spiritually dead.

Every unconverted person, therefore, walks according to the flesh, a servant of sin (to use the expression of Romans 6). To be sure, there are forces at work that create for him a level of internal conflict at times: the presence of law and order in the land, the teaching of godly parents or others, even one's own afflicted conscience. But these are not strong enough to deliver the unbeliever from the dominion of the flesh.

But when a person is born again, the Spirit brings that person to life (to a knowing and vital relationship with God) and comes to dwell within. Consequently, the regenerated person has a new and spiritual nature, one that "lusts" in an entirely different direction and enables the believer to choose and perform what is right. I understand Paul to be saying that the converted person is thereafter under the dominion of that new, Spirit-dominated nature and walks accordingly—just as I understand 1 John to say the regenerated person avoids sin: not perfectly but characteristically.

Thus, verses 19-23 provide the basic contrast between the two ways of life. The lives of those who walk according to the flesh (unbelievers) are characterized by the works listed in vv. 19-21; they do not inherit the kingdom of God. The lives of those who walk according to the Spirit (the regenerate) are characterized by the fruits listed in verses 22-23; they are already in the kingdom of God. On both sides, Paul does not mean occasional activities or attitudes but characteristic *practice* (as in 1 John 3).[25]

Does that mean every child of God *always* avoids every one of the works of the flesh and *always* manifests all the mature fruit produced by the Spirit? While our experience tells us this is not the case, Paul does not bother to say so. (The Scriptures hardly undertake to assure us it is acceptable for us to sin!) But he implies the possibility of wrongdoing, on the practical side, by introducing us to the conflict of natures within the believer (v. 17) and then exhorting us who are *alive* in the Spirit to *walk* there also (v. 25).

In other words, we walk in the Spirit; now let us walk in the Spirit! As is often true in Paul's letters (and not his only), the injunction takes the form: we are (indicative), now we must be (imperative). While I will not pursue this at length,[26] Ephesians 4:17-5:17 and Colossians 3:1-15 proceed along these lines. In both passages, we have the "new man" contrast with the "old man." And in both Paul effectively says: "You have put off the old man and put on the new man; now live like it! Put aside the old man and put on the new man" (Ephesians 4:22-24; Colossians 3:9-10).

As Eduard Lohse expresses this (commenting on Colossians), "This admonition demands of the Christian that he actualize what has already happened … and that, in obedience, he enter into the new life given him in baptism."[27]

One of the keys to understanding such passages, in harmony with these in Romans and Galatians, is not to confuse the "old man" and "new man" with the "flesh" and "Spirit." The two pairs are very different. In Ephesians, Colossians, and Romans 6, the "old man" is the unregenerate person, the person who used to be.[28] The "new man" is the person after regeneration. Each is the whole person, in two different relationships to God and two different spiritual conditions.[29] While the "old man" had only the fleshly nature and walked accordingly, the new, converted person has both a depraved nature (the "flesh," best not to call it the "old nature" to avoid confusion) and a spiritual nature (the "Spirit"). A saved person *is* a new person who has both a fleshly and a spiritual nature. And every saved person both walks according to the Spirit and is enjoined to walk according to the Spirit.[30]

One more thing Paul says in Galatians 5 is important for this discussion: "Those who are Christ's have crucified the flesh with its passions and desires" (v. 24). Once again, these words speak of *all* the regenerate as they who "are Christ's."[31] So when Paul says in Galatians 2:20, "I have been crucified with Christ; it is no longer I who live, but Christ lives in me; and the life which I now live in the flesh I live by faith in the Son of God," he is testifying on behalf of *all* true Christians, not some spiritual elite. We may not all live "the crucified life" as well as he did, but we all live it—and God will judge how well!

I do not recall what well-known preacher was reported to say, "It's funny that you can commit suicide in any number of ways, but you can't crucify yourself. When you've hammered the nail into one hand, you can't do the other one!" He was speaking graphically, of course, to make an important point. A child of God does not need to "crucify himself" in order to live the "Deeper Life." Every real Christian has been crucified with Christ: that happened when he put saving faith in Christ and so was identified with Him in all the redemptive effects of His death, burial, and resurrection. At that point of faith, the "old man"—the person who used to be—died, was crucified with Christ; and the "new man"—the converted person—came to life to live as one raised from the dead, freed from enslavement to the flesh, sin, and death. When we were baptized—put under and brought up again—we gave witness to this set of truths; see Romans 6:1-14.

I may add, Romans 6 plays a large part in Keswick discussion, but that chapter, too, depicts the contrast between saints and sinners, not between two levels of saints. See the discussion of Romans 6 in chapter five, which need not be repeated here. Barabas appears both to recognize this and to miss it, saying correctly, "Being now made free from sin" (Romans 6:18) is "true of all Christians." But he hastens to add this is a *legal* or *judicial* freedom, and one has to "claim" it for it to become *experimental*, a claiming that is "stepped into by simple faith."[32] On two accounts, I must reject this: first, this is very far removed from anything Paul urges in Romans 6; second, as I have tried to show in chapter five, Paul is referring to the *experience* of all the regenerate in the chapter, contrasting them only with the unconverted. Indeed, it has been the purpose of this book, up to now, to describe what it means in the New Testament to have eternal life: the faith that saves is a faith that manifests itself in committed discipleship (Jesus in the Synoptics) and in the consistent avoidance of sin (1 John) and acts of loving, trusting obedience (James, Hebrews). These are descriptions of *all* those who are born again. Barabas, on the other hand, has a wonderful discussion of the demands of Jesus in His call to discipleship, but he errs, I think, in taking this to mean a call to Christians to consecration, rather than a call to become Christians.[33]

For this reason, the Keswick description of defeated (or average) Christians rings hollow. If, indeed, most Christians are living in the manner described by McQuilkin (above), one may ask how successful God has been in His redemptive work! Barabas approvingly quotes Ruth Paxson to say, "The vast majority of Christians stop short in their experience of the blessings of salvation with the joy of forgiveness of past sins and with the hope of Heaven in the future. But the present is a forty-year wilderness experience full of futile wanderings, never enjoying peace and rest, never arriving in the promised land."[34] What sort of Christianity is that?

I have asked myself, speculatively, why proponents of the Keswick position have accepted such a low view of what it means to be a Christian. The leading Keswick spokesmen have included some extraordinary and powerful preachers: men like F. B. Meyer, Alan Redpath, Andrew Murray, W. H. Griffith Thomas, Graham Scroggie, Donald Grey Barnhouse, A. T. Pierson, G. Campbell Morgan, R. A. Torrey, and others[35]—men whose understanding of the Scriptures is not to be taken lightly. As I cast about for possible reasons, it occurs to me to wonder if, on the one hand, they came to their conclusions because of a widespread low level of spirituality and indifference to holiness of life within the churches they were familiar with. I can only ask questions about this: if so, did they think it better to deal with this problem as a manifestation of "carnal Christians" rather than unsaved church members? Had they accepted too quickly the idea that a mere profession of belief in Jesus is all that is required to become a Christian, regardless whether that profession manifests genuine commitment to obedient discipleship? Again, I can only speculate.

I do know, however, their descriptions of defeated Christians sound to me like unregenerate persons, and descriptions of persons who receive the Keswick "blessing" (consecration) sound very much like descriptions of conversion.[36] I tend to think the descriptions of defeated Christians will also sound like unregenerate persons when measured against New Testament descriptions of Christians. I could not help noting what struck me as a telling way of wording things in McQuilkin's discussion. Twice on the same page, he changes words from "Christian" to "church member."[37] Which does he mean, Christians or church members? They are not one and the same.

On the other side of the same coin, the Keswick descriptions of the victorious Christian life sound very much like the New Testament descriptions of what it means to be genuinely converted. Thus, Barabas quotes from the original issue of *The Christian's Pathway to Power*, the more-or-less official organ of Keswick: "We believe the Word of God teaches that the *normal* Christian life is one of uniform sustained victory over known sin."[38] The only problem with this statement is that the Word of God, as we have seen in 1 John, teaches this is true of *every* child of God! McQuilkin advances the same unnecessarily limited view when he states that Keswick teaches "the possibility of consistent success in resisting the temptation to violate deliberately the known will of God"[39]—which appears to describe a lifestyle 1 John 3:6 and 9 say is true of every regenerate person. Similarly, Andrew Murray, quoted with approval by Barabas, said, "very many Christians at conversion know almost nothing of taking Christ to be their Master."[40] But if what we have seen in chapter two is correct, no one can become a Christian without taking Christ to be Master!

Furthermore, there is a logical problem involved in the Keswick position: if victorious Christian living, *as something that can be distinguished, by definition, from the deliverance that occurs at conversion,* was provided for in the atonement, then every person who accepts the atonement of Christ by faith should receive it at the moment of conversion. In that case, every Christian should experience victorious Christian living and be aware of it. It would then be erroneous to suggest that many believers are living in spiritual defeat.

Therefore, as I said, I cannot find a New Testament basis for affirming that *Christians* need to lay hold by faith on victorious Christian living, which is common coin in Keswick presentation. In the passage from Barabas just cited, the original writer—Evan H. Hopkins, apparently—said a child of God "may step into" this "life of faith and victory" "not by long prayers and laborious effort, but by a deliberate and decisive act of faith."[41] Where in the New Testament is such a post-conversion act of faith invoked? Keswick preachers are right, of course, to insist that freedom from the dominion of sin is indeed provided for in the redemptive work of Christ and to be apprehended by faith. The sermons in Stevenson's anthology contain reference after reference to the idea that *Christians* need, now, to count on that as a fact to be grasped by faith and rested on. But this is exactly what happens at true conversion. McQuilkin comes almost to this realization when he says "that the solution for defeated, failing, sinning Christians is to return to what took place at salvation." Even so, he retains the categories of Keswick thinking when he adds, "Just as repenting, believing sinners received life by God's grace, so now the yielded, trusting saint will receive abundance of life by God's grace."[42] If people experienced what McQuilkin describes when they were converted, and now experience it no longer, one must painfully ask what happened to them?

Thus McQuilkin clearly shows he believes there are regenerate persons (and not just a few), whose lives are little if any better than they were before conversion, who need—as when they were converted—to exercise faith in Christ for their deliverance. I think he does not recognize the implicit contradiction between this and what he said earlier: "Just as a lost person can do right but cannot consistently choose to do right, so a saved person can do wrong but cannot *consistently* choose to do wrong (1 John 3)."[43] If it is true a saved person cannot consistently choose to do wrong, then by definition there cannot be defeated Christians who "yield to temptation more often than not"—to use McQuilkin's own description, referenced above.

It is obvious, in practice, that different Christians live at many different levels—not just two—of relative victory and defeat. Exegetically, we have seen above that all Christians are walking according to the Spirit and not according to the flesh. But we already know both from experience and from the New Testament (as in 1 John 1:8-2:2), that Christians are guilty of sin from time to time and in varying degrees. If victorious Christian living were provided for in the atonement and obtained at conversion by faith, then one wonders how to reconcile actual Christian experience with that idea of victory. The differences among Christians lead to doubt we can define a victory already possessed by all Christians in any meaningful way other than the way the New Testament itself describes the Christian life: the way that has been defined in the preceding chapters in this book.

To put this another way, I have the same problem with Keswick thinking on this score that I do with those who say physical healing was provided for in the atonement. If that is the case, every believer should automatically be healthy from the moment of conversion on. The Bible nowhere—directly or indirectly—indicates that the provisions of the atonement can be separated into different benefits that require separate acts of faith at different stages of the Christian experience.

Likewise the Bible nowhere suggests that after coming to saving faith a person needs to exercise faith again in order to experience Christian victory. But this appears to be the Keswick teaching; and while it is true that Keswick teachers do not espouse the doctrine of entire sanctification as a second work of grace, they are practically requiring a second work of grace for the Deeper Life.

Perhaps I should qualify the way I am presenting the Keswick view of things. It may be that they are not so much saying one must consciously claim, by faith, a victorious level of life provided for in the atonement. Perhaps they are saying, instead, that the victorious life is already the possession of the one saved by faith, who then simply needs to be informed, and to believe that this is part of what the atonement provided for him. I remember well a speaker known for his Keswick approach who used the following illustration. During one cold winter the local river froze over and one fellow, not being exactly sure how thick the ice, decided to try walking across. Carefully he ventured forth, testing the ice, gingerly sliding one foot ahead of the other and gradually putting all his weight on it before repeating the process. Suddenly a group of teenagers in a car shot out on the ice and sped across without hesitation. The man straightened up and strode confidently the rest of the way. The point, of course, is that once he knew the ice was plenty thick, he could walk on without worry.[44]

So, is that Keswick thinking? That we simply need to be informed that victorious living is ours in the cross, and once we are informed we can proceed without fear of defeat? Not quite, I think, for then there would be no "defeated Christians" for Keswick teachers to describe. There would be no need for a crisis of faith; knowledge alone would be required. And the knowledge would not change one from defeat to victory, only make one aware of the victory already possessed. But that brings us back to the problem of the great variety of Christian experience.

In fact there is no other provision of the atonement that, once saved by faith, we need even to know about in order to possess. A person may know very little Scripture and have no theological training. He may not have learned about justification, adoption, union with Christ, regeneration, and sanctification—either instantaneous, progressive, or final.[45] But learning about them changes nothing in one's experience. When a person is saved by taking Christ as Savior, all those benefits come automatically, aware of them or not. Learning about them may bring great joy and strength, of course, but it does not bring the benefits themselves.

I may add my personal testimony. When I first began to hear Keswick preaching I was positively impressed. Frankly, I often struggled in my Christian life and this seemed to offer a way to instant victory: just put faith in Christ for your victory as you did for your salvation, I was told. And I tried. And of course they said that was the problem: I must quit "trying." Just believe, they said. And I wanted to, but my own weaknesses kept interrupting. It is not your weakness but His ability that is involved, they told me. But it was mine I was grappling with, and no Scripture gave me a solid faith that another level of victorious living was mine for believing. And now, sixty-five years later, I still struggle (Galatians 5:17)—and I still walk in accord with the Spirit (Romans 8:4).

For various reasons, then, I do not find that Keswick teaching offers a helpful approach to dealing with the problem of sin in the Christian life.

The "Holiness" Concept of the Christian Life

Does the Holiness Movement offer helpful answers to questions about sin and the Christian life? The purpose of this section is to focus on this possibility.

In the United States, what is called the Holiness Movement harks back to the mid-nineteenth century and to an emphasis—principally within Methodism—on the Christian perfectionism of John Wesley. I do not propose to review the history of this movement.[46] As it developed, there came a time when smaller Methodist denominations emerged, determined to reemphasize truths they felt were being neglected in mainline Methodism. This, in turn, led to the existence of various "holiness" denominations that no longer called themselves Methodists, including various branches of the Church of God, the Church of the Nazarene, and others.[47] Without going into all the implications and variations of Holiness teaching, I summarize briefly. The Holiness concept of sin and the Christian life is that one who has been converted to faith in Christ may subsequently experience a "second definite work of grace" that produces "entire sanctification" or "full salvation." The terminology used to describe this state varies, but for most it means that the person thus sanctified has been freed from the effects of depravity and thus enabled to live without any conscious sin—in "sinless perfection," in other words. Wesley apparently thought of this as a state of "perfect love," of entire abandonment to the control of the Spirit of God. Some speak of the "eradication of the sinful nature." But all think of this as a crisis experience a Christian should seek and when it is obtained gives complete victory over sin.

Perhaps Wesley's own view (which is not entirely like that of all in the Holiness movement) is best seen in his sermon on "Christian perfection." Melvin Dieter has drawn from this and Wesley's other works in his description of the movement. Dieter indicates that the key truth for Wesley was that God had promised to deliver His people "from all willful sin" and this "sanctification" was meant to take place before one's death, thus bringing a person back to the state of holiness experienced by Adam and Eve before sin entered the world.[48]

For Wesley and Holiness theologians, then, God's "remedy for the sickness of systemic sinfulness" is "*entire sanctification*—a personal, definitive work of God's sanctifying grace by which the war within oneself might cease and the heart be fully released from rebellion into wholehearted love for God and others."[49] The "war" referred to is the very struggle between flesh and Spirit delineated in Galatians 5:17 (discussed above) and the deliverance from that war, from the dominion of sin, can be accomplished "by the same faith in the merits of Christ's sacrifice for sin that initially had brought justification."[50] Dieter adds that while this experience could theoretically come at the same time as one's justification, believers typically appropriate this "in a distinct crisis of faith sometime subsequent to justification."[51]

My purpose does not include pursuing this understanding of Holiness teaching at greater length. I should add that Wesley, like most who hold this view, did not take this experience to mean that entirely sanctified Christians could not afterward fall back into sin. His views on human freedom were such as to keep open this possibility. Nor did he discount the need for a continuing growth in grace by the entirely sanctified believer.[52] In its essence, however, and regardless how nuanced, the view of Wesley and Holiness teaching is that the sanctified believer is delivered from the effects of original sin and its resulting depravity; he is as good as free from the tendencies of "the fleshly nature."

The basic question, then, is whether *sanctification* is best or biblically conceived as an instantaneous and complete work available to a Christian and promises something not gained by mere regeneration. If it is, that may well answer many questions about the possibilities of sin in the life of a regenerate person.

No doubt, the best way to approach this is to obtain a thoroughly Scriptural view of sanctification. It has become common to describe sanctification as having past, present, and future aspects: initial sanctification which takes place at one's conversion; progressive sanctification which takes place throughout one's Christian life; and final sanctification which takes place when one is transformed for the afterlife. Is this biblical? As the following survey will tend to show, this threefold distinction does not directly arise out of biblical exegesis; it has more the nature of a theological construct. Even so, it is more or less useful as a means for discussing the various aspects of sanctification.

"Sanctify" and "Sanctification" in the New Testament

My first purpose is to survey the usage of these two words in the New Testament. After all, if we are studying the nature of sanctification it seems logical to examine closely the word(s) that mean this. Though I found this approach to be not as helpful as I hoped, I will share the results.

The verb usually translated *sanctify* in the Greek New Testament is *hagiazo*, for which the lexicons give such meanings as *make holy, set apart, consecrate, sanctify*. The closely related noun (*hagiasmos*) is variously translated as *holiness, consecration, sanctification*—viewing this as an active work in progress or accomplished. There are also (although not as important to our study) two other related words: another cognate noun (*hagiōsunē*) identifying *sanctification* (in the abstract) as the state of being holy, and a cognate adjective (*hagios*) meaning *holy, dedicated to God*. The apparent concept underlying all four (and a few other less common forms) is the idea of being set apart, especially being set apart for God. The result is that anything set apart for God is, by that definition, "holy."

What is called for here, is to survey the places where the verb and first noun—the adjective is too broad and varied to provide much help—describe the Christian's experience. The verb occurs slightly more than two dozen times and the noun ten times, though several of these do not bear directly on the subject at hand.

Christians as "Saints"

Perhaps the place to begin is with the fact that every regenerate person is, by virtue of becoming God's, sanctified, set apart to God. This is the reason the word *saints* (plural form of the adjective: "holy ones") is common in the New Testament as an identification of believers. This usage (already common in the Old Testament for those who know God, as in Psalm 30:4) first appears in the New Testament in Acts 9 (vv. 13, 32, 41). It is frequent in the epistles (more than fifty times), being often used in the addresses (Romans 1:7; Ephesians 1:1), or in sending greetings (2 Corinthians 13:13; Philippians 4:22), or in general references to the body of believers (1 Corinthians 6:2; Colossians 1:12).

It seems likely that this brief form of identification probably developed from a longer expression characterizing those who know God as "those who are sanctified." This fuller phrase occurs in Acts 20:32 and 26:18, both of which (in the words of Paul, quoting Jesus in the second) promise believers "an inheritance among those who are sanctified." In both places, the phrase seems to mean nothing more than "the saints."[53] Regardless, in both places the verbal idea is in the Greek perfect tense, viewing a settled state of being. And in both it is clear they refer to the regenerate in general, not to some more sanctified part of the church.

This is a helpful starting point: every child of God is by nature a *saint*, a *sanctified* one. And while this no doubt represents what the believer presently *is*, at any time, it must surely be grounded in initial sanctification. Upon being born again, one is sanctified, set apart as God's.

Sanctification in the Book of Hebrews

Hebrews uses the verb *sanctify* more than any other book in the New Testament—seven times in all,[54] six of them referring to Christian sanctification.[55] Interestingly, four of these are passive voice, viewing the regenerate as those for whom God works sanctification; the two that are active voice (Hebrews 2:11; 13:12) speak of God as the sanctifier.[56] The point is that Christian sanctification is the work of God.

In the four instances that describe sanctification as the experience of a believer, two seem clearly to point back to conversion. These are in 10:10: "By that will we *have been sanctified* through the offering of the body of Jesus Christ once for all"; and 10:29: "Of how much worse punishment ... will he be thought worthy who ... counted the blood of the covenant by which he *was sanctified* a common thing?"

DISCIPLESHIP AND SANCTIFICATION | 145

Commenting on 10:10, Morris contrasts the way the author of Hebrews uses the verb *sanctify* with the way Paul uses it: "For the apostle [Paul], sanctification is a process whereby the believer grows progressively in Christian qualities and character. In Hebrews the same terminology is used of the process by which a person becomes a Christian. … The sanctification meant here is one brought about by the death of Christ. It has to do with making people Christian, not with developing Christian character."[57] (But on Paul, see below.)

The first of these is in the Greek perfect tense,[58] which presents the perspective of a settled state of being. The second is aorist, which views the action in the verb, more simply, as a whole. Contextually, both are explicitly tied to the atoning work of Christ.[59] One may say, then, that both look back even before the individual's conversion to the sacrificial death of Christ in history: "God has sanctified people, that is, claimed them for himself, by means of the blood of Christ."[60] Even so, when one exercises saving faith in Christ the latter's sacrifice becomes part of the believer's history.[61] These two statements focus on the "past" tense of sanctification: "a sanctification that has taken place once for all."[62] Add to this the fact that Hebrews 13:12, one of the active voice uses, indicates that Jesus "sanctified" His elect when He died on the cross.

The other two references to the regenerate person's sanctification in Hebrews have a different sound and may refer to the "present" tense of sanctification. These are 2:11: "Both He who sanctifies and those who *are being sanctified* are all of one, for which reason He is not ashamed to call them brethren"; and 10:14: "By one offering He has perfected forever those who *are being sanctified*."

Both of these (as well as "He who sanctifies" in 2:11) are in the Greek present tense, which has the perspective of viewing an action while it is in progress.[63] There are at least three possible ways of understanding this (especially 2:11), as mentioned by Ellingworth.[64] Some take it to be timeless.[65] Others understand it to mean that each Christian, individually, is in the process of being sanctified.[66] Yet others think the verbs picture all believers throughout Christian history as a group, with each sanctified in his own time, rather than the history of the individual.[67] Both are plural, and plural verbs are sometimes used that way.[68] Ellingworth suggests that one reason for the present tense is to "avoid the possible implication that Christians had already reached their goal."[69]

Either way, however, what is very clear is that the verbs are referring to all the regenerate and not to some among them. The first and third understandings, just above, do not speak directly to progressive sanctification. Even so, to describe believers as "those who are being sanctified" (NIV: "those who are being made holy") is "progressive," one way or the other. For that matter, it is possible that some of these statements look especially to the future when the goal of sanctification is fully attained.

It seems certain, then, that the inspired writer of Hebrews spoke of initial sanctification. He may also have spoken directly of progressive sanctification or by implication of final sanctification. Indeed, Hughes may be right in his opinion that in Hebrews the verb *sanctify* "is descriptive not of one aspect of the Christian life but of the total experience, from regeneration to glorification."[70] Regardless, two things are clear. First, the author never used the word except as it applies to *all* the regenerate. Second, he never indicated by that word a crisis experience some may gain subsequent to or separate from conversion.

Sanctification in Paul

Taking Paul's letters in their probable chronological order, I begin with Thessalonians. The noun (*hagiasmos*) occurs four times: 1 Thessalonians 4:3-4: "For this is the will of God, your *sanctification*: that you should abstain from sexual immorality; that each of you should know how to possess his own vessel in *sanctification* and honor"; 1 Thessalonians 4:7: "For God did not call us to uncleanness, but in *holiness*"; and 2 Thessalonians 2:13: "God from the beginning chose you for salvation through *sanctification* by the Spirit and belief in the truth."

None of these speaks with enough precision to enable us to discern between one aspect of sanctification and another.[71] The first three seem most likely (like *holiness* in Hebrews 12:14, above) to refer to the practice of holiness: "to live a holy life" (4:7, NIV). The last one probably looks back to initial sanctification, given that it is so closely linked to "belief in the truth"; it would be possible to refer it to final sanctification, which would require that "salvation" also be taken in the sense of final salvation.

But what is clear in all of these is that sanctification is the experience of all the children of God and not just some. Again, nothing in context suggests a "second work of grace."

The verb (*hagiazō*) appears in Paul's concluding prayer in 1 Thessalonians 5:23: "May the God of peace Himself *sanctify* you completely, and may your whole spirit, soul, and body be preserved blameless at the coming of our Lord Jesus Christ."

This might appear, at first glance, to offer support for the Holiness position, if Paul is praying for his Christian readers to experience entire sanctification in this life. And the verb is aorist tense, looking at the action as a whole. On closer examination, however, the phrase "at the coming of our Lord Jesus Christ" most surely makes this a prayer for final sanctification—which fits the aorist tense as well.[72] In all likelihood, the second clause ("may your whole spirit, soul, and body be preserved...") is explanatory of "sanctify you completely."[73] This fits well with the eschatological focus of this letter.

The verb appears four times in 1 Corinthians, two of which relate to our study, as follows:[74] in 1:2: "To the church of God which is at Corinth, to those who *are sanctified* in Christ Jesus, called to be saints"; and in 6:11: "And such were some of you. But you were washed, but you *were sanctified*, but you were justified."

The first of these is Greek perfect tense and is being used the very same way as in Acts 20:32 and 26:18, discussed above. Here the close tie with the essentially synonymous "saints" makes the connection clear.[75] The second is Greek aorist and the context makes clear it looks back on the conversion experience of all the Corinthian Christians. Their sanctification took place at the same time their sins were washed away and they were justified: "one fundamental transformation that has occurred for those who now belong to Christ."[76]

The noun appears in 1 Corinthians 1:30, which reveals that Jesus "became for us wisdom from God—and righteousness and *sanctification* and redemption." The reference is too general to make anyone's case, but again the close association with righteousness and redemption would argue it looks back to the initial sanctification one comes to possess by identification with Christ by faith.[77] Fee, in fact, refers to sanctification (in all three: 1:2, 30; 6:11) as "a metaphor for Christian conversion," although a metaphor with ethical implications: "They must also bear the character of the God who has thus set them apart."[78]

In Paul's letter to the Romans the noun occurs twice:[79] in 6:19: "Just as you [formerly] presented your members as slaves of uncleanness...so now present your members as slaves of righteousness for *holiness*"; and in 6:22: "Now, having been set free from sin...you have your fruit to *holiness*." As in the usage in Thessalonians, both of these appear to focus on the practice of holiness in the Christian life.[80]

The verb appears once in Ephesians 5:25-26: "Christ loved the church and gave Himself for it, that He might *sanctify* it and cleanse it with the washing of water by the word, that He might present it to Himself a glorious church." Here the verb (aorist) looks to a complete work as a whole, but it refers to the church rather than to individual believers' experience. Even if that distinction should be discounted—the church is made up of individuals, after all—it remains that this refers either to initial sanctification at the time of the "washing" referred to (more likely), or to final sanctification when the church is presented to Christ as His pure bride. Either way, the reference is to the whole church and not just to a part of it.[81]

In 1 Timothy 2:15, the noun is used in reference to the Christian wives who "will be saved...if they continue in faith, love, and *holiness*, with self-control." Once again, the meaning seems to be the practice of holiness.[82]

The verb is in 2 Timothy 2:21:[83] "If anyone cleanses himself from the latter [vessels of dishonor or dishonor itself], he will be a vessel for honor, *sanctified* and useful for the Master, prepared for every good work." Once again, the Greek perfect views this as a settled state of being, here a state that results from self-cleansing and qualifies one for service. The focus is on being set apart to God for His purpose and use, thus devoted to or consecrated to God: "as a purified implement is prepared for use in worship."[84] This deals more with specific circumstances than the experience we call sanctification in general.

For Paul, then, sanctification and practical holiness are closely intertwined. When he speaks of sanctification in the sense we are concerned with in this study, he usually speaks of initial sanctification and links it with other aspects of conversion. But he often refers, by the noun, to the practice of holiness, a practice God has called believers to and which ought to characterize them throughout their Christian lives. Apparently he can also speak of final sanctification (1 Thessalonians 5:23) as the goal of the Christian life. What is clear, in accord with Hebrews, is that he never uses the word to refer to some experience following conversion that only some believers achieve. Except when he refers to practical holiness (as in 2 Timothy 2:21) he consistently uses *sanctification* in ways that apply to the entire community of those who belong to Christ.

Sanctification in the Rest of the New Testament

Neither the verb nor the noun occurs very much in the rest of the New Testament, at least not when Christian sanctification is meant. The noun appears only once more, in 1 Peter 1:2: "elect according to the foreknowledge of God ... in *sanctification* of the Spirit, for obedience and sprinkling of the blood of Jesus Christ." Whatever else may be said about this, it obviously refers to all the believers whom

Peter addresses: all regenerate persons, in other words. And it seems reasonably clear, again, that the reference is to initial sanctification, linked as it is with the sprinkling of the blood of Jesus and the obedience of the gospel: "the consecration of these people that occurred when they heard and responded to the word of God effectively preached in the power of the Spirit."[85]

The verb is found three times in Jesus' high-priestly prayer in John 17; in verse 17: "*Sanctify* them by Your truth. Your word is truth"; verse 19: "For their sakes I *sanctify* Myself, that they also may *be sanctified* by the truth." In verse 19, the first, of course, refers to the sanctification of Jesus[86] and not of His disciples. But in both verses Jesus refers to the correlative sanctification of disciples "by the truth." Both for Him and for them the "sanctification," the "setting apart," is for the mission of being sent into the world; compare John 10:36. As Jack Stallings expresses this, Jesus was praying "first, that they may be purified from sin" and then "that they may be set aside and consecrated to the task of world evangelization."[87] Consequently, while this use of *sanctify* is grounded in the fundamental meaning of the word, the application is more specific than to general Christian sanctification, progressive or otherwise. Debating whether this was exclusively for the disciples then present or for the disciples of all time would seem pointless; either way, the passage certainly does not speak of what Holiness doctrine calls "entire sanctification." The verb occurs in seven more verses I have not identified above or in attached notes, though none of them speaks of the general sanctification of believers.[88]

What I conclude from this survey of the usage of *sanctify* and *sanctification* in the New Testament is the following:

(1) The most clearly-established usage is of *initial* sanctification, what we sometimes speak of as the "past tense" of sanctification.[89] This is that setting apart of the believer at conversion when he becomes God's and is by virtue of that fact holy, sanctified, a saint.

(2) Less clear, but probable, is the use of the word to describe what we call *progressive* (the "present tense") of sanctification. But this is so little spoken of when the word itself is used that one must build an understanding of what this involves from other passages of Scripture where the word is not present. In that case, some terms other than "sanctification" may be at least as appropriate—terms like growing in grace, for example (as in 2 Peter 3:18; compare 2 Peter 1:5-10).

(3) Also infrequent, but enough to justify the usage, are references to *final* sanctification (its "future tense"), sometimes called glorification. This obviously

refers to the point at which the believer's "holiness" is made complete and permanent, with all the effects of depravity and the curse permanently eliminated. Whether the New Testament writers meant us to include this under the doctrinal heading of "sanctification" is not certain, but the concept is clear and the usage is convenient.

(4) It appears to be indisputably clear that the word itself is not used in the New Testament in ways that suggest a second-level experience the regenerate are invited, but not required, to seek and obtain. Indeed, Dieter acknowledges, "Adherents of this understanding [the Holiness view of sanctification] recognize that there is no explicit exhortation to seek sanctification as such in the New Testament."[90] McQuilkin, representing the Keswick position, admits the same thing: "It might be added that Scripture contains no exhortation to have nor teaching about a crisis experience subsequent to regeneration and necessary for sanctification."[91] These, I think, are telling admissions, and they are broad enough to refer not just to the *word* "sanctification" but also to the *concept* of sanctification as a crisis experience that can be defined as different from conversion.

Except when some specific instances of the practice of holiness are referred to (consistently using the noun and not the verb), then, "sanctification" is something that is the experience of all the regenerate and not an option. It is significant and interesting, I think, that if someone wishes to build a doctrine of entire sanctification as a second definite work of grace from the New Testament, he will be forced to do so from passages where the word *sanctification* does not appear! These conclusions are biblically based, and they are adequate to assure me that the classic Holiness teaching is not correct and therefore does not solve the problem of sin in the Christian life.

Between initial and final sanctification, the New Testament is most concerned to instruct believers in the practice of holiness and to nurture our spiritual development—which may conveniently be called progressive sanctification. As has become clear in the preceding chapters, especially the chapter on 1 John, the New Testament, while it makes clear Christians do not make a practice of sin, makes no claim that Christians never sin. Until the sinful nature has been eradicated (at final sanctification), the struggle Paul depicts in Galatians 5:17 remains with us to keep us from glib conclusions about sinlessness. At the same time, the provision for forgiveness and cleansing from our sins John sets forth in 1 John 1:7-2:2 continues to encourage us to confess our sins to our Father who is faithful and just.

Before any final conclusions about the problem of sin are reached, however, we must turn our attention to that very subject, in the following chapter.

ENDNOTES

[1] Interestingly, they are usually among those of us whose theological position is that it is possible for a true believer to turn away from God and be lost!

[2] Neither term is very precise.

[3] Pronounced *kessick*.

[4] Those who do not agree with my summary may well deny that my evaluation fits them.

[5] For a brief treatment of the movement, see "Keswick Convention" in *Evangelical Dictionary of Theology*, ed. Walter A. Elwell (Grand Rapids: Baker, 1984), 603-604. For more detail, see Steven Barabas, *So Great Salvation: The History and Message of the Keswick Convention* (London: Marshall, Morgan & Scott, 1952, 1957), 15-28; the "message" part of the book is organized by these five emphases. A book of sermons from Keswick groups them according to the first four of the five emphases listed: sin in the believer, God's remedy for sin, consecration, and the Spirit-filled life. See Herbert F. Stevenson, *Keswick's Authentic Voice* (London: Marshall, Morgan & Scott, 1959, reprint 1962).

[6] The Keswick emphasis on missions is well known and greatly appreciated.

[7] Perhaps the wording more often is along the lines of the "blessing" of the Keswick experience. See Stevenson, 13-22, 25-30, 137-43, 247-53, and 403-10, for descriptions that introduce each section of sermons.

[8] Barabas, 71-73, rejects both a gradual and a crisis eradication of the sinful nature.

[9] Melvin E. Dieter, "Wesleyan View," Anthony A. Hoekema, "Reformed View," Stanley M. Horton, "Pentecostal View," J. Robertson McQuilkin, "Keswick View," John F. Walvoord, "Augustinian-Dispensational View," *Five Views on Sanctification* (Grand Rapids: Zondervan, 1987). All subsequent citations will use only the author's last name and page number.

[10] McQuilkin, 151-52.

[11] Barabas, 54. It seems clear to me that all these expressions, biblical based in themselves, directly miss biblical usage that all Christians walk according to the Spirit (Romans 8:4), sin is no longer master (Romans 6:14-18), and receiving spiritual truth is a mark of Christians (1 Corinthians 2:14). See further below.

[12] Anthony A. Hoekema, 189, agrees, "there is no biblical basis for the distinction between 'carnal' and 'spiritual' Christians."

[13] In the N.T., *walking* is frequently used as a metaphor for one's manner of life.

[14] Barabas, 137, speaks of the possibility a Christian "will act or walk according to the flesh."

[15] I realize that this clause (technically, a participial phrase in Greek) is not in the critical text in v. 1; nothing at issue here is different whether it appears both times or only in v. 4. Either way, the words "who do not walk after the flesh but after the Spirit" describe *all* those who have been born again.

[16] John Stott, *Romans: God's Good News for the World* (Downer's Grove, InterVarsity, 1994), 224. Douglas Moo, *The Wycliffe Exegetical Commentary: Romans 1-8* (Chicago: Moody, 1991) agrees that in these verses Paul "describes the Christian life-style as being directed by, and under the control of, the Spirit rather than the flesh." See also Leon Morris, *The Epistle to the Romans* (PNTC;

Grand Rapids: Eerdmans, 1988), 304: "The believer does not walk 'according to the flesh' …[but] *according to the Spirit*."

[17] And yet Barabas, 76-83, in a lengthy discussion of the role of Romans 7 and 8 in Keswick, finds the "normal" (victorious) Christian life in Romans 8, as opposed to the defeat in Romans 7.

[18] If Romans 7:14-25 is descriptive of *Christian* experience (as I think), then v. 14 also uses *carnal* to modify a Christian; but there the reference is to the depraved, fleshly nature of every Christian, regardless how mature.

[19] Anthony C. Thiselton, *The First Epistle to the Corinthians: A Commentary on the Greek Text* (NIGTC; Grand Rapids: Eerdmans, 2000), 289. Thiselton and others are right in emphasizing that Paul does not here *justify* this immaturity as though it is permissible for believers to be "carnal Christians." See also Gordon D. Fee, *The First Epistle to the Corinthians* (NICNT; Grand Rapids: Eerdmans, 1987), 128, and 125, for the additional suggestion that the Corinthians, in their super-spirituality, judged Paul's teaching to be "milk," and that Paul is saying they need to "abandon their present 'childish' behavior altogether so that they may appreciate the 'milk' for what it is, 'solid food'."

[20] The difference between the Greek *sarkinos* (v. 1) and *sarkikos* (v. 3) need not occupy us here. If Paul meant them to differ significantly, it is difficult to be sure how; either way, the Corinthians were "carnal" by both terms. Compare Fee, 121, n. 1, and Thiselton, 288, who disagrees with him and views the difference as "one of morphology rather than semantics."

[21] Richard B. Hays, *First Corinthians* (Interpretation; Louisville: John Knox, 1997), 49.

[22] John MacArthur, *The Gospel According to Jesus: What Is Authentic Faith?* (Grand Rapids: Zondervan, 2008), 279.

[23] Timothy George, *The New American Commentary, Vol. 30: Galatians* (Nashville: Broadman & Holman, 1994), 385.

[24] Ronald Y. K. Fung, *The Epistle to the Galatians* (NICNT; Grand Rapids: Eerdmans, 1988), 250-51, discusses three views. (1) This refers to the successful restraint of the flesh. (2) It refers to good desires being overcome by the desires of the flesh. (3) And (as he prefers) it means the believer cannot simply do as he pleases but must choose either for the flesh or the Spirit. George, 387, prefers the middle view. Both agree, "The work of the Spirit in the believer's life does not set the believer free from the warfare between flesh and Spirit" (Fung, 251), which is the main point after all. F. F. Bruce, *The Epistle to the Galatians: A Commentary on the Greek Text* (NIGTC; Grand Rapids: Eerdmans, 1982), 244-45, does not come down clearly for one view or the other.

[25] "Do," in 5:21, is *prassō*, a close synonym of *poieō* (1 John 3) in this sense; Fung, 260: "not an occasional lapse but habitual behavior."

[26] I have touched on this in the discussion of Romans in chapter five.

[27] Eduard Lohse, *Colossians and Philemon* (Hermeneia; Philadelphia: Fortress, 1971), 142. Lohse's view is, however, more "mystical" than mine.

[28] Harold W. Hoehner, *Ephesians: An Exegetical Commentary* (Grand Rapids: Baker Academic, 2002), 598-602, discusses the matter thoroughly and concludes (602) the "old person" (in all three passages) "refers to the unregenerate person," and the "new person" to "the individual who has become new in Christ" (610). He argues (602) the putting on and putting off in Ephesians 4:22, 24—in agreement with Colossians 3:9-10—have "already been accomplished," and yet the readers are commanded to put off sins and put on godly characteristics on this grounds. Peter T. O'Brien, *The Letter to the Ephesians* (PNTC; Grand Rapids: Eerdmans, 1999), 328, agrees that Romans 6:6 and Colossians 3:9 mean, by the "old person," "the whole personality of a person when he is ruled by sin," and "the definitive break with the old person has been made in the past." But he thinks the

words in Ephesians look more to the present and have a hortatory force. The difference will not affect my point.

[29] James D. G. Dunn, *The Epistles to the Colossians and to Philemon* (NIGTC; Grand Rapids: Eerdmans, 1996), 220-21, describes the "old man" as a figure that is "clearly a way of indicating a whole way of life ... prior to and without Christ," and the "new man" as "a whole personality." He takes the aorist "put on" in Colossians 3:10 as the "event of the conversion-initiation past."

[30] Some interpreters press on the old man-new man distinction the structure of first Adam-second Adam Christology, which does not seem likely, here. Others emphasize a corporate significance, especially for the "new man." See Robert W. Wall, *Colossians & Philemon* (IVPNTC; Downers Grove: InterVarsity, 1993), 142-43. What of this implication is to be found here is surely secondary, not primary; even so, the new life is lived as part of the Christian community.

[31] Thus, Fung, 274: "It is a distinguishing feature of all Christians ... that they have crucified the flesh. ... Hence, they must (as a fact) be living by the Spirit and they must (as an obligation) be led by the Spirit." He understands the temporal reference to be to one's conversion or baptism and so to "participation in the crucifixion of Christ." Herman N. Ridderbos, *The Epistle of Paul to the Churches of Galatia* (NICNT; Grand Rapids: Eerdmans, 1953), 209, agrees that this refers to a past "moment of time ... in which ... the dominion of the flesh over them was broken." Likewise, Bruce, 256, thinks the aorist "probably indicates their participation in Christ's historical crucifixion." It is difficult to understand how George, 405, can take 5:24 to refer to "the process of mortification, the daily putting to death of the flesh." The aorist verb "did crucify" does not lend itself well—George must take it as gnomic, but he does not say—to this interpretation.

[32] Barabas, 90.

[33] Barabas, 118-120.

[34] Barabas, 68.

[35] Sermons by all of these appear in Stevenson. One must not assume all these men held exactly the same views on all the related issues.

[36] See Barabas, 123-127, for example.

[37] McQuilkin, 151.

[38] Barabas, 84.

[39] McQuilkin, 155.

[40] Barabas, 112.

[41] Barabas, 84.

[42] McQuilkin, 166.

[43] McQuilkin, 162. (Emphasis mine.)

[44] I have heard that other Keswick speakers have used the same illustration.

[45] See the discussion to follow.

[46] For a brief summary see "Holiness Movement, American" in *Evangelical Dictionary of Theology*, ed. Walter A. Elwell (Grand Rapids: Baker, 1984), 516-518. Parts of my summary reflect that article.

[47] Closely linked is the history of the Pentecostal movement, holding (with some oversimplification) that the evidence of this experience of sanctification (a crisis linked to "baptism in the Holy Spirit") is the gift of *glossolalia*, of speaking in tongues. My purpose does not include interaction with that view, since it typically (but not in all cases) involves the same Holiness concept of sin and Christian living.

154

48 Dieter, 15.

49 Dieter, 17.

50 Dieter, 17.

51 Dieter, 18. While Wesley thought more in terms of development leading to and following the crisis of entire sanctification, contemporary Holiness views may emphasize more crisis and less development. See Dieter, 39-45, for discussion of this and other varieties of thought subsequent to Wesley.

52 See Dieter, 13-14.

53 John B. Polhill, *The New American Commentary: Acts* (Nashville: Broadman, 1992), 429: "The reference ... reflects Paul's favorite designation of Christians as 'the saints,' ... who have been 'sanctified,' i.e., 'set apart' as God's people in Christ." Darrell L. Bock, *Acts* (ECNT; Grand Rapids: Baker Academic, 2007), 718, paraphrases 26:18 as "the reception of a place with God and his saints." Similarly, David J. Williams, *Acts* (NIBC; Peabody, Mass.: Hendrickson, 1985, 1990), 420, reduces it to "a place among the people of God."

54 The noun *hagiasmos* also appears once, in Hebrews 12:14, but in the sense of the practice of *holiness* rather than the believer's experience of sanctification.

55 The other is Hebrews 9:13, which refers to the sanctification wrought by animal sacrifices in the Old Testament.

56 Which person of the Godhead is meant is worth discussing but need not occupy us here.

57 Leon Morris, "Hebrews," in *The Expositor's Bible Commentary*, vol. 12 (Grand Rapids: Zondervan, 1981), 99. See also 107, where he takes the same view of 10:29 as "the initial act of being set apart for God."

58 A periphrastic construction using the Greek perfect participle.

59 Paul Ellingworth, *The Epistle to the Hebrews* (NIGTC; Grand Rapids: Eerdmans, 1993), 505, on 10:10, notes the "continuing state of believers depends on the once-for-all offering of the body of Christ."

60 Ellingworth, 541 (on 10:29).

61 Romans 6:4 likewise looks back on the believer's conversion and baptism as identification with the death, burial, and resurrection of Christ.

62 F. F. Bruce, *Commentary on the Epistle to the Hebrews* (NICNT; Grand Rapids: Eerdmans, 1964), 236 (on 10:10).

63 This perspective seems clearer in the NKJV translation quoted than in the King James Version (KJV) "they/them who are sanctified," which might be understood by the English reader as perfect tense. The NASB puts the progressive rendering in the margin as an alternative; the NIV handles one in one way and one in the other.

64 Ellingworth, 511, in commenting on 10:14.

65 Bruce, 44: "a general truth" that applies in 2:11 to the action of any consecrating priest. See also 241 and n. 73 there.

66 Stanley Outlaw, *The Randall House Bible Commentary: The Book of Hebrews* (Nashville: Randall House, 2005), 46, expresses this view.

67 Morris, 101, takes this view; he rejects "progressive sanctification" here because "the idea of sanctification as a continuing process does not seem to appear in Hebrews." That is arguing in a

circle. Homer A. Kent, *The Epistle to the Hebrews: A Commentary* (Winona Lake: BMH Books, 1981 printing), 193-94, mentions the second and third options without choosing between them.

[68] Such a usage is often called "iterative."

[69] Ellingworth, 511.

[70] Philip Edgcumbe Hughes, *A Commentary on the Epistle to the Hebrews* (Grand Rapids: Eerdmans, 1977), 103.

[71] Charles A. Wanamaker, *The Epistles to the Thessalonians* (NIGTC; Grand Rapids: Eerdmans, 1990), 150, 153, 157, notes that *hagiasmos* can "denote either the process ... or the outcome of that process"; he leans to the first for 4:3, to the second for 4:4, and to a more holistic view for 4:7 ("the sphere where God's sanctification takes place"). F. F. Bruce, *Word Biblical Commentary: 1 & 2 Thessalonians* (Waco: Word Book, 1982), 82, views *hagiosunē* (3:13) as holiness as a state of being and *hagiasmos* (4:3-4) as the process by which one is made holy—the antithesis of "uncleanness" (*akatharsia*, 4:7). Likewise Gene L. Green, *The Letters to the Thessalonians* (PNTC; Grand Rapids: Eerdmans, 2002), 190. On 4:7 (85) he notes, "by calling his people God sanctifies them in the sense of setting them apart for himself," and therefore believers "must manifest their sanctification in the ways of daily life." He adds, "the climax of sanctification appears in 3:13; 5:23, 24"—thus blending the past, present, and future. Leon Morris, *The First and Second Epistles to the Thessalonians* (Grand Rapids: Eerdmans, 1991), 119, similarly blends at least the past and present; and on 3:7 (125) he observes that God has "called them to be set apart for him, that is, to live in sanctification." On 2 Thessalonians 2:13, Bruce, 191 observes that the ongoing process of sanctification will be finished at the Second Coming. Even so, he notes the link with "belief in the truth," which inclines me to say if the *present* work of the Spirit is meant Paul must have been thinking of the readers' conversion when that work *began*. Likewise Morris, 239, after noting that sanctification in this verse "is to be understood of the work of the Holy Spirit in making the whole person holy" (reflecting 1 Thessalonians 5:23), proceeds to express some surprise that "belief in the truth" is stated after sanctification.

[72] It would also be possible, viewing the aorist verb as culminative, to think Paul is praying for the completion of their progressive sanctification; but the focus of the prayer may be more narrowly eschatological. Bruce, 129, however, thinks specifically in terms of the finished work of sanctification in 5:23. By contrast, Morris, 183, thinks more in terms of the whole work of sanctification "which will exist at the Parousia." So also Wanamaker, 206, thinks of the aorist verb as "embracing the whole process."

[73] Bruce, 129; Wanamaker, 206; Green, 267, agree that this prayer reflects Paul's desire that the readers' sanctification be brought to completion. Green, 267, says, "the focus of v. 23 is on the complete sanctification of the believer in anticipation of the coming of the Lord," but adds, "The emphasis ... falls on the entire work of God in their lives."

[74] The other two are in 1 Corinthians 7:14 and refer to the setting apart of an unbelieving spouse by the Christian husband or wife.

[75] The view of Thiselton, 76, that the perfect, here, means "a past event with present effects which remain" is too much dependent on an old view of the Greek tenses, but it does provide the perspective of a state of being where one is set apart or consecrated to God, with this kind of holiness as "received, not achieved" (Thiselton, quoting Conzelman).

[76] Hays, 98; also Thiselton, 76: "the transitional and transformative event of the reader's coming to faith."

[77] Hays, 33, however, apparently takes it to mean, here, "holy living," but as "made possible by God's act of delivering us from slavery (redemption) through the cross." Either way, Thiselton, 193, is

right to approve of the words of C. T. Craig: "In no passage in Paul does [sanctification] describe an advanced state of Christian living."

[78] Fee, 32, 86, 247.

[79] The verb occurs in Romans 15:16 but does not refer to the Christian experience of sanctification.

[80] Moo, 421, 424, regards both as references to "the process of 'becoming holy.'" But on 6:19 he leans more to "the active meaning of *hagiasmos*," which fits practice better than process; the two, of course, are not separable. Morris, 265-66, and Stott, 185-86, agree with Moo; all three are contrasting the process with the final state, the latter being the way some interpreters view sanctification in these two verses.

[81] O'Brien, 526 (citing D. G. Peterson), emphasizes, "It is the *church* … which is sanctified through Christ's death. … The verb refers to the church being brought into 'an exclusive and dedicated relationship with God, as the holy people of the New Covenant, … not to an ongoing process of sanctification." Rudolf Schnackenburg, *Ephesians: A Commentary* (Edinburgh: T & T Clark, 1991), 249, agrees. Hoehner, 752, referring to "sanctify" and "cleanse," says, "Temporally both actions occurred at the cross."

[82] Philip H. Towner, *The Letters to Timothy and Titus* (NICNT; Grand Rapids: Eerdmans, 2006), 236: "'Holiness' indicates separation from sin and probably implies sexual purity"; he compares 1 Thessalonians 4:3-4, 7). George W. Knight III, *The Pastoral Epistles* (NIGTC; Grand Rapids: Eerdmans, 1992), 148, takes this to refer, more generally, to "a state or process in which women must continue as a condition for salvation."

[83] It also occurs in 1 Timothy 4:5, referring to foods that are "sanctified by the word of God and prayer."

[84] Towner, 542. Knight, 419, agrees: "one set apart for God and his service."

[85] Karen H. Jobes, *1 Peter* (ECNT; Grand Rapids: Baker Academic, 2005), 70. I. Howard Marshall, *1 Peter* (IVPNTC; Downers Grove: InterVarsity, 2003), 31, agrees: "Right from the beginning of their Christian experience the Spirit was active in their lives to set God's seal on them as his people and to initiate the new way of life that should characterize the children of God." Paul J. Achtemeier, *1 Peter* (Hermeneia; Minneapolis: Fortress, 1996), 86-87, is not as specific: "the setting apart accomplished by the Spirit," but he goes on to refer this to Christians as "ones … set apart for God."

[86] As also in John 10:36, though there it is the Father who sanctifies Him, here it is self-sanctification.

[87] Jack W. Stallings, *The Randall House Bible Commentary: The Gospel of John* (Nashville: Randall House, 1989), 241.

[88] Matthew 6:9; 23:17, 19; Luke 11:2; 1 Peter 3:15; Jude 1; and Revelation 22:11.

[89] Some call this "positional" sanctification. While I do not object to the term, it probably reflects the "transaction model" of Christianity that I fear falls short of New Testament Christianity.

[90] Dieter, 32.

[91] McQuilkin, 55.

Chapter Eight

DISCIPLESHIP AND THE PROBLEM OF SIN

On the theoretical side, the problem of sin in the life of a child of God requires grappling with what the Bible says on the subject, and some of the things it says *seem* to contradict some other things it says.[1] In chapter four I have examined what John said in his first epistle, "Whoever abides in him does not sin" (1 John 3:6), after he indicated earlier (1 John 1:8-2:2) that we cannot truthfully claim to be sinless, even after we are born again. The conclusion I reached there—John means Christians do not *practice* sin—seems to be the right one, and it meshes well with the conclusions of the rest of this book: saving faith expresses itself in the loving obedience of a committed disciple of Jesus Christ, an obedience that, however, falls short of sinless perfection.

This does not solve all the practical problems, however. Given this understanding of what John means, how can we define *practice*? To put this personally, can I reconcile my own Christian life with that? It cannot be true that I never sin, but is it even true that I do not *practice* sin? If the Bible means a regenerate person does not sin habitually or characteristically, the question becomes, how much can I sin and still be assured I am regenerate? Whether about others or myself, I often wrestle with that issue. Furthermore, as I have indicated in the previous chapter, I have not found any of the forms of "second blessing" theology to help with the problem.

Other issues are closely interwoven with this. What is sin? What are the effects of depravity in the life of one who exercises saving faith in Jesus Christ? How does one obtain a solid assurance of eternal life? What, and how effective, is sanctification (as discussed in the preceding chapter)? Can we reach a level of at least relative sinlessness—and, if so, how do we define and achieve it? Other questions could easily be added.

The issue of apostasy also comes up in such discussions. If "once saved, always saved," how does committing a sin affect a professing Christian? Is it so that a born-again person can live indefinitely in the depths of sin, unrepentant? Or is it so that a person who is really saved will not return to a life of sin, even temporarily? (And if the latter, again, just how much sin may he commit?) Of if personal apostasy from a regenerate state is really possible, is a believer lost at the first sin? (And if not, how many does it take?)[2]

This chapter has as its purpose to pursue some of these issues, at least in their fundamental nature. Our primary effort, of course, should be to understand what the Bible says on the subject. And, following that, we will want to try to understand our own experience in the light of the Word of God.

What Is Sin?

I vividly recall a pastor who said, in my presence, "I have not sinned in forty years." I do not relate this in order to criticize him; I was then (and still am) very sure he was entirely sincere. Furthermore, I knew him well enough to know he was, indeed, a good and conscientious man, living above reproach. I certainly could not have found him guilty of any sin.[3]

There was also a student of mine (who would have shared the thinking of that pastor), who was very troubled by any implication that Christians sin. One day, when class discussion was skirting the edges of that issue, he asked me: "Brother Picirilli, can you go without sin for one minute?" Of course, I understood where that would lead. If I answered that I could, the next question would be something like, "Well, if one minute, how about five? And if five minutes how about fifty times five? And if that long, why not for days or weeks or years?" And, of course, there is some logic in that.

My answer came all too quickly. "Can you go one minute without breathing?" I responded. Perhaps I should be ashamed of that, I am not sure. I would not call it all that fair, though it squelched the objection for the moment. If my answer has any truth to it at all, it is simply just because one can do something for a defined period does not necessarily mean he can do so indefinitely. On the other hand, the problem is the analogy with breathing would tend to imply one cannot live without sinning! That, in turn, would mean sin is required, and something about that implication does not smell so good!

I suspect the root of the problem, here, is that the pastor who professed to have avoided sin for forty years, as well as the student who would have thought that pastor's view to be right, had a concept of sin somewhat different from mine. Regardless, the important thing is not the concept of sin any of us has but what the Bible has to say about sin. We should survey the body of the New Testament in enough depth to assure ourselves we have a biblical understanding of sin.

New Testament Words for Sin

I begin with a treatment of the most common Greek words translated *sin* (or some equivalent) in the New Testament.[4]

1. The *hamartia* word-group

The first is the common Greek verb *hamartanō*, meaning something like *miss the mark* and thus variously translated as *transgress, (commit) sin*. In the same root family are the noun *hamartia, sin*, and the substantival adjective *hamartōlos, sinner* (*sinful one*), as well as a few other less common words.

Interpreters typically seize on the meaning *miss the mark* and allow that to shape their understanding of the meaning of sin, an idea often reinforced by the illustration of a target that one aims at and misses.[5] While that has some value, the biblical notion involved is that the "mark" (if it is that) involved is the revealed will of God. Sin is "to act contrary to the will and law of God."[6] Nothing about the word's New Testament usage suggests one was aiming at such a good thing to begin with.

This is the sense of the noun *hamartia*, for example, when the Pharisees accused Jesus, "You were completely born in *sins*, and are you teaching us?" (John 9:34). They were implying "that he had not adhered rigorously to all the conventional requirements of the OT law"[7]—as that law was interpreted and implemented in the rabbinic traditions. They easily labeled anyone who violated the standards they upheld as a "sinner" and freely accused Jesus of consorting with sinners—as in Luke 19:7, referring to Zacchaeus the tax-collector: "[Jesus] has gone to be a guest with a man who is a *sinner*."

The word does not always involve something committed directly against God. In Matthew 18:15, for example, Jesus gives advice on what to do "if your brother *sins* against you" (cf. Luke 17:3). While this could imply some transgression of the law of God involved, it may simply mean a violation against morally right behavior toward others. Peter urges the Christian slave that there is no credit involved in bravely enduring a beating that resulted from his own "sinning" (1 Peter 2:20),[8] and it is not likely a slave-owner in the Greco-Roman world would beat a slave for sinning against God. Thus the New King James Version (NKJV) translates "for your faults," and the NIV "doing wrong." The idea is the slave had transgressed his master's known standards.

Furthermore, as in person-to-person relationships, to "sin" may violate the proper standards involved in one's relationship to the believing congregation: Paul urges that a "divisive person" should be rejected, "knowing that such a person is warped and *sinning*" (Titus 3:11). Indeed, one may "sin" against his own body (1 Corinthians 6:18).[9] But in all such contexts there may be an underlying consciousness that what is right reflects, after all, the law of God.

It may be that Romans 3:23 gets close to being a definition of sin in this sense: "All have sinned and are falling short of the glory of God." Whether *definition* is the inspired intention or not, it seems clear that falling short of the standard that reflects God's glory is sin; I will discuss this further below. Regardless, Romans 7:13 makes plain the connection between sin and the law of God: "Sin, that it might appear sin, was producing death in me through what is good [the law of God], so that sin through the commandment might become exceedingly sinful." We may directly compare Romans 3:20, "By the law is the knowledge of sin."[10]

Nor are human beings the only ones capable of sin as a violation of the law of God. Fallen angels sinned in this sense (2 Peter 2:4), as did the devil himself (1 John 3:8).

What seems clear, then, is that sin is by its very nature a violation or transgression of the revealed will of God, His law: "essentially … the rejection of the claim of God by self-assertive man."[11]

2. The *anomia* word-group

Even more explicitly, this group of words regards sin as against or indifferent to—or as outside the realm of submission to—law. The verb is not used in the New Testament, but very common are the noun *anomia*, *lawlessness*, *lawless deed*, and the adjective *anomos*, *lawless*.

Though usage, rather than etymology, reveals the meaning of a word (in Greek as in any language), the concept of "law" is built in to these words (made up of *nomos*, *law*, negated by the alpha-privative); and usage confirms this meaning. The law involved, however, does not necessarily have to be God's law or the Mosaic law.[12] The word applies to any behavior that is in "complete disregard for the laws or regulations of a society,"[13] thus it "simply means sin or unrighteousness."[14] Consequently, one may argue whether Peter (Acts 2:23), when he referred to the "*lawless* hands" that crucified Jesus, was thinking primarily of God's laws or more generally of people who were not law-abiding. Likewise the lawlessness that characterizes the present age (Matthew. 24:12) may be taken either narrowly or broadly, but even if the latter a basic disregard for the law of God (broadly conceived) is the underlying reason. This is even more obvious when the word is translated "transgressors" in Luke 22:37 to identify those between whom our Lord was crucified. Here the word gets close to what we mean by *outlaws*.

Regardless, when lawless behavior is sin in the sense being discussed here, it is a willful indifference to the law or rule of God (in general, not necessarily the Mosaic law). This is surely the sense of the word in Romans 6:19 when Paul contrasts one's pre-conversion *lawlessness*[15] with righteousness (though, of course, that lawlessness might have taken a broader form in indifference to the laws of society as well). Indeed, Paul—speaking very generally—represents the word ("unrighteousness" in the AV) as the opposite of righteousness (2 Corinthians 6:14). In this same sense Jesus exposed the lawlessness of the scribes and Pharisees as hypocrisy since their indifference to the law of God involved what was in their hearts and stood in contrast to their professed, public zeal for the law (Matthew 23:28). Either the noun or adjective occurs three times in 2 Thessalonians 2: in verse 3, the "man of *sin*";[16] verse 7, "the mystery of *iniquity*"; verse 8, "that *Wicked* [one]"; apparently the word is especially appropriate to describe the nature of the Antichrist.

The point of this word-group, then, is similar to that of the preceding group: sin is not keeping the law of God, a willful violation of His revealed will. Richard Trench may have been right to observe that where there is no revealed law one may be guilty of sin as *hamartia*, but not of sin as *anomia*, but even he proceeds to acknowledge that lying behind revealed law is the law written on the heart of natural man (Romans 2:14-15), so that "as this in no human heart is obliterated quite, all sin, even that of the darkest and most ignorant savage, must still in a secondary sense remain as [*anomia*]."[17]

3. The *adikia* word-group

Like the previous group, this one also is constructed to suggest the negating of something (the alpha-privative attached to the root that means *righteousness*). The verb is *adikeō*, translated variously *do wrong, act unjustly or unrighteously*, or even *injure*. The cognate noun is *adikia, unrighteousness, injustice, wrongdoing*. There is also a cognate adjective, *adikos, unjust, unrighteous*, which is less common. Gottlob Schrenk observes that, first, the New Testament use of the root rests on "the OT antithesis of righteous and ungodly," and that, second, in the New Testament it "means 'unjust' in the specific sense, especially with reference to rulers and judges."[18]

The fundamental idea in these words is of doing what is not right or righteous or just, and so of wronging someone, whether man or God.[19] It is possible that in 1 Corinthians 6:1 the meaning is weakened to that of an *unbeliever*: one not a genuine Christian and therefore "by implication possibly unjust or not in a right relation with God."[20] If so, this is apparently the only place in the New Testament where that is the idea. Everywhere else, it at least means to hurt someone (as in Luke 10:19) or treat others unfairly and so to wrong them, as in 1 Peter 2:19 when a slave is *unjustly*[21] punished.

Indeed, the verb seems most at home in the New Testament in contexts involving unjust treatment of other human beings. In 1 Corinthians 6:7-8, for example, Paul admonishes his readers to accept injustice (being wronged) in preference to doing injustice to (wronging) others by taking them to court before the "unjust" judges (v. 1, as above).[22] Even so, both the verb and the noun are used to refer to unrighteousness in general, thus to wickedness or wrongdoing. In Revelation 22:11 this is the sense: "He who is unjust, let him be unjust still." Even more broadly, there can be no *unrighteousness* with God (Romans 9:14);[23] the wrath of God has been revealed as against all *unrighteousness* of men, who suppress the truth in *unrighteousness* (Romans 1:18). Love does not rejoice in such *unrighteousness* (or *injustice*, 1 Corinthians 13:6[24]; the NKJV translates *iniquity*, as in Luke 13:27; James 3:6; and several other places).

The words in this group, therefore, depict especially unfair or unjust treatment of others: wronging them. But they also are used of any conduct that is not right: wrongdoing, wickedness in general.[25] In 1 John 5:17, then, we find that "all *adikia* is *hamartia*," which although it does not precisely equate the two terms lends itself to a fairly broad understanding of the word.[26]

4. The *parabainō* word-group

The verb *parabainō* means *transgress*. The cognate nouns are *parabasis*, referring to the act of *transgression*, and *parabatēs*, referring to the person who does so, the *transgressor*. These words do not occur often in the New Testament but are nonetheless helpful in understanding the nature of sin.

The fundamental idea involved is of deviating or turning aside from a defined way.[27] Once again, then, the concept reflects the existence of the law of God as the divinely-ordained path and someone's turning aside to a different way. The meaning is, then, "to act contrary to established custom or law, with the implication of intent — 'to disobey, to break the law, to transgress, disobedience, transgression.'"[28] Thus Friedrich Hauck defines the noun as "sin in its relation to law, i.e., to a requirement or obligation which is legally valid or has legal force."[29]

This meaning shows up clearly in Matthew 15:2-3, for example, when the Pharisees and scribes presented to Jesus the accusation that His disciples were "*transgressing* the tradition of the elders" and Jesus responded to ask why the accusers were, in fact "*transgressing* the commandment of God." Similarly, 2 John 9 refers to the person who "*transgresses* and does not abide in the doctrine of Christ."[30] Consequently, Paul—thinking about situations when "people are confronted with clearly defined, verbally transmitted laws and commands"[31]—can say forthrightly that "where there is no law, there is no *transgression*" (Romans 4:15).[32] Thus the word stands side by side with "disobedience" in Hebrews 2:2.

Whenever this word is present, then, the idea of a law which is broken is not far away; indeed, specific identification of the law is usually at hand. Thus Romans 2:25 says, "If you are *a breaker* of law,[33] your circumcision has become uncircumcision"; and James 2:11 clarifies that even if one keeps every law but one, and breaks that one, he is "a *transgressor* of the law."

This word-group, too, views sin as a departure from the way of life defined in the revealed will of God, His law: "violation of the law given or sanctioned by God."[34] The word appears to have the inherent notion that this is deliberate.

5. The *ponēria* word-group

The verb in this family is not used in the New Testament, but the noun *ponēria*, *wickedness*, *sinfulness*, and the adjective *ponēros*, *wicked, evil, bad*, are common. At the core of various translations of these words is the idea of badness, indicating that something is not what it ought to be. The adjective, for example, can indicate physical defects or infirmity, as when fruit is "bad" (Matthew 7:17-18) and so rotten or spoiled. Thus the "evil eye" in Matthew 6:23 is something that causes inadequate vision (double vision?).[35] But ethical badness is the usage that has significance for the discussion here. Moral corruption is the idea, and this is the way the words are most often used.

In this sense, either a person or a deed may be characterized as wicked, perhaps indicating especially enmity against or rejection of God.[36] The noun, for example, may appear in the plural to mean evil deeds (or instances of wickedness) in general and be listed with other specific forms of sin, as in Mark 7:22: "thefts, covetousness, *wickedness*...." ("wicked acts" would work well as a translation[37]). Compare Acts 3:26, where the NKJV translates "iniquities." In Luke 6:35 God the Father is pictured as being kind to "evil" persons, a likewise general description. The word can naturally refer to wickedness as motive, as in Matthew 22:18, "Jesus perceived their *wickedness*" and replied accordingly. The quintessential "wicked one" is, of course, Satan himself, as in 1 John 2:13-14 and often in the New Testament—probably including the clause in the Lord's Prayer, "Deliver us from the evil one" (Matthew 6:13).

It is difficult to improve on strong terms like *wicked* or *evil* (or even *bad* or *morally corrupt*) to capture the idea at the heart of this word.

6. The *kakia* word-group

Words in this group are likewise general in meaning, similar to those in the preceding group. The verb is used occasionally, though only in Luke-Acts: *kakoō, mistreat, injure*. The related noun is *kakia, wickedness, badness, malice*; and the adjective is *kakos, bad, evil, injurious*.

In the New Testament, there are times when the words in this group seem essentially synonymous with the corresponding words in the previous group. If there is a difference, it is probably to be discerned in the fact that words in this group often express wickedness more specifically in the intention to cause harm: "the quality of wickedness, with the implication of that which is harmful and damaging."[38] Those in the preceding group more generally point to the state of moral corruption out of which such intentions spring. Interesting, in this light, is the fact that the two words are used together in 1 Corinthians 5:8: "Let us keep the feast ... not with the leaven of *malice* and wickedness,"[39] where they stand in explicit contrast to "sincerity and truth." Walter Grundmann suggests the word, when used in an ethical sense, points to the destruction of fellowship.[40]

But rendering the word by "malice" may be an attempt to be too specific—unless the context makes clear this is the idea in a given place, and that is difficult to be sure about. In Acts 8:22, Peter urges Simon (the former sorcerer) to "repent of this your *wickedness*, and pray God if perhaps the thought of your heart may be forgiven you." There was apparently nothing malicious about Simon's wickedness. In 1 Peter 2:16 believers are warned against using their liberty in Christ "as a cloak for *vice*," again without suggesting malice specifically; indeed, the appeal is for manifesting a submissive spirit in dealings with others, as servants of God.[41]

Malice, then, is a specific form of sin and not so much a word for sin; it may well be that at times, the words in this group name that particular sin. But they also identify sin in general at times, as when Jesus commends the church at Ephesus that it "cannot bear those who are *evil*" (Revelation 2:2; compare Philippians 3:2). Thus the adjective is used very broadly, in the New Testament, to indicate evil or wicked thoughts (Mark 7:21), evil desire (Colossians 3:5), an evil deed (Romans 13:3), and evil associations[42] (1 Corinthians 15:33). The word often stands in contrast with the equally broad and general word for "good" (*agathos*).

In summary, while the word at times at least implies conscious malice, it also serves as a more general word for wickedness, evil, or badness—for what is *wrong*, in other words. When this is the case, pressing for a distinction between this wickedness and that of the preceding group of words is probably fruitless.

New Testament Passages that Define Sin

Perhaps it would be better if I spoke of these as passages that point to the nature of sin. They are not formal definitions. For that matter, I do not propose to treat every such passage in the New Testament, only those that are general enough in what they say, and pointed enough in saying it, that they help us understand the essence of sin as sin (and not so much to be able to name a variety of sins).

1. 1 John 3:4: "Whoever commits sin also commits lawlessness, and sin is lawlessness."

One need not quibble over whether this is meant as a formal definition of sin—it probably is not—in order to appreciate that it points directly to the nature of sin as sin. The first two words given brief analysis above are placed on either side of the predicate "is." The subject is *hamartia* and the predicate nominative is *anomia*. This obviously means, at least, that it is the nature of sin to express itself in lawlessness. Where there is one, there is also the other. As Daniel Akin observes, "This truth is universal. There are no exceptions."[43] I understand him to mean that this is descriptive of all sin.

Indeed, as we have seen above, both words imply violation of the revealed will of God, the law by which the kingdom of God is ruled. As we saw in chapter four, when the contributions of 1 John to our study were drawn out,[44] one of John's purposes is to make clear the difference between two "families," the children of God and the children of the devil (3:10). The children of the devil are characterized by sin that expresses itself in disobedience to the lawful rule of God (not necessarily the Mosaic law).[45] The children of God are different in that respect; they are not so characterized.

At the heart of sin is disobedience to God: active, knowing disobedience. This represents a rebellious attitude and at times may imply one's identification with the ultimate rebel, Satan himself. (See the treatment of 1 John 3:4 in chapter four.) But, even so, this "lawlessness" is the nature of *all* sin, not simply the more serious sins. All sin is "a willful disregard for God. ... a rebellious revolt against God's will. ... in its very nature is 'synonymous with being of the devil' (v. 8) and 'the opposite of being just' (v. 7)."[46] This is as much true of the sins of the regenerate as of the sins of unbelievers. All sin reflects, as James Montgomery Boice expresses it, "the spirit of lawlessness itself," a "definition" that "means that sin is simply the desire to have my own way."[47]

2. James 4:17: "Therefore, to him who knows to do good and does not do it, to him it is sin."[48]

In context, James appears to be dealing with what we might call a relatively minor matter: proceeding on a venture without saying "If the Lord wills."[49] Of course, things are not quite that simple. James' antagonist has apparently gone to a city to engage in business dealings without even consulting God (v. 13), and so is wrongly motivated. Furthermore, the venture itself seemingly shows no awareness of what is truly and permanently of value, ignoring the fact we have no promise of tomorrow. So the issue is not merely a matter of sprinkling one's speech with "Lord willing" but of undertaking every venture in life in pursuit of and submission to God's will: the "good one ought to do is to plan with a consciousness of God."[50]

Even so, there is no active sin involved here, at least not as we often define sin. And there is the point: not doing a good thing one knows to do is sin.

This has every appearance of being a general principle rather than the statement of one specific sin. If we said, "stealing is sin," we would readily agree; at the same time, we would know this is not a definition but a mere citing of one specific form of sin. But to say that "knowing to do good and not doing so is sin" is more than one specific instance of sin. It points to the essence or substance of sin. In multiple forms, when we fail to do what is right and good we have sinned.

To express this in a familiar way, there are sins of omission as well as sins of commission. Even so, the distinction between them is not all that absolute: each involves the other. One looks at sin from the perspective of what it is, the other from the perspective of what it is not. It is the pursuit of lawlessness; it is not the pursuit of what is good. In the specific case addressed by James, the failure to consult God or follow the kind of motivation He requires led to an ill-advised business venture governed by wrong values.

3. 1 John 5:17: "All unrighteousness is sin."

This too is broader than stating a specific sin or even a specific category of sins, and it involves the third word-group treated above, *adikia*. Sin is doing wrong, "a violation of God's standard of what is right."[51] Sin always wrongs someone, God or man—and usually both. Sin is living in indifference to the righteous rule of God that governs us in all our relationships and deeds.

4. Romans 14:23: "Whatever is not from faith is sin."

I did not have this passage in mind when I began this survey, but as I read every verse in the New Testament that makes a statement about sin, I decided I could not ignore it. It, too, has something important to say about the essence of sin.

In context, Paul has been dealing with a very specific problem: eating foods that were on some other believers' forbidden list and so risking the danger of causing others to fall into sin. Though he says much more than this (which I will not touch on here), one thing he says is we had better not do anything we cannot perform in "faith."

The issue, of course, is precisely how he is using *faith* here. Does he mean it in the usual sense, that one can act only in ways justified by full faith in God? That way, one must be able to act in confidence before God, out of a believing trust that what God has said is right. Morris apparently takes the words in this sense: "Faith is a humble reliance on God ... for salvation and for the living out of the implications of that salvation. What cannot be justified by being in accord with our relation to Christ is sin."[52]

Or does Paul use *faith*, here, in a slightly different sense, perhaps equal to inner "confidence" or "assurance"? Stott takes the view that Paul means to violate the conviction of one's conscience, which "although ... it is not infallible, it is nevertheless sacrosanct, so that to go against it (to act *not from faith*) is to sin."[53] It is true enough that this is opposite to the "doubt" Paul sets over against the "faith" here. Actually, the meaning of the word rendered "doubt' is debatable, and this is not the place to explore all the details and possibilities. It is enough to say it apparently means to "be at odds w[ith] oneself, doubt, waver."[54]

But is it necessary to make an absolute distinction between these two possible meanings of faith? I think not. The point, after all, is that a believer's assurance or inner confidence about a way of action is grounded in the Word of God, and confidence in God yields confidence in one's actions when they are in accord with that Word.

Again, then, Paul's added observation is not meant to be limited to the specific issue he is discussing. It provides an important principle that is always applicable. We may express it this way: whatever cannot be done with an inner confidence (in good conscience) that it is right, because one trusts what God has said about right and wrong and wills to obey God, is by its very nature sin. And sin always has that character.

So What Is Sin?

In light of the discussions above, then, what is sin? Now I mean to focus (though briefly) on specific matters. In the New Testament, what things have the words or statements we have examined applied to them? What sorts of things are identified as sin, wrongdoing, lawlessness, transgression, or unrighteousness? What does the New Testament identify as active or passive disobedience to God? What things cannot be done in good faith and confidence before him?

I do not mean, of course, to describe in detail the panoply of sin, the whole catalogue. Nor do I mean to enter into disputed matters, like whether the Sabbath law has an abiding principle that applies in this age of the gospel. But I am satisfied it is important to explore at least some of the *categories* of sin that ought to be part of the consciousness of all the children of God.

1. Doing What God Has Forbidden

Here I will be most brief, assuming there will be no disagreement. When we do anything God has forbidden in His revealed will, we sin.

NP AND THE PROBLEM OF SIN

Start with the Ten Commandments. I will not delve into dispensational issues here, except to say it seems clear to me the things these forbid are as forbidden now as ever. And I am satisfied the way to say this properly is this: they are not wrong because they were in the Mosaic law but were in the Mosaic law because they are part of God's permanent Moral law. Idolatry is sin, as are profanity, murder, adultery, stealing, lying, and covetousness.

The New Testament confirms, of course, that such acts are wrong. The lists of sins that appear here and there make this obvious. In Romans 1:29-31, for example, we find specific sins of disobedience named, including sexual immorality, covetousness, murder, deceit, violence, and disobedience to parents. And Paul's inspired words of condemnation for such deeds are unsparing. Galatians 5:19-21 is similar, where are named adultery, fornication, idolatry, sorcery, murders, drunkenness, and several other things, all of them standing under Paul's stern announcement that "those who practice such things will not inherit the kingdom of God" (v. 21).

There is no need to proceed along these lines; anyone who takes the Scriptures seriously will agree. (Even so, the church could use a good dose of this sort of medicine!)

2. Sins of the Heart

One does not get off so easily, however, by treating the sins mentioned in the previous section. The Bible moves quickly to make clear that outward observance of the law of God is not enough to avoid sin. Even in the Old Testament, it was already clear that one may be just as guilty of a sin if it is in the heart, though outwardly restrained. Indeed, the tenth commandment, against covetousness, speaks to what is in one's heart.

The New Testament firmly fixes this principle, building on the foundation Jesus laid in the Sermon on the Mount. His set of "You have heard it said, but I say to you" expressions has this as its very point. One may avoid the act of adultery, for example, but the person who looks with lust on another is already guilty of sin (Matthew 5:27-28). Similarly, as 1 John 3:15 says, "Whoever hates his brother is a murderer." Furthermore, John may well be implying that to withhold from a brother in need what one could supply him is one form of such "hatred" (v. 17). Rejection is at the heart of hatred.

Indeed, every sin is made such by virtue of the internal motive involved. Physical actions are evil when evil motives prompt them. (A surgeon may cut deeply into a person without being guilty of sin; one who intends murder cannot.)

Awareness of this principle makes one loathe to profess sinlessness. It may be easy to affirm that one has never committed adultery so long as that person considers only the act; but living without sin requires that one's motives and intentions, one's desires and looks, be guiltless and pure.

3. Sins of the Spirit

Another problem is that, even in the biblical lists of wrongdoing, outright transgressions of divine prohibitions (like theft, adultery, and murder) appear side by side with sins of the spirit. I intentionally did not include some of these when I cited, above, the lists in Romans 1 and Galatians 5. In Romans 1, alongside sexual immorality and murder, are such sins as envy and pride (vv. 29-30), and even being unloving, unforgiving, and unmerciful (v. 31). Galatians 5 includes jealousies and selfish ambitions.

It is not easy to be sure one is free from such sinful attitudes. Once again, we are brought face to face with the fact that sin lies in the heart. Jesus said it well in Mark 7: "From within, out of the heart of men, proceed evil thoughts, adulteries, fornications, murders, thefts, covetousness, wickedness, deceit, licentiousness, an evil eye, blasphemy, pride, foolishness. All these evil things come from within and defile a man" (vv. 21-23).

We must face up to this truth. *Pride* is a sin, at the top of the list of seven things the Lord hates (Proverbs 6:16-19). And pride takes many forms, whether an indifferent superiority (moral or otherwise!) over others or a self-sufficient independence of God.[55] *Jealousy* and *envy* are sins (in the lists just cited), nurtured in our hearts and leading to any number of evils like bitterness within or spiteful, injurious treatment of others. *Disgruntled complaining* is a sin, one that contributed heavily to the downfall of ancient Israel in the wilderness ("murmuring" in 1 Corinthians 10:10). It goes hand in hand with *discontent*, reflecting a covetous dissatisfaction with one's circumstances, warned against both in Hebrews 13:5 and 1 Timothy 6:6-10. Indeed, this last passage makes clear that *the love of money* is a root from which spring all sorts of evil. (And sometimes those who do not have money love it even more than those who do!)

The list could be lengthened greatly. Sins of the spirit are every bit as wicked as sins violating the Ten Commandments, whether pride, jealousy, bitterness, lustful desire, discontented complaining and criticism, even "sowing discord among brethren" (Proverbs 6:19), the seventh thing God hates. For that matter, some of these sins are in fact violations of the ten: lust breaks the tenth, for example (Romans 7:7).

4. Sins of Omission and Shortcoming

The more we examine specific kinds of sin the more uncomfortable we become. But we must not spare ourselves, and the truth is we sin at least as much by what we leave undone as by what we do—if there is a difference.

Negative lists like the Ten Commandments provide convenient codes for public conduct; but God's law is finally positive and at least as concerned with the inner self. Even the Old Testament recognized that what God's law requires is, "You shall love the Lord your God with all your heart, with all your soul, and with all your might" (Deuteronomy 6:5) and "You shall love your neighbor as yourself" (Leviticus 19:18). Jesus indicated that these are God's two great commandments. By implication, at least, they summarize the whole law of God (Mark 12:28-34).

What then? Any failure to love God with one's whole being is sinful disobedience. So is falling short of sincerely and wholeheartedly loving others. For that matter, the two are closely related. Back to 1 John 3:17: "Whoever has this world's goods and sees his brother in need, and shuts up his heart from him, how does the love of God abide in him?" Answer: it does not, and he is guilty of breaking both of the two primary commandments!

Consequently, any failure to do what God commands is sin; and here omission and commission join. Loving God with one's undivided being is a *command*, after all, and failure to do that is disobedience. So is failure to "Go therefore, and teach all nations, baptizing them in the name of the Father, and of the Son, and of the Holy Spirit, teaching them to observe all things that I have commanded you" (Matthew 28:19-20). All the way from the individual church member to the broadest echelons of church life, we sin in failing to evangelize those about us and abroad.

Other positive commands include "Rejoice always, pray without ceasing, in everything give thanks" (1 Thessalonians 5:16-18) and "Do not quench the Spirit" (1 Thessalonians 5:19). Such obligations rest on us as part of the revealed will of God for Christian living, and failure to obey them fully is sin.

Thus, when we fail to pray or rejoice as we ought we have sinned. When we do not worship or witness as we ought we have sinned. And since we lack any neat biblical formulas to define "ought" in all such cases, it is easy to deceive ourselves into thinking we have kept these commands. How easily we deceive ourselves! That, too, is sin.

So what does a person mean when he says, "I have not sinned in forty years"? Or in forty minutes, for that matter? As sincere as my pastor friend was, and as much respect for him as I have, I am left to think that his concept of sin is different from mine—and from that of the Bible.

So Do We Have to Sin?

Must we therefore sin? Can a regenerate person not avoid sin? Or, to put this differently, does the Bible lead us to say it is required of us that we sin? And if so, why is this so? Or can we, as my student thought, go for one minute (and so for more than one) without sin?

I think we must start with the observation that the Bible never undertakes to justify us in sin, to say sin is a "normal" part of the Christian life, or to reassure us that, after all, we are not able to avoid sin. The biblical stance is the very opposite: sin is never justified or excusable, on any grounds. By its very nature, sin is abnormal. Whenever sin is mentioned, the appeal is consistently to avoid it—with the expectation of successful obedience.

And yet, as we have just seen, the biblical standard for obedience to God is set so high that one cannot help wonder whether any human being other than Jesus has ever "kept" it for any meaningful measure of time.

How can these two stances, both apparently biblical, be reconciled? Furthermore, if it is indeed not possible for us to live without sin indefinitely (and I am neither assuming nor denying this), what *is* possible? What does the Bible teach? These questions bring us back to the fundamental problem. We are face to face with the issue of sin in the Christian life, although the survey above has given us a better idea as the kinds of things we have to deal with. Do the regenerate sin? How much? Must they?

Confronting the Issue

All of this brings us to the root issue: How can we define or describe the place of sin in the life of the regenerate? To express the problem in its most pointed terms, how can we reconcile two things that appear to have become clear from all the preceding discussion in this book? Here are the two sides that need to be brought together in some way.

1. On the one hand, we have seen that the lives of those who are born of God are not characterized by sin. This has been established on more than one basis in the New Testament. For one thing, 1 John 3 makes clear they do not sin. According to the discussion in chapter four, this does not mean perfect sinlessness. It does mean, however, that sin is not the habit and character of a child of God. John may or may not mean more than that, but he apparently means no less. A true Christian (to put it positively) is characterized by the keeping of the Lord's commandments and the avoidance of sin. Regardless how one reads 1 John, that much seems clear.

This also seems to be clear in the preceding discussion of discipleship. A disciple is one who has answered the call of Jesus to follow Him and in doing so has turned away from every other loyalty and committed himself to loving obedience of Jesus as his Lord. This is what faith means. The epistle of James is just one source in the New Testament, among others, that defines faith as expressing itself in obedience. Even without 1 John, then, we would gather from all this that a Christian—a disciple—though not sinless, is characterized by obedience and righteousness rather than by disobedience and sin.

2. On the other hand, our discussion of sin (above) has led to the implication that sin involves more than knowing violations of God's moral law. We can hardly claim, regardless how mature spiritually we are, to be free from the sins of the spirit and sins of omission. Neither the Keswick nor the Holiness teaching appears to point us to an experience of sanctification that will "take away our bent to sinning"—to use the words of Charles Wesley.[56] This appears to mean we are always less than everything we ought to be. Our natures are too much tainted with the effects of the fall for us to feel free of guilt at some level. As Galatians 5:17 indicates (discussed above), we are still in "the flesh"; that is, we have a depraved and sinful nature that is always pulling us in the wrong direction. When we are honest with ourselves, we sense we have "wand'ring hearts," that we are "prone to wander, ... prone to leave" the God we love.[57]

Is it *a sin* to be depraved, to have a sinful nature? Perhaps not, but it is, by definition, *sinful*, so that we can never say truthfully we are not sinful persons. This is our dilemma. How can we say with 1 John 3 we characteristically do right and avoid sin, on the one hand, and at the same time admit we are sinful beings and may never be without some measure of sins of the spirit and omission? If I say I am sinful and often sin in spirit or by omission—regularly "falling short of the glory of God," to borrow from Romans 3:23—have I contradicted the assertion of 1 John 3:9 that the person who has been born of God does not practice sin? How can we reconcile these two?[58]

The writers who contributed to *Five Views on Sanctification* (whom I have cited in the discussion of Keswick and Holiness teaching in the preceding chapter) appear to be aware—to some degree, at least—of the issue of avoidance of sin. McQuilkin, representing the Keswick perspective, discusses the state of the Christian who has by faith laid claim to "the victorious life." He notes that sin can be defined "as the deliberate violation of the known will of God" and the victorious Christian has "the ability not to sin in that sense."[59]

McQuilkin proceeds, however, to add that sin can "also mean any falling short of the glory of God." He pointedly asks, "Is it wrong to fall short in disposition and attitude of the glorious character of Christ? To this he responds, "If sin is defined to include this falling short unwittingly, Keswick does not teach that a person ever in this life has the ability not to sin."[60]

Subsequently, McQuilkin observes there is a valid and biblical distinction between deliberate (or presumptuous) sin and unwitting sin, a distinction clearly drawn in the Old Testament. But he readily acknowledges that both are sin and it is often difficult to distinguish the two.[61] He emphasizes that "any falling short of the glorious perfection of God Himself (e.g., Romans 3:23)" is not merely evidence of human finitude but *sin*, and "according to that definition, no one is perfect, even momentarily."[62] Even so, regenerated persons, having been freed from the legal control and tyranny of the sinful disposition, "have the ability consistently to choose the right."[63]

I was left somewhat unsure how McQuilkin applies all this to his Keswick experience, and that matters little for the present discussion. What he has made clear, however, is the issue of how one defines sin. He is confident that the word means both deliberate violations of God's will and any falling short of the perfect character of God as manifested in the person of Christ. He does not attempt to reconcile the latter with 1 John 3. His discussion of that passage sees John as claiming only that Christians do not practice deliberate sin.[64] He does not explain how John's claim that we do not practice sin is justified in light of his acknowledgement that consistently falling short of God's glory is sin.

Melvin Dieter represents the Holiness perspective in the *Five Views*. Responding to McQuilkin, he insists that "it is perfectly possible to define sin in Wesleyan terms of 'willful transgression against the known will of God.'"[65] Apparently, he is not willing to hold that "falling short" of God's glory is sin. Still, his view of entire sanctification, were it true, would mean that in at least some sense the sanctified Christian is freed from that disposition to sin that contributes so strongly to the falling short that plagues us.

Anthony Hoekema's response to McQuilkin expresses dissatisfaction with his view from yet another angle, focusing on McQuilkin's definition of sin. Unlike Dieter, Hoekema agrees with McQuilkin that both deliberate sin and failure to measure up to God's standard in Jesus Christ are sin. Then he asks, pointedly, since that failure is a *known* failure—and so a known sin—how McQuilkin can claim (for the victorious Christian) a "uniform sustained victory over known sin."[66] "Does not God require us in His law to love Him will all our hearts, souls, and minds, and to love our neighbors as ourselves (Matt. 22:37-39)? Can any one of us keep this broadest requirement perfectly? ... Is not such sin against a *known* law of God?" He continues—helpfully, I think—to ask about our *motivations*: "Do we ever do anything from perfectly pure motives? Do we perform our 'good works' *solely* out of love for God and the neighbor?"[67] Thus Hoekema argues that the Holiness doctrine has a weakened view of sin "by limiting it only to deliberate sin"; he argues also that "the Bible teaches that no one can claim to be free from sin"—citing 1 John 1:8-9, Matthew 6:12, and the struggle depicted in Galatians 5:17.[68] He approves this quotation from Herman Bavinck: "In every deliberation and deed of the believer ... the good and the evil lie, as it were, mingled through each other."[69] So far, so good, but if Hoekema makes any effort to match this with 1 John 3:6, 9, I missed it.

I have not pursued this in order to raise, again, the question of sanctification, but to demonstrate that at the root of our problem lies the definition of sin. If sin is only a conscious and deliberate violation of the revealed will of God, then we can satisfactorily understand 1 John 3:6, 9 to mean Christians do not characteristically commit such sins. In that case, when a Christian sins he does so as an exception of sorts, and he needs to repent and ask forgiveness, as in 1 John 1:8-2:2. But if sin is any falling short of matching the standard of God's perfection shown in the human nature of Jesus Christ, then it is easy to reckon ourselves guilty of sin often (if not always) and much harder to say that (as in 1 John 3:6, 9) we do not sin. To borrow from Hamlet, there's the rub!

What way may we turn to defuse this? Are there options we can consider? I mention three possible considerations.

1. Perhaps we can adopt the limited definition of sin as willful violation of the known law of God. That way, as noted, the reconciliation with 1 John 3 would be easy enough. That way, sin is worshipping an idol or committing murder or adultery and theft. But, as already noted, neither our Bible nor our consciences will allow for this narrow approach to sin. We have been told clearly that covetousness in the heart is already idolatry (Ephesians 5:5), that hatred is murder (1 John 3:15), and that lust is adultery (Matthew 5:28). Although this has been explored earlier in this chapter, I may add that several of the sins listed in Galatians 5:19-21, which disqualify a person for the kingdom of God, are sins of the spirit, including uncleanness, hatred, wrath, envy, and emulation. Hoekema (as cited above) is surely right in agreeing with Jesus: the two greatest commandments are to love God with all one's being and to love one's neighbor as oneself (Matthew 22:37-40). Then any failure to do this is a "knowing" violation of the law of God! And who of us can claim to be practicing such love as fully as God commanded? Are we not then guilty of sin at every turn?

2. Perhaps I have given in too quickly here. Is it possible the so-called sins of omission, at least, are not sins after all? As noted above, some identify our "falling short" of the glory of God as sin. Is it possible they are too sin conscious, that they are exaggerating our sinfulness? Are those who regard "falling short" as sin accusing us of not measuring up to divine *perfection*? Indeed, does God hold us accountable for failure to measure up to what He is?

Surely, that must not be the case. Even in his innocence, Adam was not God. He was in the image of God (or, perhaps more accurately, he *was* the image of God), but even before the fall he was not able to measure up to God's own perfection. We need not measure our holiness, then, by the character of God Himself, but by the standard of Adam before the fall—or, perhaps better, by the standard of the man Jesus, the Second Adam. In fact, however, this does not resolve the problem. We do not measure up, at any moment in our lives, to the innocent Adam or the human Jesus. Our "falling short" is not a falling short of divine perfection but a failure to achieve what God created us to be in perfect obedience to His revealed will, and our sinful nature—our depravity—appears to deny us the possibility of correcting that failure.

The understanding of Romans 3:23 is involved here: "For all have sinned, and come short of the glory of God" (AV). The "have" with the first verb (aorist tense in Greek), "sinned," does not go with the second verb, "come short" (present tense in Greek). Read it thus, "All have sinned and do come short (or "are coming short") of the glory of God."[70] The question concerns the second part: is it another way of stating universal sinfulness, or is it possible this coming short is not sinful? Does it mean all of us, the saved included, continue to fall short? What is "the glory of God" to which we measure up so inadequately?

I take the last question first. "The glory of God" is probably the glory God designed us to reflect when He created us in (or as) His image: "a declension from the 'image of God' in which human beings were first made."[71] Indeed, that may be the glory we see "in the face of Christ" (2 Corinthians 4:6), who is everything a human being ought to be (compare 2 Corinthians 3:18). This may well be the "likeness of Christ," toward which God is working to bring us into conformity (Romans 8:29-30). At least, when that full conformity is achieved we will no longer fall short of the glory of God (Philippians 3:21; 1 Corinthians 15:49). Regardless, the phrase looks to the future for fulfillment; this is clear from Paul's statement that we "rejoice in hope of the glory of God" (Romans 5:2).

Then the answer to the middle question, to be sure, is that even the regenerate continue to fall short of that glory. The commentators speak ambiguously about this. Moo says, "Even Christians 'fall short' of that goal until they are transformed in the last day by God";[72] but he also says this is a "statement of the condition of all people outside Christ."[73] Morris refers to the entire verse as a "clear statement of universal sinfulness," but he also (in commenting on the second clause) says, "Sinners fall short of it. ... They [apparently meaning "sinners"] continually come short of God's glory."[74] Osborne comments, "While in one sense both unbelievers and believers lack this glory, the emphasis here is entirely on the unbeliever."[75] Schreiner apparently agrees, noting that the emphasis falls on "all," and "recalls the argument of Rom. 1:18-3:20" that both Jews and Gentiles stand guilty before God; he takes the second verb to be gnomic (universally true), "indicating that all people always fall short of God's glory."[76] I am inclined to agree Paul is referring to universal sinfulness rather than to the continuing failure of those who are born again to achieve full conformity to the image of God. Even so, as several of these commentators have acknowledged, the statement must finally include even the redeemed, at least until their final glorification.

But is this shortfall *sin*? That is the key question, and on this point the commentators have very little to say—perhaps assuming the answer is obvious. Osborne appears to think so, saying the present-tense "fall short" (1) "shows the present results of the fact of sin," (2) is the reason "none are worthy of [God's] grace," and (3) indicates "they cannot meet the standard of God's righteousness."[77] In this way, he ties the two verbs together in such a way they explain each other. Mounce also links the verbs in this way: "All have sinned and in so doing have fallen short of 'God's glorious ideal.'"[78]

This points us in the right direction, I think. The two clauses are parallel, representing two ways of expressing our sin. It is for the sin represented in both verbs that we need the righteousness and justification that surround verse 23 and serve as the divine solution to the sin problem. Even if Paul intended to describe only those who are outside Christ, then, it seems clear that "falling short of the glory of God" is an expression of sinfulness. And there is little doubt we who have been born of God continue to come up short of the glory God intended that we display.

3. Or perhaps we can re-interpret 1 John 3: 6, 9 to refer only to deliberate sins of commission. Some things can be said in favor of this. For one thing, as I have noted above and in the discussion in chapter four, in context John is discussing the difference between Christians and the unsaved. He expresses that difference in terms of the *practice* of righteousness versus the *practice* of sin. Then it would be possible, with some justification, to think John is referring to behavior that is *observable* and so to active sins of commission that are visible to others: things people *do*, in other words. We can discern the difference between the children of God and the children of the devil by how they *behave*: that is, after all, John's point.

This limitation—if that is what it is—need not affect the conclusion reached in chapter four: 1 John 3:6, 9 refer to ongoing *practice*, to the habit and character of a person's life rather than to instances of conduct considered individually. All we need to do is clarify that this will be *observable* practice, since that is what is required to tell the difference between the two categories of humankind.

So how can we reconcile the affirmation of 1 John 3:6, 9—that the regenerate do not practice sin—with the understanding that all our failures to be everything God designed us to be are sin? I cannot give a final word that is completely satisfactory. But I think the solution may lie in two considerations. *First*, what I have just said is helpful: John is thinking contextually of observable, sinful behavior, and this is most obvious when it involves willful violations of the known law of God.

And yet, I do not think this is the *whole* solution since I think John did not consciously mean to distinguish between different kinds or levels of sin. I believe he also meant the regenerate do not practice sins of the heart or sins of omission— even if those are not so useful in helping us tell the difference between Christians and unbelievers.

A *second* consideration is needed, then, and it is this: we must not exaggerate the sin of "failure" to be everything God meant us to be. To put this in relatively narrow terms, our failure, say, to love God with our whole being is a multi-faceted thing. Some of that failure, at least, represents an inability that in our human-ness and fallen-ness we cannot rise above. To express this personally, so long as I am in this body I will never be able to love God with a perfectly undivided heart. Regardless how much I think I mean it when I tell Him that I love Him and want to do everything He asks, there will be some falling short, some mixture of motives, some failure to deliver which makes my commitment less than perfect.

The question is whether this is "sin." It is "sinful," I think, although that may not be finally different. It is a manifestation of both my depravity and my human inability to rise to perfection. It is a necessary result of my sinful nature, in other words. And only if some form of Holiness doctrine could offer us a truly biblical deliverance from this sinful bent could we expect to be "sanctified" from this failure. In this narrow sense, then, I do not think John would have consciously included failure to love God perfectly in his affirmation that Christians do not practice sin. There are, after all, some grounds for distinguishing between the necessary limitations that we sinful human beings cannot rise above and "deliberate" or "willful" sins.

On the one hand, we must not expect too much of ourselves. We will not be perfect until final sanctification, and any falling short of that perfection is evidence of our sinfulness. Some of this we cannot rectify, even though we must be held accountable for what we did to bring ourselves into this sorry state. On the other hand, we must not congratulate ourselves too glibly. It may well be that whenever there is some mixture of motives that makes my love for God less than perfect, that mixture involves *selfishness* in my fallen state, and selfishness is at the heart of sin. Most certainly, whenever we allow selfishness to issue in some choice that manifests failure to love God wholeheartedly, that decision—and the action that flows from it—is sin. Surely, it is the kind of sin, even if not a violation of one of the Ten Commandments that John would have included in his claim that Christians do not practice sin.

My conclusion is two-sided, involving both what is clear and what is not so clear. What is clear is that sin is broad and deep and includes much more than deliberate transgressions of God's stated moral law. It involves our failure to love God and others as He has commanded us. It involves the moral depravity we cannot rid ourselves of in this life. That means it is also clear we continue to be sinful beings, all our lives long and after we have been born again. First John 1:8 and 1:10 speak to us loudly: If we say we have no sin, we deceive ourselves. If we say we have not sinned, we make God a liar.

What is not so clear is how we reconcile our ongoing, sinful failure, to measure up to what God intended us to be, with the biblical picture of a regenerate person. The regenerate person is descibed with the following characteristics:

- One freed from the dominion of sin (Romans 6),
- A disciple who has turned away from sin and given unconditional allegiance to Jesus as Master (Luke 14:26-27),
- One who keeps the Lord's commandments (1 John 2:3-4),
- One who does not practice sin (1 John 3:6, 9), and
- One who consistently expresses faith in acts of obedience (James, Hebrews).

I have no completely satisfactory explanation. We must be content to say we can be committed disciples of Jesus, practicing obedience and avoiding sin, in spite of the continuing sinfulness rooted in our very nature that continues to pull away at us in the direction God forbids. Apparently, our continuing depravity does not contradict our continuing commitment to follow Jesus. As long as the habit and character of our lives, as manifested in our practice—our deeds, that is—is a consistent expression of "the obedience of faith," our sinful failure to be everything God designed us to be does not disqualify us.

The sinful nature continues to attempt to draw us away from Him, but as in Galatians 5:17, the Spirit within us continues to provide us the stronger counter-attraction to deny the flesh and obey the Lord. Indeed, is that not exactly what the New Testament provides for us and urges on us? "You are, now be."

ENDNOTES

[1] We who believe in the inspiration of the Scriptures are convinced, of course, that there is no real contradiction.

[2] As indicated earlier, it is not my purpose in this book to deal with the differences between Calvinism and Arminianism on this subject.

[3] I could, however, have responded (as Anthony Hoekema does, to a similar claim) by asking how he knew he had not!

[4] In each study I will identify only the main words involved in a given word-group; each group may include some additional words of less frequency in the New Testament. (While it would be interesting to expand this to include the words for sin in the Hebrew Old Testament, I am satisfied this is not necessary for my present purpose.)

[5] *Exegetical Dictionary of the New Testament*—hereafter EDNT, eds. Horst Balz and Gerhard Schneider (Grand Rapids: Eerdmans, 1990), 1.66, notes that the words originally meant a missing of the mark or failure to achieve a standard but in the Bible take on a distinctively religious dimension meaning to transgress.

[6] Louw and Nida, *Greek-English Lexicon*, I:773.

[7] Louw and Nida, I:755.

[8] The words are, literally, "...if, *sinning* and being buffeted, you endure?"

[9] Hays, *First Corinthians*, 106, thinks of this, appropriately, as doing "damage" to one's body as the temple of the holy God. Fee, *The First Epistle to the Corinthians*, 262, also appropriately, refers to 6:13: "the body is for the Lord."

[10] One may also compare Romans 5:13, which (regardless what else it may be saying) apparently affirms that "sin" is not calculated as "sin"—in the sense of transgression of law—except when there is a revealed law for it to violate. The passage is difficult. See Morris, *The Epistle to the Romans*, 232-33; John Stott, *Romans: God's Good News for the World* (Downer's Grove, InterVarsity, 1994), 149-154, who speaks of the law's role as "defining and identifying sin"; Moo, *The Wycliffe Exegetical Commentary*, 341-45, who regards the law's function as to highlight, if not stimulate, disobedience as rebellion. But varying interpretations do not affect the point here: a basic function of revealed law is to make sin known in its full particulars and seriousness.

[11] Walter Grundmann, TDNT, I:316.

[12] Therefore EDNT 1.106 defines an *anomos* person as "*one for whom there is no such thing as a—or the—law.*"

[13] Louw and Nida, I:758.

[14] TDNT IV:1086.

[15] AV, "iniquity"; some versions, appropriately enough, "moral anarchy." Morris, 265, quotes Godet's definition: "contempt of the standard of right written in the law on every man's conscience."

[16] Some manuscripts have *anomia*, some *hamartia*, prompting TDNT IV:1086 to say that the first "has no meaning other than" the second.

[17] Richard Chenevix Trench, *Synonyms of the New Testament* (Grand Rapids: Eerdmans, 1958), 244.

[18] TDNT I:151.

[19] EDNT 1:31 notes that when used intransitively the root "denotes a specific incongruity with divine or human law."

[20] Louw and Nida, I:124. Fee, 232, adopts this meaning. Anthony C. Thiselton, *The First Epistle to the Corinthians: A Commentary on the Greek Text* (NIGTC; Grand Rapids: Eerdmans, 2000), 418, 424, renders "a court where there is questionable justice." Hays, 94, thinks it a given that the judges at Corinth would be "biased in favor of the wealthy" and so by definition unjust.

21 The adverb *adikōs* is used here.

22 Thiselton, 437, thinks the verb, here, "conveys a double nuance of *you injure* and *you deprive others of rights.*"

23 Morris, 358, observes, "It is simply not possible for … God to act unjustly"; he cites Genesis 18:25: "Will not the Judge of all the earth do right?"

24 Perhaps "rejoices in the truth" should be taken as the opposite; see Fee, 639. Thiselton, 1054-55, offers a more extensive discussion of "taking pleasure in wrongdoing" that may include such attitudes as malicious joy, gloating, censoriousness, or a sense of superiority.

25 Moo, *Wycliffe Commentary*, 97 (on Romans 1:18) discusses and rejects—rightly, I think—the hard and fast limitation of *adikia* to the wronging of others, expressing hesitant approval of Cranfield's view that it is "a violation of God's just order."

26 See the discussion of this verse in chapter four.

27 Again, the etymology is in harmony with this meaning. The words are derived from *bainō, go,* and *para, aside.*

28 Louw and Nida, I:469.

29 TDNT V:739.

30 Instead of *parabainōn*, here, the critical text has *proagō*, "goes ahead," which is similar in meaning in suggesting one who goes beyond the limits set by a specific command.

31 Morris, 207, regards this as "the right word for overstepping a line"; Stott, 131, thinks of it as "a deliberate trespass."

32 Moo, *Wycliffe Commentary*, 282: "The law turns 'sins' into 'transgressions,' and creates, accordingly, even more judgment."

33 Morris, 140, n. 150, quotes J. Schneider (TDNT V:741) who defines this as referring "to someone who 'transgresses a specific divine commandment.'"

34 EDNT 3:14.

35 But it is possible, with some interpreters, to regard the "bad eye" here (cf. Luke 11:34) as metaphorical for a moral blemish and so a wicked or covetous or avaricious eye; see Günther Harder, TDNT VI:556.

36 See the discussion in TDNT VI:554-62. The article in EDNT 3:134-35 may be correct in connecting an element of *depravity* to the meaning of the word.

37 Walter Bauer, *A Greek-English Lexicon of the New Testament and Other Early Christian Literature*, as translated and adapted by William F. Arndt and F. Wilbur Gingrich (Chicago: University of Chicago Press, 1959; hereafter *BAG*), 697, suggests "malicious acts"—which may or may not be too specific.

38 Louw and Nida, I:754.

39 Thiselton, 406, notes that some interpreters attempt to make a distinction between the two words, with the second being the evil that results from the disposition, but he is probably right to observe that the two terms "are used as synonyms on occasion, and any difference of this kind is vague and certainly not uniform." Fee, 219, regards them as synonyms "which gather under their umbrella every form of iniquity."

40 TDNT III:484.

41 Likewise in Matthew 6:34, "Sufficient unto the day is the *evil* thereof," where the word may mean little more than "trouble" (TDNT III:483).

[42] In context, the "bad associations" may be with people or speeches that deny the resurrection; see Fee, 773. The translation of Thiselton, 1254, "belonging to bad gangs," seems exaggerated.

[43] Daniel L. Akin, *The New American Commentary: 1, 2, 3 John* (Nashville: Broadman & Holman, 2001), 139.

[44] In chapter four, I discussed the view of Colin Kruse and Robert Yarbrough that 1 John 3:4 serves to limit John's discussion to that category of sin that can be called *anomia*. See there for references and my reasons for rejecting that view.

[45] I. Howard Marshall, *The Epistles of John* (NICNT; Grand Rapids: Eerdmans, 1978), 176-77, follows those who suggest that *anomia*, here, stresses more "the idea of opposition to God" than lawlessness, specifically, but acknowledges this idea "is inherent in disregarding his law." He apparently regards this as characterizing *all* sin.

[46] Akin, 141.

[47] James Montgomery Boice, *The Epistles of John: An Expositional Commentary* (Grand Rapids: Baker, 1979), 85.

[48] Interpreters debate possible sources of this saying. That need not occupy us here.

[49] Martin Dibelius, *James*, tr. Michael A. Williams (Hermeneia; Philadelphia: Fortress, 1975), 231, 235, calls this "a general precept concerning sins of omission." He errs, I think, in suggesting the saying is unrelated to the context which speaks of sins of commission rather than omission. Ben Witherington III, *Letters and Homilies for Jewish Christians,* who judges this "may be an isolated proverb or maxim," is more on target to say, "James may be alluding to the failure to pray and place one's plans into God's hands."

[50] Peter H. Davids, *The Epistle of James* (NIGTC; Grand Rapids: Eerdmans, 1982), 174.

[51] Akin, 211; he links 3:4 with 5:17 in such a way as to suggest both are descriptive of the nature of sin as sin.

[52] Morris, 492.

[53] Stott, 368.

[54] *BAG*, 184.

[55] The case of Uzziah, described in 2 Chronicles 26, is very instructive in this regard.

[56] In the hymn, "Love Divine, All Loves Excelling."

[57] From "Come, Thou Fount of Ev'ry Blessing," by Robert Robinson.

[58] If Paul, in Romans 7:19, is expressing himself *as a regenerate person*, does he contradict John in saying he "practices" (*prassō*) the wicked thing he does not will to do? The question is worth pursuing (even though the obvious answer is that he does not), but it depends on the thorny problem of that passage.

[59] McQuilkin, 156. I would disagree only in that I would say this is true of all Christians, not just those who have experienced the Keswick "blessing."

[60] McQuilkin, 156-57.

[61] For the best resource I have read on the subject of unwitting sin (or "sins of ignorance") versus willful (or "presumptuous") sins, see F. Leroy Forlines, *The Quest for Truth: Answering Life's Inescapable Questions* (Nashville: Randall House, 2001), 467-488. I had thought to explore this matter in this chapter but decided it would take me farther afield than would be helpful.

[62] McQuilkin, 172-73.

[63] McQuilkin, 174.

[64] McQuilkin, 172.

[65] Dieter, 186.

[66] Hoekema, 188.

[67] Hoekema, 188 (italics original).

[68] Hoekema, 83-84.

[69] Hoekema, 188.

[70] It is possible to read the aorist in other ways: (1) as a reference to Adam's sin in which everyone participated; (2) as timeless (gnomic), meaning "all sin." This need not be pursued here; my main interest in this discussion is in the second (present tense) clause.

[71] Moo, *The Epistle to the Romans*, 226. Osborne, *Romans*, 95, cites the apocryphal *Assumption of Moses*, 21:6, where Adam says to Eve, "You have deprived me of the glory of God." Forlines, *The Randall House Bible Commentary: Romans* (Nashville: Randall House, 1987), 83, lists five understandings of the phrase and opts for the meaning "the approbation/approval of God." Schreiner, *Romans*, 187, leans to the view that all fall short of giving God glory.

[72] Moo, *The Epistle to the Romans*, 227.

[73] Moo, *The Epistle to the Romans*, 226.

[74] Morris, *The Epistle to the Romans*, 177.

[75] Osborne, 95.

[76] Schreiner, *Romans*, 186-87.

[77] Osborne, 94.

[78] Mounce, *The New American Commentary: Romans*, 115. His unexplained rendering ("have fallen short") of the second verb strikes me as questionable, but this does not affect the point I am making.

Chapter Nine

DRAWING IT ALL TOGETHER

What remains is to synthesize the findings of the several chapters and then to draw out the most important implications for the way we function in the presentation and administration of the gospel.

The Contributions of the Preceding Chapters

The Contribution of Chapter One and Pauline Soteriology

The transaction model of salvation elucidated by Paul provides the most central and most basic understanding of what one must do to be saved. Salvation is an entirely gracious work of God, performed for those who exercise faith in Jesus Christ. It is not by works. It is, instead, the holding out of *empty* hands to receive what God has offered in Christ, by His own sovereign willing to save those who believe. The very fact that Jesus has paid the price of our redemption rules out any possibility that the expression of our faith—the obedience of faith—can be offered to Him as a "work." In the "salvation history" that moves from the Mosaic system to the age of the gospel, we learn the law was never intended to offer a way to salvation. Instead its role was as a "pedagogue" to lead us to Christ for justification by faith (Galatians 3:24), thus serving the purposes of faith.

This means we never do anything to offer merit to God. We never deserve saving grace, never receive it as a reward for what we have done. Otherwise, we would lay claim to some part of the glory or credit for our salvation. To God alone is all the glory. Salvation is from beginning to end, from initiation to conclusion, God's work.

Faith is therefore nothing more than a condition to be met, established by the Giver, in order to receive a free gift. Salvation, from the human perspective, is by faith. Even so, it is a condition God has sovereignly laid down. As 1 Corinthians 1:21 indicates, it is the eternal pleasure and counsel of God to save those who believe.

Whatever else we may glean from this study must not contradict this. Indeed, nothing we draw correctly from the Scriptures will do so.

The Contribution of Chapter Two and Jesus' Call to Discipleship

When Jesus was asked about the way to receive eternal life, He answered in terms of repentance and discipleship. His call to discipleship required the hearer to *leave* whatever a person was obligated to or served. In doing that, a person breaks away from the claims of anything or anyone else to require his obedience. As a result, the person "enrolls in the school of Jesus" and commits to *learn from* and *follow the lead of* a new master.

The Great Commission (Matthew 28:19-20) puts this in these terms: one becomes a disciple of Jesus by submitting to baptism in His name and committing oneself to learn and obey what He has taught.

What this means is that faith expresses itself in a repentant commitment to the Lordship of Jesus as the one who gives directions for the conduct of his life. Does this contradict the truth of salvation by grace through faith? No, but it provides a fuller understanding of the nature of the faith that saves. One who believes in Jesus commits himself to a life of loving, trusting obedience of Him. Unless this is fundamentally true in the experience of a person, faith is not present.

The Contribution of Chapter Three and Jesus' Teaching in John

The Gospel of John makes clear that both Jesus and the disciple-author understood that eternal life is obtained by faith. The verb *believe* is at the heart of the record, and everywhere one is reckoned to be a follower of Jesus by this measure.

Even so, John's Gospel makes very clear that not all "belief" qualifies one for salvation. We sometimes meet, there, a shallow and merely intellectual belief that does not result in discipleship. This Gospel signals to us that the faith that saves is a full-orbed faith that expresses itself in committed discipleship.

The Contribution of Chapter Four and the Teaching of First John

Like his Gospel, John's First Epistle also makes clear that salvation is by faith. At the same time, however, John insists that faith expresses itself in practical ways.

To put this positively, faith expresses itself in obedience to the commands of Jesus. Anyone who claims to be a committed follower of Christ but does not keep Christ's word is exposed as a liar. To put it negatively, faith expresses itself in the avoidance of sin, given that sin is an expression of a refusal to submit to the lordly rule of God. Anyone who claims to be a committed follower of Christ but whose life is characterized by sinful conduct is likewise exposed as a liar—as is anyone who does not practice love for a fellow believer or hold to apostolic doctrine about Jesus Christ. A sinful lifestyle is incompatible with saving faith.

The Contribution of Chapter Five and a Re-examination of Paul

As one would expect from the preceding, even Paul is well aware that Christian faith issues in doing what is right in the sight of God. Indeed, in Romans 2, in his most theologically developed epistle, he clearly echoes a teaching that runs throughout the Bible: a person who does righteousness will stand before God justified. And in Romans 6-8 he describes the person saved by faith as one who has been set free from the dominion of sin to the service of righteousness.

Paul understood that a faith without works is hollow and ineffective. God's purpose in salvation by grace is to bring the believer to the practice of righteousness, and faith expresses itself in breaking loose from the dominion of sin and living under the dominion of Christ.

The Contribution of Chapter Six and the Linking of Obedience to Faith by James and Hebrews

If any of the preceding seems to be contradictory, James helps us see more clearly the solution the other chapters have pointed to. The faith that saves is inevitably visible in the obedience of those who have it. If one wishes to "see" the faith of Abraham or of Rahab, for example, one looks at their obedience to what God said.

Hebrews likewise touts this linking, showing that disobedience is, at root, unbelief and consequently obedience is, at root, the exercise of faith. By faith, those who submit to God act. Faith expresses itself—and in that sense *exists*—in obedience. Indeed, even Romans, with all its emphasis on salvation by faith, focuses on the act of faith as an act of obedience, likewise implying the larger truth that obedience involves both receiving the gospel and living under the authority of the Savior.

Faith is expressed in obedience and obedience is the exercise of faith. This is the reconciliation of the two models of what one must do to be saved: salvation is by faith alone, but this faith expresses itself in obedience.

The Contribution of Chapter Seven and a Study of Sanctification

The path of discipleship does not offer us a crisis experience by means of which we can escape the problem of sin. All attempts to provide that have failed. Holiness, therefore, is not obtained by a Keswick or Holiness "second blessing." The regenerate person will continue, from new birth to physical death, to labor against the tug of the flesh and the accompanying possibility of sin. Even so, the child of God walks in accord with the Spirit.

The Contribution of Chapter Eight and a Study of Sin

Indeed, sin must be understood to be always "at the door," and an important part of this is to recognize that sin is not only the conscious violation of some prohibition of God. Sin includes undisciplined desires and feelings—sins of the spirit, in other words. Sin includes the failure to do good whenever we have awareness and opportunity for it—sins of omission, in other words. Sin includes all the ways we fail to love God with our whole being and to love our neighbors as ourselves. We are always falling short of the glory of God, which must include the glory He originally designed us for before the fall.

Over against this, two things must be recognized, both of which bring us back to First John. One is that there is provision for our forgiveness when we sin—by the propitiation accomplished by Jesus Christ and conditioned on our repentant confession. This reminder plainly instructs us not to think of ourselves as entirely above the possibility of sin. At the same time, neither does this provision make room among professing Christians for lives characterized by sin.

Once again, we are led to the conclusion that saving faith expresses itself not so much in sinless perfection as in a characteristic avoidance of sin. The disciple of Jesus—the regenerate person—is one who experiences a characteristic victory over sin, and when he stumbles he repents and claims forgiveness on the basis of the blood of Jesus. This is holiness, and all those who are born again practice holiness (Hebrews 12:14).

The danger in all of this, of course, is that there is only a thin line between this understanding and a heretical view of "the obedience of faith." Being the self-centered people we are, it is all too easy to confuse the gospel at this point. We must therefore remain on guard lest we begin to regard our obedience as in some way earning God's approval and therefore serving as grounds for His granting us eternal life. Then we become self-congratulatory and see our works as something they are not.

The obedience that expresses biblical faith is nothing more than a trusting and loving response to God's free grace granted us in Jesus Christ and to what He has said. Jesus alone has earned the reward of salvation, to Him alone is all the glory. The Protestant insistence that our deliverance from sin is by Christ alone, by grace alone, and by faith alone remains secure.

Implications for How We Present and Administer the Gospel

The thesis of this book can, of course, be regarded as commonplace, as something we already understood. No doubt, in some measure, we did. It can also be understood as something new and radical, something that requires serious adjustment in how we function. There is something of that, too, in this.

At the very least, the thesis demands we rethink how we do things in order to be sure we get the gospel right.

Implications for How We Present the Gospel to the Unsaved

Not long ago I visited in the hospital with a man who was dying, the father of a younger man I had been dealing with (whom I will mention again below). He seemed very interested when I mentioned being prepared to stand before God, and this gave me the opportunity to remind him (he was raised in church) of basic gospel truths. I used the famous Romans Road and a few other Scriptures. He was responsive and "prayed" to accept Christ. The next week, I called his sister with whom he was staying and asked when I might come and visit with him. I was taken aback by her reaction. She had heard about my visit and wanted me to know that she did not think that some simple "sinner's prayer" (her words) was sufficient, and if that was all I had to offer she would just as soon I stay away. I did not know enough about her church to evaluate her meaning, but when I assured her I thought becoming a Christian meant more than a mere "God be merciful to me, a sinner," and I wanted to instruct her brother more, her attitude changed. Before he died, I had three more opportunities to visit him in her home—she listened carefully, by the way—and share much more of the New Testament with him. At each step along the way, I felt he understood what it meant to receive Christ as his Lord and Savior, and that he did so. I certainly hope so; he died within a month.

Our churches (if they are instrumental in bringing people to Christ at all!) can bear full witness to a succession of people who "accept Christ," are baptized, and join the church—and soon return to the sort of lives they led before, lives of indifference if not outright wickedness. The tragedy is that many of them at least halfway believe they are saved, and we helped them to that conclusion!

Anyone who ever goes out on church outreach visitation knows what to expect. In many homes of the unchurched in an American community—surely, at least half in the South—one encounters a husband or wife, or both, who profess to be Christians but who almost never go to church. And if one took the time to dig more deeply into their lives, it would become clear that many of them pursue a sinful lifestyle in one way or another. For that matter, even our more-or-less regular Sunday attenders-at-church include a significant number of people who are addicted to one or more sinful, fleshly practices. Any discussion with them leaves the clear impression that they think little about their wrongdoing and see themselves as Christians.

Something is wrong with this picture, and we are complicit in it, in the way we present the gospel.

I realize I must tread softly here. The last thing in the world I would want would be to compromise the pure gospel of salvation by grace through faith in Christ and His meritorious, redemptive work. But if the New Testament survey presented in this book is correct in any significant measure, we need to realize that the biblical gospel does not confront people in the terms we sometimes call "easy believism." When people asked Jesus "What must I do to inherit eternal life?" He did not say, "Just believe Jesus died to save you and you will be OK." And even if He had responded in such a fashion, it is clear what He would have meant by *believe*.

That is the key, I think: we must make sure, when we present the gospel, that our hearers understand what the faith on which eternal life is conditioned really is. We must make sure they hear the call to discipleship.

Another way of saying this is that we must cease separating *repentance* from faith. Jesus did not do this, and neither should we.

I am not necessarily suggesting radical changes in how we deal with sincere seekers. The Romans Road remains eminently usable. So does Acts 16:30 or Ephesians 2:8-9. I sometimes present the gospel using Ephesians 2:1-10; I used it with the man whom I described above. But when I got to verse 10, I made sure he understood his commitment to Christ was at its very heart a commitment to the "good works" God has "ordained"—pre-defined—for His children to practice.

In short, we need to make sure we present faith as obedience to the call of Christ to repent and put one's full trust in Him. When we stop to think, this makes perfect sense. Faith is, after all, a personal trust and not a merely intellectual belief. Most practitioners of evangelism will agree to that much.

The nature of faith, in any set of circumstances, is determined by the nature of the one whom we are called to trust. If my physician, prior to surgery, says, "Just trust me," that means I submit to surgery. Faith in that case is accepting his scalpel. If he says a certain medicine will cure a disease, my trust in him will take the form of getting the prescription filled and following the directions. If a friend who owes me money says I will have to trust him for it, the extent (and limitation) of my faith is obvious.

Nothing short of such responses as these is faith. So if my *God* says I must trust Him as my *God*—given what it means to have a *God*—my trust by definition entails obedience. I may trust my father or my boss or a friend, and disobey them, but one does not deliberately disobey a *God* he trusts.

Nor will it work with the Savior. The Lord Jesus addresses us and says, "Deny the claims of everyone else you love, deny your own claims on yourself, leave all of that and come, take up the instrument of your death and follow Me, learn from Me, obey the things I teach you, commit to Me, take My yoke on you, turn from your sins, trust Me, I will lead you home." Then nothing short of doing that will express faith.

Discipleship is the word, then. I have resolved that I will not again present the gospel to a sincere seeker (or an insincere one, for that matter) without making sure the person hears the call of Christ to discipleship.

I do not expect shortcuts to genuine conversion. Even now, I tend to think many people who come to know Christ in reality do so in more than one step. To be sure, there is some point when a person steps out of the kingdom of darkness into the light of the saving knowledge of Christ. I still believe in instantaneous conversion. I just do not think I always know exactly when that conversion occurs in the experiences of the people I observe or minister to. It may well be that some who make a profession of faith do not really understand the gospel call, and as they learn more in church and Sunday school and Christian circles they come to *real* faith. Perhaps we can do no better than to present the call to individuals to "receive Christ as Savior," knowing full well that often as they hear more they will come to a better understanding of who Jesus is and the nature of His call, and so to a more meaningful and genuine commitment. If so, however, we must be aware that "receiving Christ" is little more than a first step.

Either way, I am convinced that both in personal work and in our preaching we need to present the gospel call to a faith that expresses itself in repentance and in the obedience that demonstrates true discipleship. Indeed, our preaching is the most important presentation of the gospel we make, and it must make clear what Jesus calls us to and what it means to respond to that call in repentance and faith. Furthermore, the practice of the pastor in all his teaching relationships, whether corporately or individually, must be to model and express discipleship as the only genuine form of Christianity—the *full* gospel, in other words.

Implications for How We Administer Assurance of Salvation

This is, of course, closely related to the preceding point and builds on the same situation within (and without) the church and on the same conclusions. We need not deceive ourselves: we do in fact administer assurance of salvation. In doing so, I fear we hand out "assurance of salvation" much too easily—and will be all the more accountable for it.

To begin with, we tally up the people we have "won to Christ" far too quickly and shallowly. Long ago, I quit "cutting notches in my gospel gun." I do not count a person as converted to Christ until that person has shown some continuing evidence. Not long ago I spent many hours over a period of several months dealing with a young man in college—the same young man whose dying father I mentioned above. As our conversations progressed, it came naturally to present the gospel and pray with him. I succeeded in leading him in the right prayer, the one we are all taught to use. But I held off from counting him as a convert. I could tell he did not understand very well; he had absolutely no church background. I told my pastor I was not confident. I succeeded in getting him to come and talk to the pastor, and at the end of a service, he walked the aisle. The pastor asked me to deal with him in the prayer room, and again he acknowledged himself a sinner and asked Jesus to save him. The next week he went away to college. I continued to write, email, and call him. For all my efforts, he would not go to a church near his dorm, even though I had a pastor there get in touch. And when he returned home, I continued to pursue him, but never got him back in church. He has told me flatly he is not a Christian. I was not surprised; I never considered him one.

Sometime after that I "led to the Lord" (as the expression goes) the husband of my wife's hairdresser, a man whose doctors had not given him long to live. I gave him the gospel as well as I could, and he seemed eager and ready. I did not have to lead him in the sinner's prayer. His voluntary prayer seemed so genuine and well expressed I was moved while he prayed. Subsequently, in a hospice residence, he asked his family to leave the room so he could talk with me some more. He died the next week, never having been to a church and not having been baptized. He never had opportunity to give much evidence of discipleship, other than a sort of "witness" to his family. So, in fact, I'm not sure. I felt more confidence in his conversion than that of the young man mentioned above, but I can only hope I gave him enough gospel that he repented of his sins, renounced every other claim on his life, and followed Jesus. Whether we "count" people has very little, if anything, to do with whether they really come to know Christ.

It may be providential that, at the very time I was beginning work on this chapter, I encountered Mark Dever, who gave me a copy of a little book I have found interesting and insightful.[1] Here are some of his observations:

> When we assume the Gospel instead of clarifying it, people who profess Christianity but don't understand or obey the Gospel are cordially allowed to presume their own conversion without examining themselves for evidence of it—which may amount to nothing more than a blissful damnation. ... Believing the true Gospel, and responding to it in repentance and belief, is the only way to be saved. ... Nominalism (being a Christian in name only) has spread in our churches like gangrene, and misunderstandings about the Gospel abound among professing evangelicals.[2]

> Praying a prayer is never offered in Scripture as a ground of assurance, nor is sincerity. Jesus tells us ... to look ... at our actions—the fruit of our lives (Matt. 7:15-27; John 15:8; 2 Pet. 1:5-12). The New Testament tells us to look at the holiness of our conduct, the love we have for others, and the soundness of our doctrine as the key indicators of our assurance (1 Thess. 3:12-13; 1 John 4:8; Gal. 1:6-9; 5:22-25; 1 Tim. 6:3-5). What this means

is that we shouldn't encourage people to feel assured in their salvation based simply on a prayer prayed, with no observable fruit of repentance in their lives. ... The only external evidence that the Bible tells us to use in discerning whether or not a person is converted is the fruit of obedience.[3]

We want [people] to become Christians because they know they need to repent of their sins, believe in Jesus Christ, and joyfully take up their cross and follow Him for the glory of God.[4]

This sounds to me like the New Testament!

There are inferences, here, for people we commonly call backsliders. We have made such a big deal out of the form of "accepting Christ as one's Savior" until we feel bound to think everyone who goes through that formula is saved. This leads to various abuses. Once upon a time, I was serving as evangelist for a union meeting in a small town. Early in the week, a young man raised his hand for prayer and I spoke to him briefly after the service, urging him, unsuccessfully, to receive Christ. The next day I was having lunch with the sponsoring pastors, one of whom had noticed the exchange. He proceeded to tell me the young man was one of his members but was seriously backslidden, living in an adulterous relationship, drinking, and so on. On the last night of the meetings, the young man stopped to shake hands with me again, and again I urged him to make a commitment to Christ. He said he was ready to do so, and I beckoned his pastor over to pray with him. The pastor's first words, calling him by name, were, "Now you don't doubt your salvation, do you?"

This is a travesty of the gospel! He had better doubt his salvation! His life would not have fit either the requirements of Jesus or the description of a regenerate person in 1 John. Why should anyone think, just because he had gone through the motions of saying the sinner's prayer, being baptized, and joining the church, that he was a disciple of Jesus? The evidence was otherwise.

This is the problem we encounter when some who are overly enthusiastic for "salvation by grace" insist that so long as a backslider has not openly and deliberately renounced Christ, he is saved. There are many things wrong with that. One is that we cannot be sure the person was ever saved to start with, and assumptions to that effect are dangerous. The other is that we may well be contradicting the very teaching of the New Testament about what it means to be a child of God. Those who are born again do not live in sin, says John. Christians have been set free from the service of sin and become servants of righteousness, says Paul. People who are overcome by sin are servants of sin, said both Jesus and Paul.

One of the implications of this arises when people construct their own version of human experience in order to establish litmus tests of others' theology. They always know someone who was "genuinely saved" but later returned to a life of drunkenness and died in an accident. The problem with this is we make too many assumptions. It may be that the person's subsequent failures indicate that he or she was never saved; in many such instances, that seems the most likely explanation. Or it may be the person has forsaken the Lord. But what we cannot do is give assurance of salvation—even in home-made constructions like this—to people whose lives do not match the Bible's description of the regenerate. Whatever we believe about security, we simply cannot afford to speak of people who are living in sin as Christians. To do so is to mismanage assurance of salvation.

On one occasion, a fellow-minister tried to pin me down along these lines. He recited the story of a serious backslider and wanted to know whether I thought that person, if he died, would go to heaven. I said to him, "Now let me be sure I understand what you're asking. Is this person you're talking about a Christian or not?" Without hesitation he said, "Oh, for sure, he's not a Christian." "Well, then," I said, "obviously if he's not a Christian and if he dies, he won't go to heaven." "Good," he said, "I thought you believed like I do." I really was not trying to trick him; it simply will not do to give assurance of salvation to people whose lives give the lie to their claim to be Christians, and even our discussions about backsliders need to be careful about that.

Ministers of the gospel who give assurance of salvation to people who are living in sin are guilty of spiritual malpractice. I am not saying we can always or easily know for sure whether any given person is truly saved, even when we think we know them well. But for us to separate assurance of eternal life from the truly obedient lifestyle of a disciple is seriously unbiblical.

Implications for the Life of the Church

This is but a short step from the preceding. There are, it seems to me, two major things to be said here. The first is we need to rethink the nature and life of the church—the local church, I mean. A church ought to be a community of faith, a fellowship of *disciples* committed to Christ and to one another. Membership in the church ought to mean membership, as well as can be determined, in the body of Christ, the church He bought with His blood. People who interpret the parable of the wheat and tares to excuse the membership of the unsaved in their churches are wrongly applying Jesus' words, and seriously so, to the detriment of the church and her witness to the world.

I do not mean to suggest a church can be perfect, or that all its members can be. But we are far too much on the other end of reality. Churches should be made up of people devoted to living out the implications of discipleship *in a covenant relationship*, and to helping each other do that in confidence of the active work of God in their lives. The meaning of church includes being in the faith together and mutual submission to one another's needs, not to mention submission to the leadership of those chosen under God for that responsibility.

What we need, along these lines—and what we often lack!—is regular teaching within the church about the importance and implications of membership. As part of this, we need to re-emphasize the importance of a "church covenant." As I see it, every church should have a written covenant that is visited regularly; but, even if one is not written, the church's pastor and other teachers should give frequent and pointed attention to what it means to be a member of the church as part of a covenant relationship. Every member of the church ought to hear frequently, and be fully conscious, that being a member of the church carries with it the implication that one is a true disciple of Jesus. It means the members will hold each other accountable for living as disciples. It means the members will actively work with each other in the pursuit of "the obedience of faith." Furthermore, it implies the church will take deliberate and well-defined steps to deal with members that stray from the ways of the Lord.

The second consideration, consequently, grows immediately out of this: the church needs to reinvent discipline. While that is too big a subject to be developed here, some basic implications are more or less obvious. One is that "discipline" does not begin when a member falls into sin. Effective discipline, in any context, is always both positive and negative, and in this matter it includes all the positive forces brought to bear on guiding the spiritual development of Christians.

Another is that when a member violates the obligations of the covenant relationship, discipline requires first that every deliberate effort be made to "restore" him or her to that relationship (Galatians 6:1). The first awareness a member is practicing wrongdoing should trigger a concerted (and previously defined) program to rescue that member.

Only after that has failed does the final factor come into play, and when it does the *congregation* should take the necessary action to expel the sinning member (1 Corinthians 5).[5] A church will be far more likely to take such action without serious tension if all the implications of church membership have been taught and understood before the case arises.

For a biblical example of this, 1 Corinthians 5 cannot be improved on. All the elements are there, as long as the text is properly understood. The incestuous member's conduct is such that he cannot be regarded as a Christian. By implication, at least, he has been entreated to repent and has refused to do so. The congregation's voice must be to put him out of the church's recognition that he is a regenerate person, which continued membership implies. This is necessary for the purity of the church, and the hope is he will yet, ultimately, be saved. Meanwhile, it may be the Lord will permit Satan to inflict yet another kind of discipline—although Satan's goal will obviously be entirely different from the Lord's goal.

This kind of action has at least two purposes, neither of which should be overlooked. One is to preserve the purity of the church. The other is to make sure the sinning member, along with everyone else, knows his or her conduct is such that he or she cannot be seriously regarded as a follower of Christ. This is done, then, with the hope the offender will recognize the implications of his behavior and come to repentance.

Not all situations that need church discipline are this serious, of course. In 2 Thessalonians 3:6-15 we learn of a very different case. The offending members are "free-loaders" and are creating disorder within the church, disrupting its fellowship and peace. In this case, the inspired advice is *not* to count the one who continues to disobey as an *enemy* of Christ but to admonish him "as a brother" and to break "company" with him. While I cannot pursue this in detail, here, the example serves to give us guidance about discipline when a member's conduct is not so serious as to deserve the judgment that the offender cannot any longer be regarded as a genuine Christian. In this case, the *peace* of the church is at stake and discipline seeks to bring about the adjustment of conduct needed to restore that.

I have mentioned, above, the need for renewed attention to the relationship that exists among members of a local church and to the *covenant* that expresses their commitment to each other. I repeat, then, that this, together with the Scriptures, ought to be the basis for discipline.

One warning may be in order: it would be easy to move from a healthy approach to church membership and discipline to an unhealthy and cultic level of interference in the lives of fellow-believers. Some Christian leaders have approached the danger of substituting their authority and opinions for the authority and will of Christ and have structured and governed their churches in a manner that borders on mind control. We walk a fine line between indifference on the left hand and total control on the right. We must learn how to "do" church in a way that does not abnegate responsibility for the lives of members without at the same time taking away the liberty of the believer to hear and obey the voice of Christ in the written Word.

Implications for the "Lordship Salvation Controversy"

In the latter half of the twentieth century, there was a storm of controversy that came to be known by this terminology. I will not attempt to trace its roots or describe the forms it took. At risk of oversimplification, I note that it probably resulted from an apparently exaggerated emphasis on salvation by faith alone on the part of some in the dispensationalist camp. They said, in effect, that the true gospel requires nothing but belief in Jesus for one to receive eternal salvation. Backing this up, they denied that any other element of perception or will—whether repentance (in the sense of turning from one's sins) or commitment to Christ as one's Lord or even the intention to obey God—was required. Indeed, they emphasized, any insistence on such things constitutes a perversion of the simple gospel of salvation by faith. Only saved people need to be confronted with the claim of Christ to be their Lord, and any decision they may make to submit to that is distinct from the decision to accept Christ as Savior. Those who followed this emphasis mockingly dubbed the view of anyone who said that to be saved one must acknowledge Jesus as Savior and Lord as "lordship salvation."

Perhaps the writings of Lewis Sperry Chafer led the way in the development of "anti-lordship salvation"[6], but it came to its fullest expression in the writings of Charles Ryrie[7] and Zane Hodges.[8] All three of these were prominent members of the faculty of Dallas Theological Seminary. My purpose, here, does not include interaction with these men, but it seems appropriate to give a quotation or two that will inform the reader of the nature of this view.

In discussing the encounter between Jesus and the woman at the well in Samaria, for example, Hodges emphasizes, "Jesus ... said nothing to her about the repair of her life." He said "nothing to her of her obligations to God's will for a very simple reason: He was there to offer her a *gift*." He concludes, "She could not have comprehended the dazzling splendor of that gift, its sublime and total freeness, had He encumbered His offer with a call to reform her life."[9] This reflects what he had already said about this incident:

> It is hard not to be impressed with the magnificent simplicity of the transaction which Jesus proposes to this sin-laden Samaritan woman. Its very lack of complication is part of its grandeur. It is all a matter of giving and receiving, and no other conditions are attached. ... There is no effort to extract from the woman a promise to correct her immoral life. If she wants this water, she can have it. It is free! ... It must be emphasized that there is no call here for surrender, submission, acknowledgement of Christ's Lordship, or anything else of this kind. A gift is being offered to one totally unworthy of God's favor. And to get it, the woman is required to make no spiritual commitment whatsoever. She is merely invited to ask.[10]

Many similar quotations, from these and other anti-lordship salvation sources,[11] could be given but seem unnecessary to my purpose. According to this view, a person sitting in an audience, who hears the preacher say Jesus died for his sins and accepts this as the truth, without doing anything else to confirm this or live out its implications, is saved. A single act of believing the gospel to be true saves, and this can never be reversed. Indeed, even the faith itself may not continue: "It is sufficient to observe that the Bible predicates salvation on an *act* of faith, not on the *continuity* of faith." For that matter, that faith may lapse permanently: "Nowhere does the Word of God guarantee that the believer's faith inevitably will endure."[12] Even so, once the person has believed, his salvation is eternally settled.

Probably the most well-known defense of lordship salvation against this view has been offered by John MacArthur. His *The Gospel According to Jesus* was first published in 1988. A second edition followed in 1993 and a third in 2008. As I have noted in the preface to this work, most of MacArthur's conclusions parallel mine, although my "exegetical theology" approach is different and has come from an entirely different set of concerns. He says, for example, "Implicit obedience to [Jesus'] commandments is the necessary, expected, and natural fruit of genuine love for Him. It is also therefore the telltale mark of authentic saving faith." "No past experience ... can be viewed as evidence of salvation apart from a life of obedience."[13]

MacArthur, of course, believes in what is often called "eternal security." But he is quick to affirm that there is no assurance of salvation for one whose life is not in accord with discipleship, regardless how confidently that person professes faith. His chapter ten—originally a sermon on Matthew 11:25-30—powerfully presents what he calls "five essential elements of genuine conversion": humility, revelation, repentance, faith, and submission. I might change a few words here and there, but this is good reading; it is worth taking to heart.[14]

It should be obvious to any reader that my basic thesis, if correct, settles once for all the issue of lordship salvation. There is no such thing as faith that does not express itself in submission to the lordship of Jesus, responding positively to His call to forsake everything else and rely totally on Him for salvation and directions for life. As MacArthur had already observed, in agreement with what I have said, "Every Christian is a disciple. ... Any distinction between the two words is purely artificial. Though introduced by sincere and well-meaning men, it has given birth to a theology of easy-believism that disposes of the hard demands of Jesus."[15]

In Conclusion: The Need for Self-Examination

My final word (except for the "Conclusion" to follow) is about what this study has meant for me and what I hope it will mean for others. To borrow the words of 2 Corinthians 13:5: "Examine yourselves, whether you are in the faith; prove your own selves."

I remember well when I became a disciple of Jesus. I was at Bible College, having gone there (not so much out of my own desires) from a church background where I was told I was a sinner and needed to confess Jesus as my Savior and be saved. I had done that, in some measure of sincerity. But in that first semester at college I was confronted, perhaps for the first time, with the Lord's call to put the reins of my life in His hands. I did, having no idea where that might lead. Furthermore, I did not care. I turned away from my own fairly well laid out plans and submitted to His. My decisions would not be determined by money or status. In effect, I "left all and followed Him." The life I have led since then—for more than sixty-five years, now—has developed from that commitment.

Except that I have to ask myself whether I have taken it back. Have I gradually taken the reins into my own hands? Am I as free, now, to follow wherever He leads as then? Are my motives as unselfish? Are money and security as meaningless as they once were?

These are questions I ask me, and in the asking, I seek to ensure that my answers are the same as they were, say, in the fall of 1949. In short, I am prompted repeatedly, these days, to give attention to being not just a "Christian," in the usual sense of that word, but a *disciple* of Jesus Christ.

We need to think in those terms.

ENDNOTES

[1] Mark Dever and Paul Alexander, *The Deliberate Church: Building Your Ministry on the Gospel* (Wheaton: Crossway, 2005). Every pastor will do well to digest what they have to say about church membership and discipline, 47-48; 59-73—although I would suggest using deacons for what he assigns to a plurality of "elders."

[2] Dever and Alexander, 43.

[3] Dever and Alexander, 53.

[4] Dever and Alexander, 57.

[5] Those who do not practice *congregational* church government may wish to re-word this, of course; even so, if the congregation is not in some way well informed and involved, discipline will not have its proper effect.

[6] See Lewis Sperry Chafer, *Systematic Theology* (Dallas: Dallas Theological Seminary, 1948).

[7] Charles C. Ryrie, *Balancing the Christian Life* (Chicago: Moody, 1969), and notes in *The Ryrie Study Bible* (Chicago: Moody, 1976).

[8] Zane C. Hodges, *The Gospel Under Seige* (Dallas: Redención Viva, 1961), and *A Biblical Reply to Lordship Salvation: Absolutely Free!* (Dallas: Zondervan, 1989).

[9] Zane C. Hodges, *The Hungry Inherit* (Portland, OR: Multnoman, 1950), pp. 25-26.

[10] Hodges, *Gospel Under Seige*, 14.

[11] Those who hold this view have since come to be known as holding what they call "free grace theology." One may "google" this phrase for additional information.

[12] Hodges, *Biblical Reply*, 63, 111.

[13] John MacArthur, *The Gospel According to Jesus: What Is Authentic Faith* (Grand Rapids: Zondervan, 2008) 32, 38.

[14] MacArthur, 116-23; see also 175-84 for his helpful chapter on repentance as a necessary concomitant to faith. Alan P. Stanley, *Did Jesus Teach Salvation by Works? The Role of Works in Salvation in the Synoptic Gospels* (Eugene, OR: Pickwick, 2007) provides an equally strenuous and more systematic defense against the likes of Hodges and Ryrie. In many ways, Stanley's conclusions are similar to mine about the nature of saving faith as expressed in obedient discipleship, although his focus is primarily on the Synoptic Gospels. I did not learn of this work until my writing was essentially complete, but I have included a few references to it in the notes. In my view, Stanley relies a little too facilely on his insistence that the works that manifest faith are, like faith itself, the gifts and work of God; but of course, this is good Calvinism. At the same time, it is good Reformation Arminianism to insist, similarly, that both saving faith and the obedient discipleship that expresses that faith are

possible only by the enabling, gracious work of God. I think he also tries too hard, when moving from one passage to another, to separate future salvation at the judgment from present salvation. To be fair, I think he is especially on target in his insistence that "salvation" is not simply a past experience but a pilgrimage; but this point could shift the focus from eschatology to one's present condition and experience. In his discussion of "Keeping the Commandments and Entering into Life" (194-202), for example, he appropriately speaks of a "clear trajectory of thought within the New Testament concerning a close relationship between *practical righteousness* and eschatology" and of "the need for obedience to inherit eternal life *in the future*" (197, emphasis his). In support, he cites 1 John 3:10, which in fact speaks of the way we may distinguish the children of God from the children of the devil *now*. It is their *present* salvation, or lack thereof, that is in view. But none of this detracts from an otherwise erudite and helpful work.

[15] MacArthur, 219.

Conclusion

So What Is a Follower of Christ?

In light of the thesis of this book, the final question is relatively simple, although the answer may not be: what does it mean to be a disciple of Jesus Christ? What characteristics are essential to the life of one who is saved, one who is truly regenerate? In other words, accepting the premise that a child of God is one who has in faith answered Jesus' call to the obedience of discipleship, what does that look like?

A full answer might require yet another book. But it strikes me as unfair to my own purpose not to attempt at least an overview. I have decided to discuss what strikes me, in grappling with the New Testament passages I have used to make my case, as four of the most basic requirements of discipleship.

Before doing this, however, I must offer an important and essential qualification: namely, that none of our Lord's demands mean that only those who are *perfect* will inherit eternal life. If that were the standard, none of us could meet it. The purpose of some of the preceding chapters—especially seven and eight on sanctification and sin, not to mention chapter four on the pronouncements about sin in 1 John—has been to show we are too much depraved to be able to claim entire sanctification and absolute sinlessness in the present world. And the Bible has too many reminders of the sinful failures of godly men and women for us to be glib about being absolutely righteous even in our conduct, much less in the inner selves only God sees accurately.[1]

I need not pursue this again, I think, except to add there is some risk in mentioning it. The danger is twofold. For one thing, we may congratulate ourselves too quickly, excusing our sins as though we cannot avoid them. There is never any excuse for sin, and every sin should make us ask whether, in fact, we are disciples of Jesus or have betrayed a lack of genuine faith. The other danger is we may doubt our salvation all too soon, forgetting that our salvation depends on Christ's redemptive work rather than ours, and even our discipleship living depends on the regeneration that has made us new persons in Christ.

Our works do nothing more than express our faith, our response in loving trust to the call of our Savior to follow Him. Nothing more? That is much, and it is enough; indeed, our works do that as nothing else can. Our works are *essential* expressions of faith. At the same time, until we have been delivered from our depravity we will not express faith perfectly. Even so, we can usually tell the difference between the exceptional failures of one who is fundamentally committed to Jesus as Lord and the characteristic failures of one who is not.

What, then, are the most basic demands our Lord makes if we are to live with Him forever?

One. The most fundamental requirement, to be a disciple, is that we place faith in Jesus and His redemptive work as the sole grounds of our salvation. This means turning away from anything we might be tempted to offer God as a reason for Him to deliver us from our sins and the coming wrath. There is no reason for Him to save us other than His own good pleasure to do so as manifested in the person and work of Christ. I repeat that faith is holding out to Him *empty* hands to receive the gift He offers in grace, acknowledging that nothing we can do will earn favor from Him. And when we do, a "great transaction" is most certainly done. Our names are entered on God's roll, the righteousness of Christ is counted ours, and we are forgiven and freed. And in the continuing exercise of this same faith that standing is fixed.

We have seen this in wonderfully clear focus in the transaction model Paul champions. We have qualified this only to the extent that we understand faith better. There is an unavailing "faith" that is mere intellectual belief and not really faith at all. Saving faith is a trusting, submitting, committing belief, one that expresses itself in obedience to the call of Christ to repent of our sins and follow as His disciples. Nothing less is faith, and one who has not rested his faith in Jesus as the only source of salvation, and as the Lord who demands that he enroll in His school, has no promise of eternal life.

Two. This means Jesus demands that a true disciple deny every other person or thing that makes a claim to direct his life. Chapter two has put down the basis for this in the teaching of Jesus in the Synoptic Gospels, including His "hard sayings."

In the end, there are not many sources that ask us to live in their service and offer us direction and meaning in life. One of these is *family*: one's parents, siblings, mate, or children. Many are tempted to live for one or more of these. Indeed, they call to us sweetly, sometimes urgently, to recognize their claims on us. They—especially parents or mate—seek to give us direction for the course we pursue and think they do so in love. No wonder Jesus spoke so firmly about this: we must deny "father, and mother, and wife, and children, and brothers, and sisters" in order to be His disciples (Luke 14:26-27). James and John *left* their father in the boat to follow Jesus (Mark 1:20).

This does not mean we are indifferent to our loved ones or their needs or that we isolate ourselves from familial relationships and obligations. Jesus is the very one who directs us to love and provide for them. Instead, this means if we have made Jesus our Lord—and if we are regenerate, we have—His claims on us take precedence. His directions for our lives are the ones we follow, He is the only one who understands us fully and knows the right way for us. This cuts to the root of what it means to follow Him as disciples. He directs our lives. Indeed, God has the right to run our lives.

Another siren call comes to us from that whole complex of influences which we may sum up as *mammon*: money and all the things, physical and otherwise, that money represents. Jesus said, "You cannot serve God and mammon" (Matthew 6:24). Paul insists the love of money is a root from which all sorts of evil spring up (1 Timothy 6:10). Levi *left* his livelihood, the tax-booth, to follow Jesus (Luke 5:28).

Make no mistake, this is a powerful appeal and it offers much. Money promises security, comfort, pleasure, and influence—to name a few of the things it teases us with. In short, the god mammon dangles before us the hope of happiness and meaning. If we allow, it stakes a claim on us and commands the direction we take.

Jesus calls us in a different direction and to an entirely different meaning for existence. He requires that we make a choice: a disciple—everyone who will be a Christian—must renounce this false god and the meaning it claims to offer. And with that go the things money indirectly buys, including security and pleasure. Jesus did not accidentally say to would-be disciples that He had nowhere to lay His head! He did not carelessly ask the rich young ruler to sell everything. He did not speak off the top of His head to direct us to lay up treasure in heaven and not on earth.

The spirit of the age, especially for those of us who are born and live in the western world, makes it almost essential to live for material things. This is the world's reality, and most of the world's citizens are deceived to think it to be *the* reality. Even after we have been converted, sincerely intending to renounce this god and live for Jesus, we find it all too easy to come again under the sway of this foolish influence. A disciple of Jesus turns quickly back to hear the voice of the shepherd (John 10:3-4) calling him to truth and sanity.

Know this, then: one who is living for things is not a Christian. What Jesus said is still in force: "Whoever of you that forsakes not all that he has cannot be my disciple" (Luke 14:33).

The third claim on our lives is the most fundamental of all and out of it grows all the voices that conflict with the claim of Jesus. This is *self*, and its claim is the hardest to deny. But Jesus is unrelenting: if a person does not hate his own life, he cannot be His disciple; if he does not take up his cross and follow Jesus, he has not answered the call to discipleship (Luke 14:26-27). As indicated in chapter two, the cross is the place of execution. Jesus demands it as a way of saying we must die in order to follow Him to eternal life.

No one finds it easy, I suppose, to escape the desire to be his own master. I want to run my life, I do not want anyone to tell me what to do. And this desire is synonymous with the human condition in a fallen world. No doubt that is the reason Jesus makes such an issue of it. He knows we have not submitted to His lordship—and in His lordship is our salvation—until we have dealt with this god we have made of ourselves, the cruelest idol of them all. The conflict over who will be our master is what all our choices reduce to. The disciple of Jesus has chosen to make Him Lord rather than to rule his own life.

Does this mean that, once saved, the conflict is over? Not quite. Every day we are faced with this choice, to have it our way or His, and every time we permit our selfish wills to rule, we are reminded of the root sinfulness of our natures from which we cannot yet be delivered. But this does not mean we wallow in defeat: the true Christian, in spite of lapses now and again, has set it as his basic course to deny himself and take up the cross of his death and let Jesus rule. This is the way we express our faith in Christ, who alone has both the right and the ability to direct the course of our lives. If this is not the general pattern of a person's life, there is good reason to doubt that such a person is a Christian after all. Indeed, the truly converted person is aware he lives in submission to Jesus.

These three more or less sum up the alternatives. We become His disciples when we submit to His lordship and deny family, mammon, and self. In practice, that means He rules us. His will provides meaning and direction for our lives. We listen to Him to discern our calling. We seek His direction about whom to marry and how to provide for our family. We follow His rules and obey His commandments. We accompany Him to a local church where we worship and fellowship with those He bonds us with. We let His standards set the values that govern what we labor for and spend our time in. We submit without grumbling to the circumstances and places He puts us in. In short, He sets the course of our lives that finds us in work and play and worship and conduct. Jesus is Lord.

Three. The call to discipleship is a call to repentance, to a deliberate turning away from sin—with the help of the grace of God, of course. There is no such thing as a salvation that offers or seeks only forgiveness for sins without deliverance. No one really asks for forgiveness who does not intend to forsake the offence. The very word *salvation* denotes deliverance from one's sins. The word most commonly translated *forgiveness* (*aphesis*) means release, and if this most directly means release from the guilt of sins, it also surely connotes a commensurate release from the dominion of sin. Paul speaks of *all* Christians as having been made free from sin and become servants of God (Romans 6:22).

Jesus made plain that repentance is the requirement for entrance into the kingdom of God. As noted in chapter two, Mark 1:14-16 reveals exactly what He preached in this regard. "The kingdom of God is at hand; repent and believe the gospel." In the parallel Matthew 3:2 (compare 4:17), only *repent* is commanded. No doubt each word—repentance and faith—is broad enough to include the other in its implications. Conversion, reduced to its most fundamental element, is a *turning*: away from sin and to God. That is repentance, and that is faith. Without this, there is no salvation.

What this means in practical terms has been opened to us by the inspired writer of 1 John 3:9: "Whoever is born of God does not commit sin." As we have seen in chapter four, this does not mean a Christian is sinless; the very same epistle affirms otherwise (1:8-10). Instead, it means the Christian does not *practice* sin. Sin is not the habit and character of one's life and that is the essence of repentance.

We may not be able to define *exactly* what this produces in every conceivable situation, but anyone who is regularly overcome by sin has no grounds for assurance that he is a child of God. Neither that person nor we who minister to him should proceed on any other grounds. It does not seem possible to affirm that such a person has repented, and a full-orbed repentance is called for. As our Keswick friends remind us (see chapter seven), Jesus has done everything needed to provide deliverance—salvation—from our sins. He calls us to experience that by faith, faith that trusts Him enough to forsake our sins and our self-mastery to submit to His lordship and follow Him.

Four. Discipleship—being a Christian—means, to put it as simply as possible, obeying the Lord. These are terms that Jesus Himself defined over and over, including in His most basic commission: "Going, disciple all nations, ... teaching them to be keeping everything that I commanded you" (Matthew 28:19-20). This is the way to make people disciples: namely, by teaching them the commandments of Jesus. This defines discipleship as (from one perspective, anyway) the *practice* of obedience, signaled by the present infinitive *tērein*, to be keeping. And this characterizes the full message of Jesus as incorporating His commandments for living. I see no way around these clear implications.

A regenerate person is one who orders his life by the teachings of Jesus. No contrary definition will do. Jesus said, "If you keep my commandments, you will abide (remain, continue) in my love" (John 15:10). Someone may take this to mean a Christian who does not keep the Lord's commands will continue to be a Christian but not experience Jesus' love. Given the number of outlandish things I have heard here and there, I can conceive someone saying such a thing, but I cannot conceive that the words will be taken seriously. Anyone who is not making a genuine and generally successful effort to live by the words of Jesus is not His disciple. John, whose Gospel recorded this saying of Jesus and who surely understood it, subsequently affirmed that anyone who claims to know Christ (or God) but does not keep His commandments is a liar (1 John 2:4). Jesus likened the person who hears and does His commandments to a wise man whose life endures; and the person who does not do so He likened to a fool whose life is destroyed (Matthew 7:24-27).

In chapter six, taking a cue from James, I have indicated that obedience is the way faith expresses itself. Interestingly, Revelation 14:12 links "keeping the commandments of God" directly to "keeping the faith of Jesus." The two are not contradictory but complementary ways of expressing the same basic commitment. One does not really *believe in, put faith in, trust,* or *commit oneself to* Jesus without intending to live by His rules. (Perhaps it would be better to speak of the *principles*

He taught, but given who He is, *rules* is a perfectly good word.) What I am saying is not an expression of legalism, given that this is a loving, trusting obedience—"the obedience of faith"—not offered up as merit or as grounds for salvation. It is what the Old Testament calls the fear of the Lord, a reverential submission to God for who He is and what He commands. When one's *God* speaks, one listens!

It would not be possible for me to isolate and identify here all the "commandments" of Jesus a disciple lives by and teaches those whom he disciples to live by. That would require an exposition of all the Gospels and the Epistles, at least. Even so, for this to be truly practical, a few examples are needed to translate the concept into practice. I can only hope that the four I have selected for brief mention here are at least among the most fundamental ones and have broad enough implications to cover most aspects of the commandments of Jesus. One who is serious about being a disciple will not find it difficult to expand on these, or to add others, based on careful analysis of the New Testament.

(1) One of our Lord's most basic requirements is that His followers live in love for God and for others. The Scriptural basis for this is well known, and I need not develop it fully. I will mention just two passages. First, almost immediately following what I have quoted above from John 15:10, Jesus said, "This is my commandment, that you love one another" (John 15:12; cf. 14:15, 21), leaving us in no doubt that Jesus meant this to be included when He referred, in the Great Commission, to observing "all things that I commanded you." Second, we have Jesus' own word that the two greatest commandments of God are those found in Deuteronomy 6:5, to love God with one's whole being, and Leviticus 19:18, to love one's neighbor as oneself (Mark 12:28-31). Jesus Himself taught that on these two "hang all the law and the prophets" (Matthew 22:40). Similarly, Paul summed up all the horizontal commandments, at least, under the heading of Leviticus 19:18 and added, "Love is the fulfilling of the law" (Romans 13:10).

I mention again what I have said already: in the Bible, *love* is not mere emotion. It means, instead, the choices we make and the actions we take that grow out of those choices. In one sense, to love God turns out to be another way of saying to choose Him in faith: to submit, in other words, to the lordship of Jesus Christ. Loving one another, however, needs a little more discussion. Obviously significant is it that the command to love one another, cited above from John 15:12 (also v. 17), is in the context of *discipleship*, a context that pervades the chapters of John that are sometimes called the "Upper Room discourse." Consider John 13:34-35: again,

Jesus speaks of loving one another as a *commandment*. Then He adds this pointed commentary: "By this shall all men know that you are my disciples, if you have love one to another." Discipleship, then, demands love for fellow disciples.

This passage also leaves us with no doubt as to exactly how seriously Jesus meant His command to love one another: "as I have loved you," He said, and those words immediately cut to bedrock. This is not a trifling standard. Jesus loved us in such a way as to give His life for us. His disciples follow His lead in this, not usually by dying for fellow disciples but by giving themselves to live for them, which may be in some cases even harder.

The practical implications of this are too many to list. To love one another this way—and there is no other way—is to devote oneself selflessly to the welfare, spiritual and otherwise, of our fellow believers. It means to rejoice with them when they rejoice and weep with them when they weep (Romans 12:15). It means to reach out to them in compassion when they hurt or when they stumble. It means to "esteem others better than" ourselves, to look out for the interests of others rather than selfish interests (Philippians 2:3-4).

All this takes on special meaning within the life of a local assembly of disciples of Christ, a matter I will return to below. Meanwhile, it should be obvious that loving others self-sacrificially will rule out the violation of all the second table of the law. Followers of Christ do not make a practice of being indifferent to the wellbeing of others (much less murder), or of depriving others of what they need (much less stealing), or of being dishonest with others (much less bearing false witness), or of being jealous about others' possessions and circumstances (much less coveting what they have). No wonder Paul said love is the fulfilling of the law.

(2) One of the most important of our Lord's commandments for disciples—if also one of the most different from the spirit of the age—is a commitment to sexual purity. Jesus Himself initiated this discussion when He revealed that lust in the heart is already adultery (Matthew 5:27-28). He said this in the context of an explosive pronouncement: "Unless your righteousness exceeds that of the scribes and Pharisees, you will by no means enter the kingdom of heaven" (Matthew 5:20)! Then, to make sure we heard and understood, He put it in extreme terms: "If your eye causes you to stumble (into lust, for one thing), better to pluck it out and cast it away than to go to hell!"

I rely, here, not on Jesus alone but also on those with whom He shared His teaching and the responsibility to instruct would-be disciples in His commands.

Between the resurrection and Pentecost He was often with the apostles, expounding His commandments to them (Acts 1:2). The Epistles also then, as "the apostolic deposit" for the faith, define Christian obedience, and this includes the letters of Paul. Hear this, then, from what was probably his very first inspired letter: "This is the will of God, [for] your sanctification, that you be holding yourselves off from sexual immorality" (1 Thessalonians 4:3). Indeed, God's Word pervasively requires sexual purity in thought, look, and act, and this means bringing our sexual nature under the discipline defined by the creator of our sexuality.

Here, as perhaps nowhere else, Christians are called to be counter-cultural. Husbands and wives are to be faithful to each other *both before and during* monogamous marriage for life, and this must be from the heart. "Blessed are the pure in heart," said Jesus. In fact, there is no other purity. When this full, marital fidelity issues from within, faithful behavior flows naturally. Furthermore, this commitment to marriage will lead directly to honoring what Jesus and Paul said about divorce. In one sense, then, given the moral sickness of present culture in this matter, it is relatively easy for disciples, following the lordship of Christ, to show what it means to be a follower of His.

Even so, sexual purity is not easy. Our hormones rage, the media titillate and entice us, our peers justify the illicit indulgence of our urges. But our Lord calls us to walk a different way, to forsake our sins and follow Him. If now and again we fail to hearken to that call—especially in the secrecy of the inner person—we must be quick to seek His forgiveness, help, and correct our way. Disciples make it their practice to live in obedience to the teachings of their Lord. Lapses are exceptions, and exceptions are not ongoing.

Some of the pollsters report that there is little if any difference between Christians and unbelievers in the area of sexual behavior, especially among teens and twenty-somethings. One reason for such reports is the pollsters do not know how to distinguish true Christians from mere professors of faith. Church members who regularly indulge in sexual misbehavior—ranging from the pursuit of pornography to living together outside committed marriage—are simply not Christians. They are not living in faith.

(3) To obey Jesus' commandments, and so to be a follower of Jesus, one must actively participate in the life of a local church. The grounds for this claim are many and important. There are exceptions to this, of course, for persons who are not able for one reason or another, but *exception* is the right word.

Did Jesus indicate that His disciples must do this? Perhaps not as directly as the other matters I am treating in this chapter. Even so, the church is His creation, as He said in Matthew 16:18: "I will build my church." And He assumed the existence of a local church to provide the context for the Christian life and relationships among fellow Christians. In Matthew 18:15-20, dealing with a matter that needs to be resolved, He taught that when personal efforts have failed one should "tell it to the church." The church, then, will speak the final word. If we had nothing else, this short instruction alone suggests a full-orbed doctrine of church life. Indeed, verse 20 speaks loudly to this effect, in one sense defining a church: "Where two or three have gathered in my name, I am there in their midst."

The apostles, whom Jesus instructed in His commandments (as noted above), were careful to establish churches at the heart of Christian experience. The book of Acts gives clear evidence of this, as even a cursory survey will reveal. I cite but one of many obvious examples, Paul's first missionary journey as recorded in Acts 13-14. As they evangelized in the region (now a part of Turkey), they planted churches in Pisidian Antioch, Iconium, Lystra, and Derbe. Returning by the same route, they taught to "confirm the souls of the disciples" and "ordained elders in every church" (14:22-23). Indeed, wherever they went, their activities revolved around local churches.

The word *church*, in Greek, is *ekklēsia*, and the word carries with it well-known implications about its nature. Among the Jews of Jesus' day, the word appeared often in their Greek translation (LXX) of the Hebrew Old Testament referring to the *congregation* of Israel. In the Greek world of that day, the word referred to an *assembly*, especially an assembly of the true citizens of a community to function for the life of the community. A church is therefore, by definition, an assembling or gathering.

The existence of a given church is the result of the active work of the Holy Spirit. Paul teaches that Christians are responsible to "keep"—guard, preserve—the "unity of the Spirit," meaning the unity the Spirit has created, and this matches his next affirmation that there is one body and one Spirit (Ephesians 4:3-4). As a result, we are "members of one another" (Ephesians 4:25)—not to mention many references to "one another" in Ephesians and the rest of Paul's letters *to churches*. In one sense, of course, all the people of God everywhere make up the church universal as the body of Christ, but it will not *assemble* until He comes. Meanwhile, each local church is the body of Christ in microcosm, and it assembles every Lord's Day to function for the sake of the disciples who participate.

This is God's will for all followers of Christ, and one of the prime apostolic directives for disciples is that they not forsake the *assembling* of themselves, but instead urge and encourage (the twofold meaning of *parakaleō*, "exhort") one another (Hebrews 10:25).

The point of all this is that when a person is converted he is not left to live the Christian life alone. The Christian way—the way of discipleship—is a corporate way, not the way of mavericks. The Holy Spirit creates a bond between Christians for the purpose of their mutual edification. If we have seen that to be a disciple means to enroll in the school of Christ to learn His ways, then the local church is where the lessons take place. The members of the church hear and learn together from Him. They worship together and the worship of each strengthens that of the others (Ephesians 5:18-21). They take responsibility for one another for the purpose of their joint spiritual development (Ephesians 4:11-16). When one stumbles, the others seek to restore that one (Galatians 6:1). They discipline one another when that is needed (2 Thessalonians 3:6-15). When the manner of life of a member comes to be such that the person can no longer be counted a disciple, and all other forms of discipline have finally failed to bring repentance, the others may need to resort to excommunication (1 Corinthians 5:1-13), as indicated in the previous chapter.

In other words, the normal Christian life is lived in concert with other believers. Jesus has designed this way for those who follow Him.

Is church "membership" in the Bible? Of course it is. Could Paul and Barnabas have ordained elders in every church (Acts 14:23), if no one knew who the members were? In Acts 15:22, could Luke have written that "the church" in Jerusalem was pleased to adopt the recommendation of James (who was obviously presiding over the meeting), if no one knew who belonged? In reference to the disciplinary action discussed in 1 Corinthians 5, how could the church there "put away" from themselves the incestuous person if they and he and every observer outside did not know who were members of that church? Such questions can be asked at great length, including whether the people in Thessalonica, knew who was part of the group called "the church of the Thessalonians" (1 Thessalonians 1:1). The entire New Testament assumes that each local church had an identity. They might not have used membership certificates as we do, but they probably kept written rolls in one form or another. And even if they did not, they knew how to distinguish between their "members" and the non-Christian Jews or Gentiles. So did those who were not Christians.

A church is a "covenant" relationship, a community of faith committed to each other. Those who follow Jesus follow Him into the life of an assembly. They need each other in order to prosper spiritually. They mutually edify, and are edified by, each other. They share mutual responsibility for each other's discipleship. They need every part of the life of a church: its strengths and weaknesses, its ups and downs, its decisions and ministries. Professing Christians who absent themselves for an extended period from the regular assembling of their church are just that: *professing*. A professed disciple who flits about from one church to another, taking what he likes from this one and that one without making a covenant commitment to participate fully in the life of a congregation of disciples of Jesus is simply deceiving himself.

(4) Finally, one of the fundamental demands of disciples is that they be watching for the coming of Jesus and live accordingly. Jesus commanded this. Mark 13:33, 35, and 37 is but one of many such expressions and it has the nature of defining what it means to be a disciple.

First Thessalonians 1:9-10 serves as an especially significant and apostolic passage to make this clear. In what might have been his first inspired letter,[2] Paul recounts the conversion of Thessalonian believers under his church-planting ministry there on the second missionary journey:

> For they relate, about you, what sort of entrance we had with you,
> and how you turned to God from the idols to be serving a living
> and true God and to be awaiting His son out of heaven, whom He
> raised from among the dead, Jesus, the one delivering us from the
> coming wrath.

This is conversion reduced to its essence. These pagan Thessalonians turned to God from idols. In other words, they repented and genuinely believed, turning away from unreality to the true God. When they turned, they did so for two purposes: to be serving God and to be awaiting the return of Jesus.

The *serving* is broad and no doubt includes both acknowledging and worshipping Him as the true and living God and living in submission to Him—

discipleship, in other words. Compare the challenging affirmation in Joshua 24:15: "As for me and my house, we will serve the Lord!"

The *awaiting* (*anamenō*) means, "to remain in a place and/or state, with expectancy concerning a future event."[3] Indeed, the expectancy implies eagerness. Both of these verbs are in the Greek present tense, which yields the perspective of seeing an action in progress. In this context, they appear to imply a continuing experience, perhaps deliberately so, in contrast to the aorist "turned" which views an act as a whole. Surely, it is correct to say their conversion yielded serving and living as a twofold way of life.

The point is that *this is apparently intended to be a statement about the meaning of conversion, of becoming a disciple of Christ.* And in that light, Paul is implying it is the very nature of a disciple to be expectantly waiting for the return of Jesus. The very fact that he includes this element in his brief statement about their conversion must surely mean it is at the heart of their turning.

The problem is that we too easily lose sight of this promise and of the impact it should have on us. Christians are intended to be "second coming people," looking for the risen Savior from heaven and living accordingly.

To live in the light of the return of Jesus to this earth will mean a number of practical things that help define a Christian, only a few of which I note here. For one thing, it means what John said, "Everyone who has this hope in Him [the appearance of Christ, as in the previous verse] *purifies* himself, even as That One is pure" (1 John 3:3). Purity of heart and life will characterize the person who is watching for Jesus.

For another thing, it means Christians will be *awake* and *sober* (1 Thessalonians 5:6, 8). The latter word (*nēpho*) originally meant literal sobriety, as opposed to drunkenness. Here and elsewhere in the New Testament it is apparently used more figuratively and broadly of moral self-control or restraint as opposed to indulgence and the lack of self-possession. People who live with awareness and expectancy for the coming of Christ will maintain control of their faculties and not give themselves over to the control of evil influences of any kind.

Titus 2:12-14 is similar but more comprehensive. God's grace teaches us to deny ungodliness and worldly lusts and to live soberly, righteously, and godly in the present age, *looking for that blessed hope,* "even the glorious appearing of our great God and Savior, Jesus Christ," who performed His redemptive work for the purpose of purifying for Himself a people uniquely His own, "zealous for good works."

Without going into detail, here are both the avoidance of sin and the practice of the works of obedience that express faith. Living with expectancy for the coming Lord provides the context and the motivation for such a lifestyle.

Much more could be added, of course, but I have intended only to point those who are serious about discipleship back to the Scriptures to learn what Jesus expects of us. On this latter point, for example, any reader with a minimum of biblical knowledge can expand on the practical effects of living with expectancy for the coming of Christ. I find it interesting, for example, that the apostles could evidently use a simple expression of this truth of Jesus' return as a strong motivator for Christian living. Philippians 4:5 provides an example: "Let your sweet reasonableness be known to all men; *the Lord is at hand.*" Similarly, James 5:9 warns, "Do not be complaining against one another, brothers, lest you be judged: behold, *the judge stands before the doors.*" The basic point is the same, but the perspective is more specific: when the Lord returns He will do so as judge.

I have treated this fact briefly in chapter two under the heading of the second-coming judgment. He comes to judge, and this is the reason His impending return—it is always impending—serves as an effective motivator for the kind of Christian living that is truly discipleship. By the same token, that sort of living is truly an expression of faith.

That sort of living is, after all, nothing more than being a Christian.

ENDNOTES

[1] Is it providential that in the very day I work on the final version of this I meditate on 2 Chronicles 6 and the marvelous prayer of Solomon delivered at the dedication of the Temple (before his spiritual lapse)? I encounter there two of Solomon's "asides," one to the effect that God alone knows the hearts of the sons of men (v. 30), and the other saying there is no one who does not sin (v. 36)!

[2] Whether Galatians was written earlier is not clear; I am not inclined to think so.

[3] Louw and Nida, 1.729.

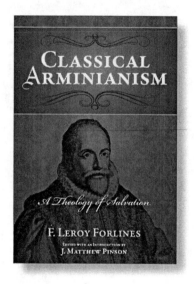

"In this book Leroy Forlines presents a lively, relevant, biblical restatement of classical Arminian theology. In a time when the choice seems to be Calvinism or "free will theism," his classical Arminianism is most welcome. Believing that theology is for life, Forlines writes for every Christian, not just for other theologians. His work appeals to the whole person, sets before us a powerful vision of God's holiness, and calls us to holy living. Every Christian who seeks to be biblically faithful will grow by reading and digesting this nourishing work."

Jonthan R. Wilson
Pioneer McDonald Chair of Theology
Carey Theological College

"Leroy Forlines is an accomplished and seasoned scholar who is the face of Reformed or Classical Arminianism, which is closer to the actual teachings of Jacob Arminius than the more widely known Wesleyan Arminianism. Forlines is, above all, faithful to careful biblical exposition as the foundation of his theology. The perspective offered by Forlines, along with like-minded theologians such as Robert Picirilli and Roger Olson, deserves to be heard on these crucial issues. Although our own perspective differs at points, we have used their books profitably at our seminary."

Steve W. Lemke
Provost
New Orleans Baptist Theological Seminary

randall house

To order, call 800-877-7030
or visit www.randallhouse.com.